Andrea,

In appreciation of our friendship with so many memories over the years!
love always,

Paula

Frank

A LIFE IN STAGES

Frank Farr

Eighty-two years of living a good life, learning,
working hard and enjoying the love of family
and the companionship of friends and colleagues

 FriesenPress

One Printers Way
Altona, MB R0G 0B0
Canada

www.friesenpress.com

Copyright © 2021 by Frank Farr
First Edition — 2021

All rights reserved.

No part of this publication may be reproduced in any form, or by any means, electronic or mechanical, including photocopying, recording, or any information browsing, storage, or retrieval system, without permission in writing from FriesenPress.

ISBN
978-1-03-911063-2 (Hardcover)
978-1-03-911062-5 (Paperback)
978-1-03-911064-9 (eBook)

1. *Biography & Autobiography, Business*

Distributed to the trade by The Ingram Book Company

INTRODUCTION

Paula Farr

I truly hope that you enjoy reading this book, as much as we enjoyed the trip down memory lane. Many of you will learn much about my Dad's life. Some of you may already know many of these stories but some may surprise you! We hope that you find it interesting and come away with an understanding of how his life evolved in stages – definitely a good life, well lived.

For as long as I can remember, I have enjoyed listening to and reading my Dad's stories. Over the years, my Dad has often written short stories to my Mom and I and as we found ourselves with more time on our hands, due to Covid, the idea of "A Life in Stages" took on a life of its own and turned into an eighteen- month project. I know I will always be thankful for this incredible gift!

As Frank's daughter, here are some of the things that stand out for me.

As a child in England, I grew up listening to my parents and my Grandparents stories about growing up in World War II. Some of my favourite memories, as a child, are from my Nan and Grandad's home in Liverpool (Mom's parents) and at my Gran's home in Leeds (Dad's Mom), listening intently to the stories about the war and those stories will stay with me forever. Time well spent with my aunt's and uncle's and cousins – everyone coming home from the pub and sitting around telling stories. Despite the obvious hardship of those war-torn years, what sticks in my mind is the feeling of a united country – friends and family sticking together, through the good and the bad. I loved the weekend visits to both of these homes and spending time with our family, they were very happy days. Our house in England was always full of friends and family – so many good memories of England!

Some of my earliest memories always seem to be in a car or on a train! We spent a lot of time driving to visit family on weekends and we spent a lot of time driving for Dad's work and visiting supermarkets. I remember many visits to supermarket openings and spending lots of time watching Dad work. I still like "facing" all of the food tins in the pantry to face the right way! I still have a huge appreciation for a well merchandised store! Many childhood memories of driving around England, Scotland and Wales visiting supermarkets.

I remember my parents driving me every Saturday to my horse riding lessons at a local stable. It's funny, at the time, I never realized that they usually stayed in the car and were not really fond of horses. I think I had asked for a dog a million times – they tried to placate me with guinea pigs, hamsters, gerbils and finally for my 10th birthday we got our first dog Lassie, who moved to Canada with us. My parents may never understand my love of animals, but they have wholeheartedly supported me in this lifelong passion.

I also grew up hearing about the "wonders of Canada", as Dad had lived in Canada for five years in his early twenties. We ended up moving to Canada when I was eleven and it still amazes me that my parent's best friends (Jim and Angela and Steve and Mary) moved here shortly after and now we have 50+ members of our three families, here in Canada. Best decision Dad ever made and I think we will always be thankful that we made that life changing move back in 1975. With relatives now spread out from England to Ireland to France to Taiwan to Italy. We have all become one Canadian family here in Vancouver.

Something that sticks in my mind is our first family trip to Canada. First to Toronto and then to Vancouver. We loved Vancouver! As an only child, I will always appreciate our family discussions and being included in life changing decisions. Everything was always a three-way decision.

As you will see through this book… my Dad worked hard, still does! Harder than anyone I have ever known. He is the most thorough, methodical person I have ever known. He seriously likes to double and triple check everything! As much as this drives me crazy, he is usually correct. Sometimes, I just wish he would do things a little faster! Lol! Some people say I am like my Dad – sadly I did not inherit this trait though and he is always telling me to slow down! I still think I'm more like Mom! My Dad always says that he has infinite patience with people but not with inanimate objects – don't ever ask him to put something together that requires tools (that's always been Mom's forte!) But he does try!

I would say my Dad to me has always been like having my own private "google", even before "google" existed. He has a love of literature, history, geography, politics, current events and jazz music like no one I have ever met and has always been a huge source of information and inspiration in that regard. Spelling and remembering names – not so much and for some reason, we are still showing him how to use his cell phone! Games night, especially Trivial Pursuit in this house can get very animated.

Dad has an amazing "calming" effect on people. I don't think I have ever heard him yell and certainly never swear at people. The one with the sense of humor in the family is definitely Mom – must be from growing up in Liverpool they say! Dad is the most positive person I have ever met – sometimes it drives us crazy! And be careful what you ask him – always put aside a couple of hours for the answer! A couple of years ago, I asked him a question about the English monarchy, within a week, I had a huge binder on my desk – he had printed off a one-page biography of every King and Queen of England going all the way back to William the Conqueror in 1066!

As unsettling as these past 16 months have been with the Covid situation, it gave us the time to work on this book together, Dad's business trips to Europe, over the past 16 months were canceled and this book became his new project. We spent more time than ever watching the news from around

A LIFE IN STAGES

the world (Covid related, political events) and having family discussions and yes – many more game nights and garden projects. I truly think we made the best of an unprecedented situation – Covid time well spent as a family!

I can honestly say that my parents have always been there for me, through the good and the bad (through sunshine and shade). I have always felt loved and included – what more could any daughter ask for. My parents were definitely not very conventional – one of the first movies they took me to was James Bond in London (after Lassie and Black Beauty of course!), on my 10th birthday cake they put little statues of The Beatles and they can certainly host a great party to this day! And just like Dad's personalized license plate – the famous "EBITDA" – he certainly taught me the meaning of "earnings, before interest, taxes, depreciation and amortization"!

So many amazing memories with my parents - from traveling around England to visit family and for Dad's work, to supporting my love of animals. Our big move to Canada, my parents surviving my crazy teenage years (and always welcoming all of my friends into our home) to working with Dad at 7-Eleven head office for 16 years and all of our parties and adventures with the 7-Eleven group. So many amazing travels around the world. We are still working together, as a family, with our current company and traveling to Casa Farr Away in Mexico. It's been a hell of a journey with more adventures still to come!

In writing this, I am reflecting on the past 16 months. So difficult for so many people, in different ways but throughout it all, Dad at 82yrs of age, has remained more positive than anyone I know. On July 9, 2021 Dad will be leaving for his first business trip to Europe since February 2019 and as much as we worry, we also understand that this is his passion (golf and gardening was never his thing!) and once again we wish safe travels to the #travelingman

I would describe my Dad as a good man, a man that has always listened to and taken care of his family. An honest man with both integrity and character who stands up for his beliefs and is always determined to succeed.

I will always be incredibly proud to say that I am Ann and Frank Farr's daughter.

With love,
Paula

DEDICATION

This book, *A Life in Stages,* is dedicated to my wife Ann. Without her love and support, most of this long and unpredictable journey would not have been possible.

It is also dedicated to my daughter, Paula. It was Paula who suggested that I commit my story to paper before the details of my life are forgotten. She has also acted as my editor and fact checker as this work has progressed. As a young child, Paula must often have wondered where I was and what on earth her father was doing. As an adult, she has been there alongside me to witness most of my challenges and achievements.

PREFACE

There are a number of reasons why I wrote *A Life in Stages*. Firstly, my daughter Paula has been asking me to do this for some time.

Secondly, a number of friends who have known me for many years, frequently suggested that I make a written record of the events of my life. Many of these friends participated in these events and have played a role in how my life has evolved.

Thirdly, I hope that my family and friends will find it interesting to travel with me down Memory Lane and to revisit the stages that my life has gone through and the themes that have shaped this eighty-two year-plus journey.

Here are some of the themes that I hope you will recognize as you read.

This is the story of a young man from a working-class background in war-time northern England, who married, had a daughter, and went on to have a successful international career, serving many companies at the highest level, while travelling the world and using his experience to help others along the way.

With a reasonable degree of intelligence, hard work, and good luck, there are no limits to what you can achieve. Always question the status quo and try to have a positive influence on those whose lives cross yours. Apart from bad health or bad luck, life is what you make of it.

Life can be so wonderful, but you have to find a focus that will enable you to achieve your potential. You cannot succeed by meandering through life. Let your decisions be guided by your values and nurture the few good friendships that can last a lifetime. We all need mentors/coaches.

When your values are clear, decision making is easy. Do not be afraid to step up to the decisions that you face in life. Try hard to make the right ones and live with the consequences. These major decisions will determine the trajectory of your life and allow you to live it fully and completely.

❖

Never forget your roots, but realize that "the station" where you start your life's journey does not have to be "the station" where you end it. The choice is yours.

❖

Intelligence Vs Intellect:

Intelligence is the ability to absorb, sort, understand, recall and use information. Intellect is the desire to use your intelligence to ask why, to question the status quo and continually seek better solutions. We all have intelligence in varying degrees. The challenge is to use your intellect to put that intelligence to its best use.

ACKNOWLEDGEMENTS

To my mother, Olive Farr, for instilling the basic values that have guided me through all these years. To Dorothy and Montague Simmons, my second parents, for seeing some potential in a young boy of fourteen and providing me with the confidence to believe that I could develop an enquiring mind and succeed in life.

To Jim Waldron and Steve Murray, friends for life, and my companions and confidants through the thirty-five years at Fine Fare, Tamblyn, and 7-Eleven.

To George and Esther Pope, my parent's in law, for the gift of Ann and for being such good friends and companions for so many years

To Nort Delaney, Don Neville, Laurie Edwards, Werner De Smidt, Wallace Monaghan, Dick Dole, Adrian Evans, Steve Krumholz, and Steve LeRoy for tolerating me in the early years, as I learned, and for supporting me during my later years of business maturity.

To Peter Flach for being a good friend, at 7-Eleven and for introducing me to the European Bank for Reconstruction and Development (EBRD), providing a challenging and stimulating final chapter to my life in business.

To Agon Gashi, Hakif Gashi, Hida Gashi, and my friends and colleagues at Meridian Corporation and Meridian Express in Kosovo, for welcoming me into their business and their lives.

To Oleg Merchenko, Serhiy Kykinov, Inna Zholob, and my friends and colleagues at Clever Stores LLC in Ukraine, for welcoming me into their business and their lives.

These people have contributed so much towards the happiness of my life. I think it was Walt Disney who said, "Anybody's accomplishments are usually due to the contribution of many hands, hearts, and minds." To the degree that I have accomplished anything in my life, I am thankful for the support that I have enjoyed. I have had the good fortune to enjoy the friendship and support of so many people. Too many to mention. I hope that I have fairly acknowledged them in the body of my story.

TABLE OF CONTENTS

iii	Introduction *Paula Farr*	103	**Chapter Eleven** *The Weston Family*
vii	Dedication	109	**Chapter Twelve** *The 7-Eleven Years – Part One 1978-1990*
ix	Preface	133	**Chapter Thirteen** *7-Eleven Travel and Vacations*
xi	Acknowledgements	165	**Chapter Fourteen** *The 7-Eleven Years Part Two 1990-1998*
1	**Chapter One** *Poor but Happy 1938-1945*	191	**Chapter Fifteen** *Bosses*
11	**Chapter Two** *Post-War England 1945-1953*	197	**Chapter Sixteen** *West Van to Morgan Creek—Building our Retirement Home*
23	**Chapter Three** *Juvenile Delinquency 1950-1953*	205	**Chapter Seventeen** *Retirement (NOT) 1998-2010*
29	**Chapter Four** *Bright Delinquents—Kneesworth Hall School—The Simmons 1953-1957*	213	**Chapter Eighteen** *Glow of Ownership—English Language*
37	**Chapter Five** *Canada—Loblaws and Buffalo 1957-1961*	219	**Chapter Nineteen** *The European Bank for Reconciliation and Development 2010-2021*
47	**Chapter Six** *Ann and Paula 1962-1964*	249	**Chapter Twenty** *Mexico and the Caribbean*
57	**Chapter Seven** *The Fine Fare Years—Part One 1961-1970*	257	**Chapter Twenty One** *Close Friends, Good Company and Many, Many Parties*
65	**Chapter Eight** *The Fine Fare Years—Part Two*	263	**Chapter Twenty Two** *Golf*
83	**Chapter Nine** *The Fine Fare Years—Part Three 1970-1975*		
93	**Chapter Ten** *Canada Again—The Tamblyn Years 1975-1978*		

269 Chapter Twenty Three
2199 179th Street, South Surrey

273 Chapter Twenty Four
On Eighty

283 Chapter Twenty Five
Epilogue: No End in Sight—Just Yet!!!!!!

287 Appendices

289 Appendix 1
Fish and Chips (Part 2)

293 Appendix 2
2020 - The Covid 19 Pandemic and Donald Trump

297 Appendix 3
My Final Staff Communication as President of 7-Eleven Canada

301 Appendix 4
Schools and Education: A Slow Start and a Strong Finish

305 Appendix 5
My Work History (CV)

309 Appendix 6
Family Tree

CHAPTER ONE

Poor but Happy
1938–1945

I was born in London at Lewisham Hospital, on Sunday, October 16th, 1938. Francis, the third child to Olive and Walter Farr.

There are two things that come to mind.

Firstly, from 1939–1945, Britain was engaged in the Second World War, and for almost ten years following the war, we had to cope with rationing and austerity measures.

Secondly, I was so fortunate to have the mother that I did. Olive Farr, poor, hard-working, self-educated, intelligent, and strong. What a woman! I don't know how, but through all that she had to overcome, she remained cheerful, provided a happy home, and instilled the values that sustain me to this day. I honestly cannot remember her saying a bitter or negative word about the challenges that confronted her during difficult times. With little education, she was worldly wise, she managed to be well informed, she knew much about opera and other arts, and she encouraged me to read, to question, and to be truthful. She also encouraged me to treat girls and women with respect.

We were a working-class family, in a relatively poor neighbourhood close to the centre of Leeds in Yorkshire, England. (At that time, Leeds had a population of 500,000.) We were certainly poor, but thinking back to those times, I have to say that I think of them as happy. With the one exception of when my father died, I cannot remember any time that I was not happy.

Starting in the Middle Ages, Leeds/Bradford was always the centre of the woollen industry. (Manchester was cotton, Sheffield was steel, Liverpool was docks and shipbuilding.) These industries have all died away, but Leeds has remained an important centre for Finance and Law. There is a magnificent statue of a mounted Edward, Prince of Wales (The Black Prince) in Leeds City Square. He is credited with bringing the woollen industry to Leeds in the mid-fourteenth century.

The population of Leeds (including surrounding areas) has doubled from the early 1950s, and now Leeds has a population of a little over a million.

FRANK FARR

We were a small family and had few close relatives. My father, Walter, spent most of his adult life in London, and I did not really see much of him. He died in 1949, when I was ten years old. He is buried in Killingbeck Cemetery in Leeds.

Because of the prominence of the woollen industry in Leeds, Textiles was a required subject in most colleges. (I later studied Textiles and Retail Organization at Leeds College of Commerce.) Before and after the Second World War, Montague Burton (The Tailors) operated the largest ready-made clothing factory in the world. The property employed many hundreds of workers and was so huge that they actually held Formula 1 car races on the grounds. Leeds has always had a large Jewish population, frequently associated with the tailoring industry. Despite the dominance of such companies as Montague Burton's, most of the trendier youths always had their suits made to measure, by one of the many local Jewish tailors. Three and half yards of cloth to make a suit!

My older brother Leslie was a loner, who left home at sixteen when I was five. I did see a little of him over the years, until he moved to Scotland in the 1960s. He died at the age of seventy-eight in 2009.

My mother, my older sister Olive, and my younger brother Michael were close, Michael and I became much closer as the years passed and we remained close until his death following a six-month battle with pancreatic cancer in 2018.

My wonderful mother lived to see her ninety-second birthday, remaining in her own home until she was ninety-one and dying of old age in 1994. She was, and still is, a source of inspiration for me.

I never met any of my grandparents. I believe that they had all passed before I was born.

My mother had four brothers. Two of them died in the First World War, I did meet the other two, Arthur, who lived in Leeds and Robert, who lived in London. My father had a brother, Billy, but I only saw him once, at my father's funeral.

Frank's Grandparents—John and Mrs. Stuart and Uncles—Arthur, Jack, and John

Family photos in Horsforth Museum/Leeds—propeller from WWI

A LIFE IN STAGES

My sister Olive and her husband, Stanley, had four children: Pauline, David, Jaqueline, and Suzanne. I have remained in touch with them and have occasionally managed to visit them in Leeds over the years. David has lived and taught school in a number of countries, but has been settled in Rome for several years, so I have not been able to meet him, although his sisters keep me up to date on how he is doing.

My family was from Leeds, but for reasons that I do not know, they moved to London some time before 1938. My mother had had an earlier child, Bobbie, who died as an infant, and my younger brother, Michael, was born in 1943, after we had returned to Leeds.

On a recent visit to Leeds, my niece gave me a photo of my sister holding me in her arms. This is the earliest photo of me, and it was taken in London, probably close to 1940 when I may have been two years old.

Frank with his sister Olive—London, 1940

The Second World War had started in 1939, and within a year, London was under nightly attack by German air raids (the Blitz). My family decided to return to the relative safety of Leeds in 1941 and this is where my memories begin.

I know that when we first returned to Leeds, we lived in a flat in the Hyde Park area and subsequently moved to Carlton Place and then Carlton Terrace, followed by Hillary Street in 1942, Cobourg Street, and then back to #14 Hillary Street. We remained at Hillary Street until 1953.

Following our return to Leeds, my father had difficulty finding work and he returned to London. My mother and father never divorced, but they did become legally separated, and in the early years, all that my mother had to manage on was the infrequent "maintenance" money that my father could afford to send. He would also send me a postal order for one shilling (twenty-five cents) and sometimes a half-crown (two shillings and sixpence). Knowing that my mother had no money, I loaned her my postal orders and she planned to pay me back later. When the amount owing grew to two pounds, we both realized that she would never have that much money, and we agreed that it should be forgotten.

Although my mother and father were legally separated and he continued to live in London, they remained on friendly terms, and my father returned home for short periods of time up until his death. My father died suddenly from a heart attack at our home at 14 Hillary Street, in May of 1949. He was only forty-nine years of age.

Walter Farr – Leeds, 1937   Olive Farr – Leeds, 1977

My memories of my father are very limited, although I do remember that I used to go down to Leeds Central Railway Station on Sunday evenings to see him off to London. He used to buy me a one-penny platform ticket, and I would run alongside his train as it pulled away from the platform.

My strongest memory of this time is that when my father died, he had less than a pound (five dollars) to his name, and my mother had to work hard and scrimp and save to keep a roof over our heads as we grew up. I made a vow to myself that I would never let that happen to my family, and I would do whatever it took to make sure that my family did not join the ranks of poor widows and orphans that are too big a portion of our society.

It is hard now to try to recreate those times. The world has changed, and we have all changed with it. Although we did not have very much, neither did anybody else around us.

When we moved from Carlton Terrace to Hillary Street, my mother rented a pull-cart for one shilling. That four-foot by six-foot cart with two big wheels and a long handle, held everything that she and the rest of us owned, and we pulled it, by hand, for about one mile to Hillary Street. This was probably our most difficult time.

During this period, I attended St. Anne's Children's School and then St. Anne's Junior School. These were Catholic schools attached to St. Anne's Cathedral. I remember that at St. Anne's Junior School, there was an adjacent shop that made fresh pikelets (crumpets) daily, and we would go and buy them for a half-penny for our lunch.

When we moved from Hillary Street to Cobourg Street, I did not know that we were moving, or where we were moving to. I went to school at St. Anne's in the morning and in the afternoon after school, my sister's boyfriend, Stanley Dickinson, met me and took me to our new home. He was a delivery boy for a local grocer, and he gave me a ride in the carrier fixed to the front of his bike. That was a bumpy ride over cobblestone streets.

After one year, we moved back to 14 Hillary Street and we remained there until the end of this chapter of my life.

14 Hillary Street

Hillary Street no longer exists, (it is now a part of the parking lot for Leeds University), but in those days it was in an area bounded by Fenton Street, Woodhouse Lane, Leeds Infirmary, and Leeds University up as far as Woodhouse Moor. On the other side of Woodhouse Lane was the Blenheim School area. Within these bounds were many pubs and numerous fish and chip shops, all of which came to play a role in my life.

The house, built around 1910, was just the same as hundreds, if not thousands, of working- class houses in the North Leeds Area. There was a "cellar kitchen" (half underground) where we spent most of our time, a "front room" upstairs, with two bedrooms above that, and an attic "loft" above that. There were four houses with a shared passage through to the next street (West Hillary Street). The four houses shared two outside toilets. The houses were "back to back," hence no back garden. We had a front garden that was six feet by fourteen, surrounded by a low wall. The iron railings had been removed for recycling as a part of the war effort.

14 Hillary St

We had a coal fireplace in the cellar kitchen, and in addition to heating the kitchen, this provided heat for the oven and for a clothes boiler. We also had a fireplace in the front room, but we could seldom afford to have a fire in that room until several years later, when my sister Olive and Stanley married, and this room became their first home. Stanley turned the attic loft into an aviary for his hobby of breeding budgies and canaries

The electricity and gas were controlled by meters. We had to feed shillings into these meters and if we didn't have a shilling we had to go without. One way around this was to use illegal metal "slugs" the same size as a shilling. When the meter man came to empty the meters, we usually got a small refund and we had to hope that the refund was big enough to cover the shortage caused by the "slugs."

The rent for this house was ten shillings per week (approx. $2.50) for most of the time that we lived there. (There was no such thing as inflation in those times.) My mother paid for this from an assortment of cleaning and cooking jobs that she managed to find during these early years.

My mother also received a "Welfare" allowance (a credit note) from the government for ten shillings per week and I remember that we had to walk a couple of miles up to the Woodhouse Moor Library, to collect it. We would then return home, where she would sit at the kitchen table, writing lists of groceries to see what she could afford to get with the credit note. This note was then exchanged for food at the shops at the bottom of our street.

Sid Cowlings' grocery shop; the fruit shop; Mullin's, the butchers; and Dyson's, the cake shop. There was also a newsagent's and a fish and chip shop.

Fruit Shop and Cake shop at bottom of Hillary Street

As you can see, we had no money, however, we were not much different from those around us. The houses were the same for a mile in every direction. By the 1950s, most working men were paid five pounds per week and most homes got by with one wage earner. The homes of those families that had two or more wage earners certainly stood out from the rest.

But despite all of this, there was a lot to be happy about. All of the young people made their own fun in the streets around us. The girls played skipping, hop-scotch, and tossing balls-up against the walls, while the boys played marbles and cricket against a chalked set of stumps on the wall. We calculated that the block at the top of the street was a quarter of a mile around and we organized foot races around this block. I could never afford the luxury of a bike. These were such enjoyable, innocent times, never to be repeated.

The Second World War

All of this took place against the background of the Second World War, which had an impact on everything. For much of the time, most of the adult men were away serving in the war. Women moved into the workforce and life was not "normal" until well after the war ended in 1945.

In those days, soldiers were everywhere. There were three army barracks close to Hillary Street. Fenton Street Barracks, Imphal Barracks (named after a famous battle in India), and Gibraltar Barracks.

Some images remain in my mind:

Leeds did suffer at least one bombing attack in 1941. Most of the bombs landed in the centre of Leeds with sixty people killed and several hundred injured. Ten houses at the bottom of Hillary Street and West Hillary Street were among the buildings hit in the air raid, but we did not move to Hillary Street until a year later in 1942. The Leeds Town Hall was also damaged.

A LIFE IN STAGES

London, Southampton, Coventry, and Liverpool all suffered much more than Leeds. However, I do remember the air raid sirens going off, usually in the middle of the night. It was many long blasts for an "Air Raid Warning" and one long blast for the "All Clear." As soon as we heard the first warning, we would all get up and head to the local air raid shelter, along with other families.

The air raid shelter was approximately 200 yards away, a plain, ugly brick building with a cold concrete floor. Some of the houses had gardens big enough to accommodate a "Bailey" shelter, dug into the ground and covered by a sheet of corrugated metal and a layer of soil. Many times, we would just head down to our cellar kitchen and hide under the kitchen table. As soon as we heard the "All Clear," we would pester my mum for a pot of fresh tea and a jam sandwich.

Every night from dusk to dawn, we had to put up the black-out curtains on all windows. If every building in the city did this, it made it more difficult for the German bombers to know where to unload their deadly bombs or to navigate their way home.

Hillary St. was cobblestoned and huge tanks routinely drove down our street causing everything to shake. The housewives were not very happy, as they had to rush out to remove the washing lines that they had strung across the street and the shaking caused pictures and ornaments to fall off the walls.

There were many American soldiers around, clearly distinguishable by their colourful and posh-looking uniforms. We soon learned that if you approached them with the familiar request, "Got any gum, chum?" they would frequently oblige with slivers of Wrigley's spearmint gum. At that time, this was not available in the shops. We soon figured out that there was a house on the way home from school that was full of American soldiers and young local women. This was too good an opportunity to pass up, and so we would knock on the door and utter our never-ending question, "Got any gum, chum?" Usually the answer was positive and, of course, being the cheeky, persistent ones that we were, we would shortly return to do the same thing again. For some reason the soldiers were preoccupied, did not recognize us, and frequently gave us more.

Allotments: Most of the parks and public spaces were converted to small allotments and given over to individual gardeners, who could grow their own vegetables to supplement the small quantity that was available in the shops. These allotments remained in use for many years and some are still there to this day.

There were two endings to the war. The first was VE Day (Victory in Europe), May 1945 followed by VJ Day (Victory over Japan). August 1945. I remember VE Day. Everybody was celebrating and most of the adults went to the local pub (the Fenton). When the pubs emptied, the drunken men were so happy that they threw any spare coins that they had to the incredulous kids watching outside. I still remember the shiny half-crown that came my way and was eagerly received.

Some of the returning soldiers placed souvenirs in their window such as Nazi flags, Nazi uniforms, and other souvenirs, to commemorate their personal story in our victory.

The Germans unconditionally surrendered in May 1945. Unfortunately, the Japanese showed no intention of surrendering, and the Allies were faced with the impossible task of invading the Japanese mainland. Between May 1945 and August 1945, the Allies dropped two atomic bombs, one on Hiroshima and one on Nagasaki, destroying both cities and killing over 200,000 people. Japan unconditionally surrendered on August 11th, 1945.

Pocket Money

I often listen with interest when I hear mention of "pocket money" or "allowances."

I know what they are, and they make sense; it's just that I never had either. I think that they mainly relate to something that your parents give you, usually on a weekly basis, from an early age and up to your first job.

However, growing up through the '40s and early '50s I never had pocket money or an allowance. The very idea was inconceivable, as my mother struggled throughout the Second World War and the years that followed, to raise a family on her own and keep a roof over our heads.

That's one of the reasons that I have never owned a bicycle and cannot ride a bike to this day. But even without an allowance my friends and I could usually go to the cinema and buy ourselves the odd treat.

Here are some of the ways that we earned our money.

Selling Firewood Bundles

We lived near the centre of Leeds and on a Saturday, we took our "bogie" (a plank of wood with four wheels) and headed off to Kirkgate Market. We collected any old wood that we could find, (old orange crates were the most popular), loaded them onto the bogie and took them to the bombed-out building at the bottom of our street. We broke them up, tied them in bundles, and set off around some of the better houses to sell our firewood bundles for two pence and sometimes six pence.

Collecting (Sometimes Liberating) Returnable Bottles and Jars

We also collected and returned bottles and jars. They were usually worth a half-penny, or one penny and sometimes two pennies.

Roundhay Park was a large and splendid park on the outskirts of Leeds (it still is), and as such was the venue for numerous festivities throughout the summer months. Sometimes we took the bogie and headed off to the park to spend most of the afternoon collecting returnable bottles.

Roundhay Park was three miles from where we lived, and to get home from the park we had to pass through a couple of the roughest areas of Leeds. We went around the edge of the notorious Gipton Estate and then we had to go along Camp Road. Camp Road was by far the worst and there were several times when we were "relieved" of our precious bottles. I still have scars on my head from the bricks that were thrown.

The other and more creative way of collecting bottles was to "liberate" them from the back yard of the Fenton Pub and then have the cheek to walk around the block and "return" them to the pub.

This was quite complicated, as we had to find somebody small enough to slide between the top of an open mesh gate and the roof of the bottle shed. (I think that we used my younger brother Michael.) He would then drag the cases of empties over to the gate and pass the bottles through to eager hands on the other side. I don't think that we ever explained to Michael that if the landlord came into the shed from the back of his pub, we would have to abandon him.

The Fenton Pub "Our Local"

Now that I have mentioned "liberating," I should also mention that occasionally we came all the way home from school during the lunch break (three miles). We'd go to the corner store and consider very seriously which ice cream treat we wanted from the very bottom of the freezer. While the assistant was diving into the freezer for our selection, we liberated bars of Van Houton Orange Milk Chocolate and Terry's Chocolate Oranges. We then went back to school and attempted to sell these treasures to other kids at half price. (These were the kids who did get pocket money or allowances.)

Recycling

Occasionally we went to some of the nicer streets and knocked on doors soliciting used newspapers or unwanted clothes. We then took them down to a central recycling depot where we soon learned the value of paper, woollens, cottons and occasionally scrap metal.

The highlight of this endeavour was when we persuaded a couple of Gypsy boys that we knew, to loan us their father's horse and cart, as their dad was away.

This was a dismal failure; the horse would not go the way we wanted. The cost of the balloons that we had purchased, to give away in exchange for used articles, exceeded the value of what we collected, and it was all over before we could make it work.

FRANK FARR

Shopping

I did have a couple of more normal ways to make money.

The shopkeeper at the top of our street had purebred dogs (golden retrievers), and he would sometimes pay me a shilling to go down to the market and buy horsemeat for the dogs.

Also, a married couple who worked at the nearby Somnus bedding factory, used to pay me to go to the local co-op during my lunch break and pick up their groceries and take them back to their flat.

So, there you have it. Somehow, we survived and prospered. No pocket money, no allowance. We were no different from most young lads growing up in Leeds during those years. We found ways to get by, enjoy life, and I think most of all, appreciate the sacrifices of our parents, raising families in difficult circumstances.

Frank with his mother Olive,
brothers Leslie and Michael – 1988

❖

"Always be a gentleman in the way that you treat women." Olive Farr

CHAPTER TWO

Post-War England 1945–1953

Although the war-time rationing and other restrictions were still in place, this was a time of relative peace, prosperity, and optimism. The 1948 London Olympics and the 1951 Festival of Britain occurred during this period.

During the war, and for number of years after, basic foods were rationed. This created some odd consequences.

We all had ration books (adult and child versions). These had coupons that had to be provided in order to purchase a weekly quantity of things such as clothing, meat, and a range of basic groceries, including sweets. Standard rations were six ounces of fresh meat and four ounces of corned beef per adult per week. We were also allotted two ounces of sweets/candies when they were available. There were also ration coupons for petrol, although this did not affect us.

These coupons had a value of their own and many schemes were cooked up by petty crooks (spivs[1]) and others to forge or counterfeit these valuable coupons.

Those of us who could not afford to use all our coupons, could sell them for cash to others who could afford them (some of the two-income households that I mentioned earlier).

There were almost no imported foods, particularly fruits, during the war, and it took several years for things to return to normal. It was not until the end of the war that I saw a banana. In fact, I had trouble visualizing a banana or a pineapple, although they had been described to me. Best butter, as we called it, was not available, and there was only one type of government-issue margarine available.

Once per month, we would go to an office in the centre of Leeds to collect our ration of powdered milk, concentrated orange juice, malt extract, and cod-liver oil, which were all intended to prevent children from becoming malnourished.

The English eat a lot of sweets on a per capita basis, and I think that it was around 1950 that the restrictions on sweets were removed and coupons were no longer required. Predictably, all the sweet shops were out of stock within days, and this situation persisted for some time. One day, an ad

---

1 Swindlers or black marketeers.

appeared in the local newspaper, advertising that Lewis's (the dominant department store in Leeds), was expecting a huge shipment of sweets on Friday. I, along with my sister and half the population of Leeds, joined the queue that circled the entire store, and we lined up for over an hour. When we got into the store, we discovered counter after counter loaded with the promised sweets. There was only one problem. They only had one type: fruit bonbons. We were grateful, but to this day, I cannot see fruit bonbons without picturing those loaded counters in Lewis's back in 1950.

Annual Events We Looked Forward to

Children's Day at Roundhay Park

There was a large, open-air swimming pool in Roundhay Park and one of my mother's claims to fame was that her father had been a swimming instructor for Leeds schools, and he had been chosen to give a demonstration of life-saving in the pool, on the day that it had opened back in the early 1900s.

Roundhay Park, in Leeds, is one of the largest city parks in England and the biggest event of the year was Children's Day, held in August. The crowds were enormous and the entertainment varied. It was a day that we all looked forward to. We used to watch some of the cycling and track and field events sitting on Hill 60, overlooking the main arena.

There was a large lake in the park (Waterloo Lake) and the big pleasure was renting a paddle boat or a rowboat out on the lake. ("Come in number 5!" was a phrase that we all learned to recognize.) I don't think that fishing was allowed on the lake, but there were lots of fish in the water around the boat area. I also remember going to the park many years later when the lake was temporarily drained. That was an odd sight.

The Woodhouse Fair (Twice a Year on Woodhouse Moor)

These travelling fairs were a big highlight and for most of us, our first exposure to "The Coaster," "Bumper Cars," "Big Wheels," and "The Waltzer." In later years, we also used to take advantage of the fair for impromptu dancing, as the speakers blared out the popular tunes of the day. One of the features of the fair was the boxing match. The promoter would offer one pound to any local lad who could last three rounds with the promoter's semi-professional boxers. The bouts were probably fixed as the local lads never won.

Those fairs were a lot of fun.

A LIFE IN STAGES

*Bonfire Night on the Fifth of November. **What a time that was**.*

In England, the tradition of Bonfire Night dates back to the time of King James I. King James succeeded Elizabeth I in 1608. This was a time of intrigue between the Roman Catholics and the Protestant Church of England, founded by Henry the Eighth, Elizabeth's father, to facilitate his divorces and his quest for a male heir.

Guido Fawkes and other Catholic co-conspirators planned to blow up the House of Parliament in London and kill King James, but the plot was uncovered and the perpetrators were hung, drawn, and quartered, with their severed heads displayed at the city gates.

"Remember, remember, the Fifth of November, Gunpowder, Treason and Plot."

Throughout England for four hundred years, the Fifth of November has been celebrated by street bonfires, and the streets of Leeds in the '40s and '50s were no exception. Although many streets had their own bonfires, our bonfire was always on West Hillary Street and three or four streets joined to make it a big affair.

During the weeks leading up to Bonfire Night, we got together in little gangs and went off hunting for anything that could be used as fuel for our fire. We called these treasures "chumps" and chumping became an excuse for liberating anything that would burn. We had to store these chumps in one of the bombed-out houses on West Hillary Street and make sure that rival street gangs didn't raid it to steal our chumps.

It was a wonderful time to get rid of old furniture. Chairs and sofas were placed around the bonfire to provide seating, until the time came for them to be thrown onto the fire as it got later into the night.

Some of the mothers would bake "parkin" or gingerbread, to eat around the fire. Potatoes would also be baked in the ashes at the edge of the fire. They were pretty dirty, (no aluminium foil in those days).

The big challenge was to see how long we could keep the fire going. It always lasted through for a second night and on one occasion, I remember it lasting into the third night. To this day, I am a little ashamed of some of the wooden items that we liberated in order to keep these fires going.

In the week leading up to the fire, we used to make up a dummy Guy Fawkes, as we called it, and wheel it around town (usually outside pubs) asking adults for "A penny for the Guy." We often raised more than we expected and hid our loot, (which we used to buy fireworks) from all of the other little groups doing the same thing. On the night of the bonfire, all the little "Guys" were placed on top of the fire before it was lit.

Bonfire Night was the biggest night of the year for fireworks. Although fireworks are much more regulated today, their use was indiscriminate in those days. It truly is a miracle that more people were not injured during these rowdy times.

One other side to all of this, was that November 4th, the night before Bonfire Night, became established as Mischievous Night. I mention this with some embarrassment, as it became an excuse for a lot of behaviour that in hindsight was pretty bad. Much of it was another excuse to raid the neighbourhood for more chumps.

Despite all this, I mostly look back on the Bonfire Night festivities as a fun time, filled with some excesses.

I think that in the country areas, with a plentiful supply of trees, bushes, etc., they had great bonfires, without the excesses that were part of the inner-city experience.

Winter

Winter was always a difficult time. We could only afford one sack of coal per week (if we were lucky), and coal was sold by weight. The coalman used to leave his truck outside overnight, so that the coal would absorb more water and weigh more. My mother hated that. We also used to throw anything that might burn into the "coal hole" to add it to the fire with the coal—old shoes, anything that would help the coal last a little longer.

The Yorkshire coal mines were in the area south of Leeds and we had several coal miners living in the streets around us. If they were underground workers, they were entitled to a large quantity of coal for free, once per month. This was usually dumped in the street outside of their houses. They and their families had to work quickly to get it inside before nightfall and the arrival of anybody who might steal some of their precious coal.

My mother's mother had taught her how to make a "pegged" rug from scraps of clothing. So, one winter pastime was to turn the kitchen table over and stretch a piece of sacking over the four legs. We would then take old clothes and cut them into diagonal strips, and this would be a winter project for all of us during those cold winter months.

The winter of 1947 was a record one for cold and snow. We used to trek for miles, finding hilly streets with fresh snow to use our cheaply made sleds.

As I write these recollections now in 2020, I realize that I am going back to 1945. That's seventy-five years ago: three-quarters of a century!

My explanations to Paula about how everyday life was in those days must seem unreal to her.

- No household refrigerators—just a stone shelf in a pantry, which meant that you had to shop daily for milk and fresh foods.

- One integrated "Black Lead Polish" fireplace—oven—copper boiler. About once per year, when the soot fell down the chimney, the whole room was covered in fine black powder and everybody had to help to clean up.

A LIFE IN STAGES

- No washing machines—just a copper boiler that relied on the coal fire for heating the water and then washing the clothes in the boiler using a "posser" to pound the clothes.

- No dryer. On a cold or wet day, clothes were hung on an indoor clothes rack, suspended from the kitchen ceiling over the fireplace. On a clear day, clothes were hung on a washing line across the street in front on the house.

- Outdoor toilets, shared by two houses—Going to the toilet in wintertime was not fun.

- No domestic telephones—arrange to call your boyfriend/girlfriend from two public phones at the same time!

- No TV—Only the radio, daily newspapers and the local cinema.

- One pair of shoes at a time, sometimes one shirt at a time, with the collar cut-off and turned around, when worn out.

But we were still happy and these really were the good old days!

I love fish and chips. I have for as long as I can remember, and I probably always will.

As you know by now, I grew up in Leeds, and despite what anybody from other parts may tell you, there are no better fish and chips to be found anywhere. I've heard people say that they used to have good fish and chips in Bradford and even in Keighley, but I'm not certain. I'm not sure who lays claim to the famous Harry Ramsden's, as it's in Guiseley and we only went there on days when we went hiking around the dales.

There were six fish and chip shops within five minutes walking distance from our house.

Usually they were run by a couple, with the man cutting the fish and chips in the back room and bringing them out to place carefully in the incredibly hot deep fryers. The lady would be busy serving customers and the two of them would bring the chips out of the boiling fat and up into the holding bins to check the fish and make sure that it was done just right. They had little red wheals up their forearms as a result of the unavoidable splashes of boiling fat (an occupational hazard). Usually they had some extra help at the busy times (lunch time and 9:00 to 11:30 pm after the pubs closed). Last orders in the pub at 10:00, closed by 10:30, and then out to the nearest decent fish and chip shop.

I remember the Fenton Street shop for asking the customers to bring in their used newspapers, and I can still hear the distinctive rip as the lady tore them into sheets for wrapping. Sometimes, if they were particularly short of paper, they would give us kids a helping of free chips for bringing in an extra-large bundle of newspapers. I wouldn't want to say where we got the newspapers from, but I don't believe that anybody came to any harm. During the war and just after, when food rationing was still in place, my mother's friend Liza used to get her weekly ration of corned beef (four ounces) cut at Mullin's Butchers, across the street, and take it into the fish shop at the bottom of our street, where they would obligingly batter and deep fry it for her.

I remember the Carlton Fish Shop and the lovely lady who ran it with her husband. She was always pleased to see us, and if we were wearing our grammar-school caps, she would ask how we were doing and usually give us an extra-large helping of scraps. If you wanted a "special," a little larger piece of haddock or cod, it was best to call out, "One special please, love," as you entered the queue, so that you wouldn't have to wait when it was your turn to be served. Scraps were the little bits of batter that floated off as the fish were cooking—most fish shops used to add a few scraps to the chips. At the Carlton Fish shop, they used to take any fish that just didn't seem right, too well done or too small, and break it into small pieces among the scraps. A good reason to go there more often.

I remember the Blackman Lane Fish Shop particularly well, with its black and green plastic-panelled décor. I could just see over the top of the counter if I stood on my tiptoes. Fish were sixpence and eight pence and chips were tuppence and four pence. Blackman Lane was the first fish shop that I remember selling those delicious Yorkshire fish cakes for three pence. (They were made by putting a thin slice of fish between two slices of potato, coating them with the fish batter, and deep frying them with the fish. When we were kids, my mum couldn't afford fish for me or my little brother Michael, so we had to settle for a fish cake and chips. I still love them and remember them with great nostalgia.

My sister Olive was eight years older than me, and if the money was there, she qualified as a grown up and had a fish with the other adults.

The frying ranges were wondrous contraptions with stainless steel compartments for just about everything and they had confident-sounding names like "ACME" and "PRESTIGE."

As I grew a little older and ventured farther afield, I came across other good fish shops, which were well run, usually by the same family over many years. My first memory of these other good fish shops was when my father took me to one by the side of Kirkgate Market. Up a small flight of stairs and you could sit down and have tea and bread and butter with your fish and chips. I was only eight or nine and I thought that it was quite posh at the time. Youngman's on New Briggate, close to the Odeon Cinema and another wonderful establishment, Nash's, up the side street just off New Briggate, opposite the Tower Cinema are two that come to mind.

Going to Leeds Modern School meant that I had to get the tram to Lawnswood, to and from school. It took me past many good fish shops that I would patronize in later years. Three that stick in my memory were: Bryan's, just behind the Headingley tram depot; Brett's, set back in an end terrace house in North Lane close to the Lounge Cinema; and one on Headingley Lane, just across from the Shire Oak Pub.

Many years later when I was managing the Fine Fare Supermarket in Crossgates, I thoroughly enjoyed the wonderful fish and chips from Coe's, another well-run establishment that was and still is, a popular fixture of the Crossgates area.

North Vs. South

No contest really, I only mention it in case somebody thinks that I've overlooked that other part of England with its own traditional foods. Have you tried eel pie or pig's trotters?

When I first returned to London, I found that strange things could be done with fish and chips: cook them in oil (rather than fresh lard) to give them a slightly odd taste,) or use unpopular fish with deceptively exotic names.

Enough said!

I'm sure that there were isolated examples of good fish and chip shops in these other places, but not the profusion that existed in Leeds in the '40s and '50s. The only other place where I found consistently good fish and chips was in Aberdeen, where there are many good fish shops and they have a lovely custom of serving additional portions of fish.

Quality

I've often heard people deride fish and chips as being typically English, poor quality food, for people with no taste. I can understand that point of view, having had some of the awful fish and chips that are so bad, they give the whole lot a bad name. Why is it that fish and chip shops in seaside resorts like Blackpool and Scarborough and around the world, have such dreadful fish and chips?

But there's something special about good fish and chips that the critics often miss. My mother used to say it all came down to the batter and keeping the fat fresh. I'm sure that she was right. Whatever it was, there is something very special about fish and chips done well. (See "Fish and Chips Part 2"—Appendix 1."

FRANK FARR

The Radio

This period of my life was before television, and in today's world it is impossible to reflect clearly on how influential radio was in those days. Listening to *Family Favourites* on a Sunday at noon was a national tradition, followed by a never-ending series of comedy shows such as *It's That Man Again* (*ITMA*), and *Hancock's Half Hour* followed by the evening news. The drama series such as *Valentine Dial: The Man in Black* could be truly scary.

Later, there was *Pirate Radio*, which had started on Radio Luxemburg, with the most popular show broadcast at 11:00 pm on Saturday night. Jack Jackson with the "Top Twenty" records. Listening to this on a hand-held radio with a "cat's whisker" antenna was quite the challenge.

Cinemas

The cinemas played a big part in our lives. There were six cinemas within a mile of where we lived and another eight cinemas in the city centre.

The Carlton and Gaumont Cinemas were typical. One main feature on Monday, Tuesday, and Wednesday, followed by another main feature on Thursday, Friday, and Saturday with another one just for Sunday. I can only imagine how many movies we saw over those years.

The Odeon, at the corner of Briggate and The Headrow was the premier cinema in Leeds. There were two cinemas at City Square. The Tatler, next door to Yate's Wine Cellar and the News Theatre, next door to the City Station. The Tatler showed mainly foreign films and I did see a couple of famous French movies that I remember: *The Wages of Fear* and *Les Diaboliques.*

The movies were classified as U (universal) A (adult) or H (horror). X-rated movies came a little later. You had to be accompanied by an adult to see an A-rated movie and I remember that we used to linger near the entrance with our admission money, asking adults if they would take us in, and then we would go our own way.

You had to be sixteen to see an A, H or X-rated movie by yourself and I remember the ludicrous time when I decided that I would try to fake it, in order to see an X-film. I think that I was fourteen and it was in 1952. The film was titled, *The Well.* I did not know what to expect but still determined, I stole/borrowed a trilby hat from my father's old wardrobe and donned a long raincoat and literally standing on my tiptoes asked for one adult ticket. I don't think that they really cared, as I received my ticket and entered the darkened cinema to see my first X-film. I was quite pleased at my daring.

Unbelievably, there was no sex or violence; it was a film about a missing child in a small, southern US town and the problem was all about the taboo subject of racial prejudice. So much for X films in 1950.

A LIFE IN STAGES

Kirkgate Market

Leeds Kirkgate Market holds a special place in my memory. I hope that they preserve it forever.

The city centre was only twenty to thirty minutes' walk from Hillary Street and no visit to town was complete without a visit to "The Market."

On the way to town, we would pass The Civic Hall, the office of the lord mayor. I remember that the only Rolls Royce that we ever saw belonged to the lord mayor, and it was usually parked outside. The license plate was MUM1.

One of Kirkgate Market's claims to fame, is that it is the site of the Original "Mark's and Spencer's Penny Bazaar." Although Marks and Sparks (as we called them) had their origins in street markets in Manchester, it was Leeds Kirkgate Market that saw the first permanent stall, located in the upper hall of the market. Marks and Spencer's still have a stall there, selling M&S memorabilia, highlighting the company's origins.

Briggate Street, Leeds—typical Saturday afternoon, 1950

I continue to have incredible nostalgia for the smells and tastes of the fresh-food hall with its Pork Butcher's Row, The Fish Row, The Fresh Meat Row, the Chicken and Poultry Row, and the many Fruit and Veg rows. There was one special "Pork Pie and Peas Shop" in the lower hall, close to the bottom end and the outdoor part of the market.

They say that the taste of food is nostalgic and it's true for me, as good fish and chips and a good pork pie and peas are still among my favourites, on those occasions that I can still enjoy them.

One of my earlier memories of Kirkgate Market was in 1942. We had no money and my mother was really

The Leeds Arcades

Many of the cities in England have arcades, but none have the quantity or quality of the Leeds Arcades. The centre of Leeds is unique in that it is a level area bounded by The Headrow, Boar lane, Vicar lane and Albion Street. Linking all of these streets is a series of wonderful arcades (Covered Shopping streets, protected from the rain and the sun) all preserved in their Edwardian/ Victorian splendour. Queens Arcade, Thorton's Arcade, Grand Arcade, Victoria Arcade, County Arcade (the home of the Mecca Locarno), Central Arcade, Schofield's Arcade, Woolworth's Arcade and Victoria Gate Arcade. The Thorton's (The Ivanhoe Clock)and Grand Arcades (The Pott's Clock) are also famous for their wonderful mechanical clocks.

scratching around for a Christmas present for me. I remember that we ended up in the market and she found a "Compendium of Games" for two shillings and sixpence. That was my present that year. Draughts, Snakes and Ladders, Ludo, some wire puzzles and maybe a couple of others. I've always enjoyed silly board games ever since.

In the '50s, retail stores did not open in the evenings and were not open on Sundays. Most people were working through the day from Monday to Friday and therefore Saturday was the big shopping day, with huge crowds in the city centre.

Holidays

For obvious reasons, we rarely had vacations. I do remember that my mother saved up to take me and my younger brother Michael on a day trip to the coastal town of Bridlington. My first sight of the sea.

When I was seven years old, together with my older sister Olive, I did get to spend several weeks in London with my father, and we still have an old photo of me feeding the pigeons in Trafalgar Square.

Frank—Trafalgar Square 1945

In 1949, I was selected to go for two weeks to Silverdale, the Leeds Poor Children's holiday camp on Morecambe Bay. I only got to stay for the first week, as at the end of it I was told that my father had died, and I was put on the train back to Leeds. I was ten years old.

I remember hearing the sound of the train on the tracks, *clickety clack, clickety clack, it can't be true, it can't be true.*

Shortly before my father died, he had been in Leeds to "give away" my sister Olive Farr, in her wedding to her one and only boyfriend, Stanley Dickinson.

I had transferred from St. Anne's Junior School to Blenheim Secondary School at eight or nine, and I remained there until I passed my Eleven Plus Exam and was granted a grammar school scholarship to Leeds Modern School.

I have two memories of Blenheim Secondary School.

There was a teacher there by the name of Frank Cooper. He was a kindly man who gave me my first encouragement to do my best. It was also Mr. Cooper who gave me the good news that I had passed the Eleven Plus Scholarship Exam and that I would be going to the grammar school in the fall.

The English school system in those days, practiced a form of "streaming." All children took the Eleven Plus exam and if you passed that exam, you were offered a scholarship place in a grammar school. This was subject to a space being available. If you failed the Eleven Plus exam, you had another opportunity at the age of thirteen. If you passed this test, you were offered a place at a technical training school. It was very rare that a child from a working-class family could attend university. Following the war, university enrolment was extremely limited.

Youth Activities

I had a very enjoyable time as a member of a local youth club and on the many hikes that were organized to visit the local Yorkshire Dales. Again, an innocent and wonderful time.

We went to Otley, Ilkley (The Cow & Calf), Bolton Abbey (The Strid), Airedale, Wharfedale, and took the occasional trip out to York

My closest friend at this time was Peter Armitage. He and I used to produce general knowledge quizzes and puzzles for the youth club members to solve. We also did a skit take-off of Fred Astaire and Judy Garland dressed as tramps and singing "We're a Couple of Swells," from the movie *Easter Parade*.

Reading

Although my early school performance, during my years at Blenheim and Leeds Modern School, was checkered, I was always fascinated by words and the English language. This was also supported by my endless search for more knowledge about geography and history.

Encouraged by my mother, I was an avid reader and I remember winning some form of prize for writing an essay about Gandhi, following his assassination in 1947. I had read about him in the papers, and I was amazed that such a little man, clad only in a what appeared to be a bedsheet, with the power of his words and personality could command such attention, meeting with the king and the prime minister.

I read everything that I could lay my hands on. Sometimes a book a day. Go to the public library straight from school, sit on the warm radiators in the library and read, take the book home to bed and read, take the book to school and read, take the book back to the library, finish it off, return it and take out another one.

I read all the typical boy's books: *Biggles* books, *The Jungle Book*, *Kim*, *Gunga Din*, Agatha Christie, *Beau Geste*, *The Four Feathers*, *Treasure Island*, *Kidnapped*, *Robinson Crusoe*, *Gulliver's Travels*, *The Saint* stories, and many more.

It was also during my time at Blenheim that I demonstrated my first sign of rebelliousness. We lived close by and I often used to go home at lunch time with Peter Armitage. This frequently resulted in us being late back to school and we were warned about this several different times.

One day, we went home at lunchtime and realized that we were going to be late back again. So we did the only thing possible and decided to *run away from home!*

We caught the tram to Lawnswood terminus, on the northern outskirts of Leeds, and then proceeded to walk off into Lawnswood Woods, with the idea of disappearing into the woods, *maybe forever!* Near the famous Adel Church, the only Norman structure in Leeds, we found a deserted campground with some wooden tables and chairs and settled in for the night.

I don't know if it was being scared by owls or awakened by hunger, but sometime around midnight, we headed back to the main road and found shelter in a phone box. That was where the police found us and returned us home to grateful but alarmed families. I never had the urge to run away again, but I do think that this was the beginning of the rebellious period of my life.

Peter Armitage lived across the street, and as he was ten months older than me, he preceded me from Blenheim to Leeds Modern School.

Peter came from a large family of ten children and although I knew all of them, Peter and his older brother, David, were the only ones that I was close friends with. I do remember that they were all intelligent and funny, living in a house full of laughter and family jokes.

Down the street from the Armitages were the Bells, another large family, but altogether different from the Armitages. I knew all the family, but only Leonard was a close friend. I call him a friend, but Leonard Bell was our protector. He was an unusually big boy, with the voice of an angel; he used to sing from the stage at the Gaumont Cinema on Saturday mornings. However, he had another side. He would fight anybody at any time, and if he fought, he really was like an animal. Most youngsters in the area were terrified of him. It was good to have Leonard Bell as your friend and the reputation of the Bell family spread across much of north Leeds.

The entire Bell family was notorious. His father and older brothers were window cleaners who had a daily routine. Clean windows in the morning, collect money, and go to the pub for the afternoon and evening, sometimes getting into a fight, and then go home. When Leonard left home, the usual admonishment from his mother was not to steal anything that he could not carry.

Me, Peter and David Armitage, and Leonard Bell—what an odd group, to form such a strong friendship that lasted for a few unusual years.

I started attending Leeds Modern School in 1950 and I was there for about three years. I did not fit in at this school. My closest friends and I were poorer than most of the other kids; we could not afford the better-quality school uniforms and we always stood out (not for the best of reasons). This was when my rebellious streak really took over.

Leeds General Infirmary Hospital/14 Hillary Street—top left corner

CHAPTER THREE

Juvenile Delinquency 1950–1953

Brian Dromey, George Lowther, Peter Armitage, and I formed a small clique that could be relied upon to break all of the rules on a regular basis, whether it was playing truant, chasing the girls from Lawnswood High School (next door), or picking fights with the prefects. We were always in the thick of it.

Leeds Modern School and
Lawnswood High School

Leeds Modern School cap
and badge—
"Fortem-Posce-Animum"

Here are some of my memories from Leeds Modern.

- Being told by my form master, Mr. Fletcher, that he could not deal with me and that if he saw me coming down the corridor, he would take another corridor to avoid me. He said that he found me to be far too argumentative. I was a twelve to thirteen-year-old child, and he was a fifty-year-old teacher, with a cap and gown to protect him—I found this strange.

- Being caught on the school roof, firing an air gun. It was a Webley, purchased by Brian Dromey and was subsequently confiscated for use by the school theatrical society.

- Experimenting by using a hammer to hit a .22 bullet in a bicycle pump tube, which was fixed to a vise in the woodworking shop. The bullet shattered a window (not appreciated).

- Detention: If we misbehaved, there were daily detentions for a half an hour after school on weekdays and if you accumulated too many of these, you had to attend a Saturday morning detention. I had to attend many of these.

- The most serious punishment was to be on the Headmaster's Report. This meant that you had a report that had to be signed by each teacher at the end of each class, and turned in to the headmaster's office at the end of each day. If the report was considered not good enough, the headmaster would give us "six of the best" strokes of a cane on our backsides. I can remember this vividly and as you might expect, I rebelled even more strongly.

Each morning at the school assembly (550 boys), the roll call of those on Headmaster's Report would be read out loud: Frank Farr, Peter Armitage, Brian Dromey, George Lowther, Derek Anthony! If I sit back and quietly think, I can hear that headmaster's voice to this day.

We were quite proud of our notoriety, but it all had to come to an end, and I believe that the headmaster, Mr. Holland, was very pleased when within a short period we were all gone from Leeds Modern School.

About this time, I became more and more of a juvenile delinquent. I think they called us "tykes" at the time.

It began slowly at first and then accelerated. I did not know it at the time, but there was a wave of juvenile delinquency that was occurring across Britain and the US.

I think that during these years, the young people were caught between the "pre-war" expectation that "young people should be seen but not heard," and the feeling of the '50s in which young people wanted to speak up and be heard.

This phenomenon was exemplified in such movies as *Rebel without a Cause* with James Dean, *Blackboard Jungle* with Glenn Ford, and the film that became a sensation in the UK: *Rock around the Clock* with Bill Haley.

I mention this, because when *Rock around the Clock* arrived in the UK, teenagers across Britain started dancing to the music in the aisles of the cinemas and would not stop, despite all of the authorities protesting. By the time it came to Leeds (I think it was at the Odeon), we were primed. When you get dozens of young boys dancing in the aisle and ushers trying to stop them and throw them out, anything is likely to happen and it did. Collapsed rows of seats and fights breaking out, were enough to make the headline news.

However, despite this youthful exuberance, my adventures with my small group of friends began to take on a new dimension—one that would change all of our lives and change mine in ways that I could never have imagined.

A LIFE IN STAGES

Firstly, without any prior knowledge on my part, four of my closest friends committed an outrage, one that I have never understood to this day. They attacked a local shopkeeper (the ice cream parlour) and robbed her cash register. This was inexplicable, since they all knew the shopkeeper and she knew them. They were quickly arrested and sent for trial. All four were sentenced to time in an approved school, and because of the violence of their offence, they were sent to The Outward-Bound School in North Wales. This was a forerunner of the franchised Outward Bound Schools that exist around the world today. In the 1950s, there was only one such school, run by ex-military men with a very strict and tough regime. Up in the morning for cold showers, rigorous exercise for most of the day, with mountain /rock climbing on weekends. These young teenagers thought that they were tough. They were soon exposed to what tough means, explained to them by people that you didn't argue with.

There was no way that I could ever have participated in such a scheme and I have never understood how this could have happened, without my knowledge, by people who were my closest friends.

My comeuppance was a little different. My best friends from grammar school were gone and I was left with David Armitage and Leonard Bell. They were both two years older than me but more adventurous and less law abiding, to put it politely.

I don't know why, but we always got in trouble on Sundays. Most businesses were closed on Sundays and living close to the centre of Leeds, as we did, what started off as adventures soon became something more.

One of the ways of showing daring was to climb things. We practiced on the unfinished Parkinson Building close by (this is the Leeds University Tower). In many cases, we climbed up drainpipes on the outside of buildings. It is one thing to climb up a rickety drainpipe for two, three, or four stories on the outside of a building and onto the roof. It is another thing entirely to lie on the roof facing down to the ground and slide back onto the drainpipe to get back to the ground.

There was one obvious solution. Break a window and come down inside the building and let yourself out on the ground floor. Unfortunately, this constitutes "break and enter" or "burglary," and this is a crime.

The first time that we were caught doing this resulted in my going to a juvenile court and being sentenced to probation. This happened twice. Undeterred, we carried on our merry way, not always being aware that these incidents were being reported to the police.

Leeds University—Parkinson Building, Woodhouse Lane

The grand finale to these adventures was on one Sunday, when we were apprehended on the roofs of some buildings behind the Ritz Cinema. At the time, we were quite pleased to be brought off the roof by a fire ladder that the police had summoned. This was about 5:00 pm. The queue for the Sunday cinema was forming, and we thought it great that people that we knew could see us being brought down to the "Black Maria" (a police van) waiting to take us off to Millgarth Police Station, where we were charged with sixteen such offences. The next stop was The Leeds Juvenile Remand Home in Lower Wortley.

Roaming around these inner-city buildings, we would occasionally come across signs on a wall proclaiming, "Ancient Lights." This was a centuries-old way of protecting the right of letting daylight into a building. One way to deal with this was to have new buildings constructed with white-glazed bricks facing the "protected" windows. We came across many examples of this as we wandered around these back-alleys in the centre of Leeds.

One last note on this day. We were not concerned about entering this tough environment, because we had the distinguished company of Leonard Bell, who proudly announced that he would beat up anybody who bothered us. How strange this all seems today.

The Leeds Remand Home was a very strict place. At night-time, we all trooped upstairs, where we changed into pyjamas and placed our day clothes in lockers, cleaned our teeth under supervision, and then went to our dormitories, which were equipped with loudspeakers so that any sound could be picked up by the night supervisors.

Two things remain clearly in my mind. One is of no real importance, and the other was life changing:

1) Onions

I have always had a problem eating onions. In fact, I will not knowingly eat onions to this day. One day we were served onions with our dinner and I declined to eat mine. This was considered an act of insubordination, and it was demanded that I eat them. I refused. They served them again for my breakfast and advised that I would get no further food until I ate the onions. I refused again. For dinner that night, I was served the dried-up onions on an enamel plate and again told that there would be no more food until I ate the onions. Out of hunger, I tried, and immediately ran to the toilets where I threw up. For daring to be sick, I received a very heavy-handed smack across my face.

The next day, I was in the Juvenile Court for a review of my case. As the review drew to a close, I asked to speak to the magistrate. He agreed and I told him about the incident with the onions. I told him that if he sent me back to the remand home, I would find a way to escape and run away.

Surprisingly, the magistrate was sympathetic. He admonished the people concerned and instructed the policeman to take me over to the canteen in Leeds Town Hall and provide me with a proper meal.

Lesson Learned

A LIFE IN STAGES

If you believe that you are right, don't be bullied by authority and
speak up for yourself, in a reasonable but forceful way!

Once back at the remand home, I felt that I was being treated in a different way and given some respect. They made me a prefect. Unbelievable but enjoyable.

2) IQ Tests

I did not know it, but at this time The Stanford-Binet Intelligence (IQ) tests were in fashion, and the authorities were puzzled as to why so many young people were in rebellion. They decided to try to identify the young leaders and see if there was a correlation between intelligence and outspoken rebelliousness. It seems that there was!

I was taken into one of the offices and subjected to this now famous test. I knew that the result must have been good, since again, I noticed a difference in attitude towards me on the part of the senior staff.

Shortly thereafter, a meeting was arranged with my probation officer, Mr. Peddie, and my mother. Mr. Peddie explained that a place had been found for me at Kneesworth Hall, an experimental residential school, located near Royston in Hertfordshire. It seemed that somebody had coined the phrase "Bright Delinquents" and by definition, I was one of them. This residential school had been recently established to accommodate "Bright Delinquents" and to provide them with a holistic education that would encourage them to play a positive role in society, as they moved into adulthood.

By now, my mother was out of her mind with worry for me. Once she understood the purpose of this proposal, She gave her consent. I am so thankful for her wise, but difficult decision.

The school only accepted boys between fourteen and sixteen, whose IQ was not less than two standard deviations above the norm. The norm for IQ measurements, starts from the average of the population being 100. One standard deviation is 15 and therefore two standard deviations would require an IQ of not less than 130. I later learned that my IQ had been assessed at 156. As I learned more, I realized that this was judged to be very high. I did not appreciate the significance of this until I was faced with some of the challenges later in my life.

This opportunity to get away from the delinquency of my life in Leeds, at the tender age of fourteen, changed my life forever.

Previously, I had still been at Leeds Modern School when King George VI died in 1952. I can clearly remember our form master (in cap and gown), coming into our class with a solemn look on his face and proclaiming, "The king is dead. Long live the queen," and we all trouped outside to see the flag lowered to half-mast.

By the time of Queen Elizabeth's coronation in June of 1953, I had just arrived at Kneesworth and I was delighted to write an essay and be rewarded with a short trip home for the coronation festivities.

There were parties in most streets. I attended one on some spare ground next to the Cankerwell Inn Pub. I can still remember the area being decorated with flags and bunting. All of the long tables were set out and the local mums were busy making food and cakes.

I am ending this chapter in 1953, as this was when my life changed for the better and a completely new life began.

❖

"The station where you begin your life, does not need to be your station at the end of your life. The choice is yours." Frank Farr

CHAPTER FOUR

Bright Delinquents—Kneesworth Hall School—The Simmons 1953–1957

Kneesworth Hall (1)

Mr. Peddie took me by train, the 170 miles to Royston, Hertfordshire. Mrs. Dorothy Simmons met us at the station and drove us to Kneesworth Hall School.

Kneesworth Hall sits in 150 acres of beautiful countryside, including a stream and a small lake. There had been fine homes on this land since the sixteenth century and the various versions of the main home had been owned by the Nightingale family for over 200 years. Florence Nightingale had grown up in this house.

The home was renovated following the Second World War and opened as Kneesworth Hall School in 1949. It was designated as a school for boys of high intelligence between the ages of thirteen and fifteen and dedicated to providing a broader and more advanced, accelerated education, designed to allow these youths to play a positive role in society as they emerged as adults. (I believe that I have lived up to those expectations).

The school, which could accommodate up to fifty boys, was under the control of Mr. Montague Simmons and his wife Dorothy Simmons. Mr. Simmons had been a schools Inspector and had played a role as a part of an international committee that had re-established the Berlin school system following the collapse of Nazi Germany.

Montague and Dorothy Simmons were both intellectuals who possessed a unique empathy for the young boys under their care.

FRANK FARR

First impressions—Lessons learned

Shortly after my arrival, I tried to learn what the new rules were. (I had just left the much stricter environment of the Leeds Remand Home.) Remember that I was a natural rebel. To my surprise, I learned that there were very few "rules." This presented a wonderful opportunity. Instead of reporting for classes at 9:00 am, I could go off to explore the woods and basically do as I pleased. I did this for a few days and then out of boredom, I decided to turn up for classes. *What a difference!*

The classes were typically ten to twelve pupils, the teachers were casual and friendly, and there was no problem in veering away from the curriculum to ask questions. Suddenly, this was fun. It was not unusual for us to stop our classes before dinner and then resume them for the evening, if the topic was particularly interesting. If we agreed, we would also continue these lessons through the weekend. This was a whole new and accelerated approach to education.

The most popular teacher that I had was Mr. Saul; his favourite pastime was completing the *Guardian* crossword each day. He enjoyed asking us to help him and we took great pleasure in doing this.

Despite this relaxed approach, there was a curriculum, and we quickly realized that we were being prepared to complete the GCE examinations that lay ahead of us. We learned that the school's board of governors included representatives of Cambridge University (not too far away) and that at least one of our young members had gone directly from Kneesworth to Cambridge University. Unbelievable.

The experience of living and learning on such a huge estate, in an intellectually aware community, at the age of fourteen, was a profound experience.

Here are some memories:

- The boys were allowed to smoke, and I quickly established myself with a side business, buying and selling cigarettes, starting with the small allowance that we earned on a weekly basis. Mr. Simmons brought this to an end, advising me that being a "tobacco baron" was not what he had in mind for me.

- Mr. Simmons would start each day with an assembly, at which he read aloud his message of the day. I remember very clearly his frequent reading from the meditations of the emperor, Marcus Aurelius. Something in those words resonated with me and I recently reread many of these works, written two thousand years ago. They still have great meaning to this day.

- As a part of our English literature curriculum, we had to study one of Shakespeare's plays on a continuing basis. I still remember many of the more famous quotations from *Macbeth, Julius Caesar, A Midsummer Night's Dream, A Merchant of Venice* and *Hamlet*. We also studied selected works by Charles Dickens, Rudyard Kipling, and Tolstoy.

- Mrs. Simmons was a violinist and a sculptress. She had a studio in the loft and we were invited to join in. I derived great pleasure from creating what I thought were masterpieces: bookends, and plaster heads.

A LIFE IN STAGES

For the first time in my life, through my visits to their flat on the top floor of this wonderful house, I experienced the luxury of wall to wall carpets, nice furniture, paintings, and sculpture. I particularly remember their Pye "Black Box" record player.

This left such a strong impression on my juvenile mind that I resolved that one day, I too would live in a nice home with carpets and furniture, complete with art, books, and sculpture.

I also discovered the next food item that I would learn to dislike. *Mustard!* One of our duties was to share the responsibility of washing dishes after meals. Standing over a sink, washing dishes from fifty or so people, most of whom had left stale mustard on their plates, I soon learned to dislike the taste/smell of mustard. I still can't stand mustard to this day.

Frank at Kneesworth Hall School 1953

Based on our results of the week, we earned a small amount of pocket money. With this we were able to take the school bus into the local town, Royston. This included visits to the open-air swimming pool and to the local cinema, The Priory. We had competition for the local girls with the trainee jockeys from the local racehorse facilities on the Royston Downs. I did have an innocent friendship with a very pretty local girl. She used to take me to her house for tea and sandwiches. I remember her for her unusual name, Ethne Buttery.

I had arrived at Kneesworth in January 1953. In May of 1954, the Simmons' decided that I should be allowed to return home on license. (probation). I refer to this as my first time as Kneesworth Hall, as I was destined to return.

On leaving Kneesworth in 1954, at the age of sixteen, I got my first job in the advertising office of *The Yorkshire Post*.

In my leisure time, I was quickly caught up in the latest fads of the day, and this included my "Teddy Boy" period. It would take too much time to document the Teddy Boy phenomenon, but basically, the youth of the day affected copies of Edwardian-style clothing, as a means of group identification, and proceeded to disrupt most of what they came in touch with. There was rowdiness, drinking, dancing, and chasing girls. All of this became a full-time occupation.

I also remember my first date with a very attractive girl from the *Yorkshire Post* office. I went by tram to the Crossgates terminus, as we were to meet at the Barnbow factory for a Saturday night dance. No sooner had I arrived at the dance, than I was surrounded by local youths who had decided that they did not want "outsiders" going out with girls from their area. I was escorted back to the tram terminal and swung over the tram lines, until a tram arrived to take me back to where I belonged, on the north side of Leeds.

Tribalism was a built-in part of our youth culture.

31

My version of the style of these times was a tailored black gaberdine suit. It had a knee-length jacket, link button, rolled silk collar, half-moon slit pockets, and tight trousers with twelve-inch bottoms. I wore black suede shoes with 1.5-inch wedge heels and rainbow socks.

My mother was aghast and said that I looked like a big black beetle.

To make matters worse, the group that I was with all had their own version of this style, but frequently in different colours. A purple suit, a lime-green suit, etc. As we roamed the streets, we would switch jackets, creating a bizarre appearance that attracted comments. This often led to the challenge "What are you looking at?" followed by some form of altercation.

I thought that all of this was just fine. But my mother was alarmed and worried that I would soon find myself in trouble again.

One day, early in 1955, I arrived home from work, to find Mr. and Mrs. Simmons at our house in Hillary St. We had some conversation and then they advised me that they were revoking my "license" and that I had to return to Kneesworth with them that night! I never saw my wonderful suit (my mother destroyed it) or the *Yorkshire Post* office again.

Kneesworth Hall (2)

My second stay at Kneesworth was short but more fulfilling. I had returned as a more senior boy, and this resulted in my being assigned more responsibility.

I organized lots of activities: dances with the trainee teachers from the Saffron Waldon Teacher's Training College, and group trips to Cambridge and the Norfolk Broads. I had a new girlfriend, one of the student teachers from Saffron Waldon.

I also created a "Record Club." This was quite good, as I collected a penny each from most of the boys and used the funds to buy records for our collection. The best part was that I got to choose the records. It was not long before the hall rang out with the sounds of my new-found friends: Ella Fitzgerald, Sarah Vaughan, Frank Sinatra, Tony Bennet, Frankie Laine, Johnny Ray, Duke Ellington, Count Basie. And of course. Louis Armstrong. What pleasure there is in such music. On one sunny afternoon, I managed to climb onto the huge cedar tree outside my dormitory window, hook-up a record player, and proceed to sunbathe while blasting out my favourite jazz records. This session did not last too long.

Kneesworth Hall School—giant cedar tree outside dorm window

A LIFE IN STAGES

Although this was enjoyable, there was a serious side to this second stay. Mr. and Mrs. Simmons had taken a more personal interest in me and wanted to ensure that when I left Kneesworth this second time, they had instilled in me all that they could.

- Mrs. Simmons invited me to join the debating group that she had in their flat on a weekly basis. These sessions were enlightening, as she often invited one or more of her distinguished friends to join in. On two occasions, she invited me to lead the debate. One was on "The Future of the British Empire." I proposed that it would last for a hundred years (I lost that one), and the other was on "The Morality of the Death Penalty." I proposed its abolition (I won that one).

- Both Montague and Dorothy told me they believed I would do well in life, but I had to remember that this involved responsibility for others. They counselled me that I should be careful in how I exercised that responsibility and to try to have a positive impact on those whose lives crossed mine.

- Mr. and Mrs. Simmons explained to me that, based on my GCE results, if I wanted to work hard and stay at Kneesworth until I was eighteen, they could try to arrange for me to apply for admission to Cambridge.

They arranged for me to be interviewed by a member of the board of governors. Dr. King was an Economics don, a master at Pembroke College in Cambridge, and a very gracious older gentleman. I went to meet him at his college across the main quadrangle and up the stairs. A note on the door read, "Dr. King lives in the cupboard behind you." Just one of those odd Cambridge eccentricities. The cupboard door opened into a stepdown to a huge room and living quarters. I spent the morning talking with him ("call me Rufus") and then he took me on an afternoon walking tour of Cambridge, showing me many of the oddities of this wonderful town.

At the end of our time, he said that he would consider sponsoring me. He explained that I would need at least four more "A" levels and that one of them should be Economics. I dreaded this, but he said that if I made a start and showed some promise, he would consider tutoring me closer to the exams.

I didn't fully appreciate this remarkable offer. In any event, I thought that I should be back home, working and supporting my mother and younger brother, as they were struggling financially. I opted to return home to Leeds.

- Montague and Dorothy Simmons were like second parents to me. I visited them on numerous occasions, including at their final home at Brockwood Park in Sussex. This was one of the four schools in the world dedicated to the teachings of Krishnamurti. Mrs. Simmons was a strong convert, and she told me that one of the key learnings was always to "question the status quo." I remained in touch with them for the remainder of their lives. After Montague died following a heart attack, I was fortunate to have one last time with Dorothy, when she visited Vancouver Island for the opening of the Krishnamurti school at Wolf Head Park near Victoria. She died peacefully in her sleep within a few weeks of our meeting in 1990.

I left Kneesworth for the second time in November 1955, and I shall forever remain in Dorothy and Montague Simmons's debt, for the guidance and care they gave me during those two stays at Kneesworth in the 1950s.

Frank–1956, Woodhouse Moore, Leeds

The experience had changed me from a "bright delinquent" into a relatively sensible young man, although it would be several years before the real lessons that I learned from the Simmons' could play any part in my life.

I still had some wild oats to sow and some life to experience. I returned to Leeds and 14 Hillary Street.

The years from November 1955–May 1957 were interesting, but mainly fun. I got a job working in Gould's Menswear store, close to the Corn Exchange, spending most of my leisure time chasing girls and going to the dance halls and subsequently to the jazz clubs that were beginning to appear.

Dance Halls

There were five major dance halls in Leeds during the early '50s. By major, I mean that they could accommodate up to 500 dancers, and they were generally open five nights per week.

The most famous one was The Mecca Locarno, in the Mecca Arcade, just off Briggate, followed by The Scala on Albion Street; The Majestic in City Square; The Astoria on Roundhay Road; and the much smaller Mark Altman's, close to Leeds Infirmary. There were several other dance venues, but these were the most established ones.

Peter Armitage and Frank—Leeds 1957

Pubs

Making our way to these dance halls on a regular basis, led to the development of a routine list of pubs to visit along the way. The Pack Horse, The Fenton, The Cankerwell Inn, The Black Swan (The Mucky Duck), The Robin Hood and The Town Hall are the ones that come to mind, but there were many others.

These were good times and it was during this time that I reconnected with Peter Armitage, met Joy, his future wife, and also met Doreen Abbott to whom I quickly became engaged.

A LIFE IN STAGES

We did this with little thought. Several of our friends had become engaged and it seemed like a good idea at the time. In those days, most young people got engaged (usually for a couple of years) and then got married, often with little expectation of what lay ahead.

Jazz and Jazz Clubs

My interest in jazz had awakened during my time running the record club at Kneesworth, and following my return to Leeds, my passion grew, almost to an obsession. Changes in union rules had paved the way for American musicians to perform in England and this caused a wave of legendary artists to perform in concerts around the country.

I could not wait to crisscross England to see live performances from such greats as Ella Fitzgerald, Louis Armstrong, the varied All-Stars that toured with the Jazz at The Philharmonic (JATP) concerts, and the incredible bands led by Duke Ellington, Count Basie, Stan Kenton, and others.

This invasion of American stars let to the growth of English bands. Ted Heath, Humphrey Littleton, Bob Collier, Johnny Dankworth, and Chris Barber, were among the more popular ones. There was also the emergence of "Skiffle bands." The most successful of these was an offshoot of the Chris Barber Band led by Lonnie Donegan.

Doreen Abbott and Frank at the Scala Ballroom, Leeds

The emergence of these local bands led to the arrival of jazz clubs, located in most cities, often in basements. The most famous was "Ronny Scott's" in London, which is still open to this day. The best one in Leeds was The Oasis. It was created by a local tuba player and located in a basement off Upper-Briggate, between The Odeon and the Assembly Rooms. I spent many late-night/all-night sessions at The Oasis.

But again, this particular phase of my life was coming to an end.

One day, shortly following my engagement to Doreen, I went to her home to find that the family was seriously considering emigrating to Southern Rhodesia. I was not too keen on this, given my understanding of politics in South Africa and the future of the British Empire, but I agreed to consider joining them. Within a month or so, they had changed their minds and were considering emigrating to Canada. After some deliberations, I agreed to join them, and we departed for Canada in May of 1957. I was eighteen years old.

There was Doreen's mother (her father had died on active duty during the war) and stepfather John, her older sister Jean, and her younger brother Derek, together with me and Keith Watters, a friend of mine.

The voyage to Canada took seven days (Southampton to Montreal) and the cost of fifty pounds was paid by an immigration grant from the Canadian Government.

35

FRANK FARR

When we left, I packed everything that I owned into a small "steamer trunk." My mother had bought it for a few shillings from a second-hand store at the bottom of our street. It was old and had seen better days. My mother disinfected it and lined it with some spare wallpaper left over from a kitchen project. She also gave me a blue-check woollen blanket, as she knew that it could be very cold in Canada. Now, sixty-four years and twenty-plus homes later, I still have that old steamer trunk and the blue-checked blanket. Dear memories of my mother and a trip to the unknown all those years ago.

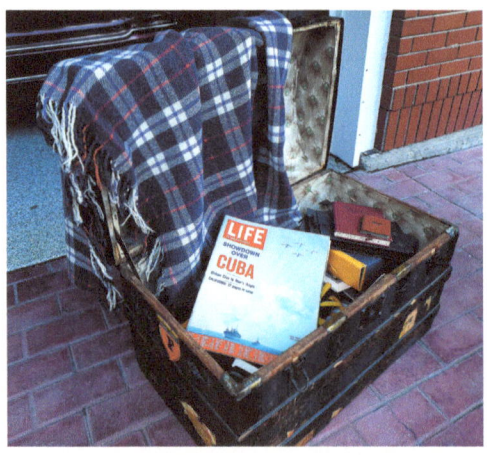

The steamer trunk and the blanket
(Frank's sole possessions in 1957)

Frank's old diaries

We left for Canada in May of 1957 and less than a year earlier, a new entertainment phenomenon had arrived in the United States, Canada, Britain, and the rest of the world: Elvis Presley. Elvis would change the face of popular music in a way that had never been done before. At the same time, back in Liverpool, a thirteen-year-old girl and her friends were also discovering Elvis. Her name was Ann Pope. She was also the proud owner of a "five shilling piece" that she had received from attending the 1953 coronation parties in Liverpool. Ann had also passed the Eleven-Plus examination and was attending Maghull Grammar School.

❖

"You will probably enjoy success and authority in your life. Please remember not to harm those over whom you have authority." Montague Simmons.

❖

"Always question the status quo. Don't set limits. There are no limits to what you may do with your life." Dorothy Simmons

CHAPTER FIVE

Canada—Loblaws and Buffalo
1957-1961

We arrived in Canada in May of 1957. What to expect?

It was a big year for immigration to Canada in 1957, mostly from Britain and Europe. The Russian invasion of Hungary, in 1956, had caused thousands to flee. Many went to England and then to Canada, along with the large number of Scots and English who had made the decision to give Canada a try.

Paid for by a fifty GBP (pound) grant from the Canadian government, we departed from Southampton, on board the *SS Homeric,* the flagship of the Italian Passenger Line.

I was familiar with the geography of Canada from looking at maps and globes, but nothing could have prepared me for what lay ahead. Our first sight of Canada was the little townships that dot the shores of the St. Lawrence River. We disembarked in Montreal, where we obtained our "pink slip," granting us permission to live in Canada. Then we went by train from Montreal to Toronto. I still remember being amazed by the sheer size of the areas that we travelled through, compared to the relatively small spaces in England.

Frank on the SS Homeric – 1957

The government had arranged accommodation for us in the Ford Hotel in central Toronto. The rooms were equipped with coin-operated radios. This was an unexpected novelty, and I think that the top records of the day were Elvis Presley's "Heartbreak Hotel," "Hound Dog," and "Blue Suede Shoes," along with a couple of songs by Pat Boone.

It was very warm at the end of May and we wandered around the streets of our new home. As you might expect, I found a basement jazz bar. The unexpected part was that the doorman was the same doorman from The Oasis jazz bar in Leeds. He had also just arrived in Toronto!

37

I can't remember the details, but Doreen and her family went to a flat in the centre of Toronto, and Keith Watters and I ended up in a bed and breakfast house on Palmerston Blvd. I did not realize it at the time, but in its prime Palmerston Blvd. had been home to some of Toronto's wealthier families; the original Weston family had lived on this street, back in the late 1800s.

We had no money and no jobs. I used to approach the newspaper boxes, pretend to deposit coins, take a newspaper, look at the jobs section, and then walk for miles looking for work. It was a time of high unemployment in Ontario.

We had been advised not to accept any job that paid less than $1.25 per hour. The first wages that I earned were after I replied to a newspaper article offering jobs at $75 dollars per week. "Meet a Mr. Richardson at one of the local hotels." The job was to sell encyclopaedias, on a door-to-door basis, on commission. Not really a good prospect, although I did sell one set, got my money ($10) and left. There was something intrinsically wrong with selling sets of twenty-five encyclopaedias to newly arrived immigrants who often spoke little English, for "Less than the cost of a newspaper per day."

Loblaws

The owner of the B&B told us that Loblaws (the local supermarket chain) were hiring. So off we went to the Loblaw Head Office (at Fleet and Bathurst St.) at 7:00 am, only to find approximately one hundred other people lined up in the street, looking for the same jobs.

The first thing that happened was a man appearing from the office to declare, "Sorry, no jobs, all gone." At this, about half of the people walked away from the line-up. Forty or so remained.

Then the same man appeared with the new message, "There is no point in you staying, unless you have retail experience." More left, but Keith and I stayed. We were the only ones dressed in suits and ties, and I think that this helped, because within a short time, we were invited in. We signed an application form and were told to report to one of the local Loblaw supermarkets the following day. The starting pay was $1.15 per hour.

Get a System

I don't know how to describe the work at Loblaws except to say that it was non-stop and almost impossible to keep up. I was assigned to look after the dairy section, and I literally ran from one task to another. When I had been there a couple of weeks, I happened to comment to another employee that the pace of work was tough. In the nicest way possible, he told me that they were going easy on me because I was new. He said that the guy who'd had the dairy section before me, also had the twenty-foot-long canned goods section. I told him that this was impossible. but his only reply was, "You've got to get a system."

There was no organized training, you either learned on the job or you lost your job. They were only required to give you two hours' notice.

Several of the other staff members offered tips on how to get things done faster. This usually came down to "no wasted motions."

On reflection, Loblaws were the ones that "had a system." High unemployment meant that nobody wanted to lose their jobs, and if you could adjust to the required pace of work, you might keep your job. I managed to figure out how to do the work. This was a medium-sized supermarket.

Within a few months, Doreen's stepfather had secured a job at Stelco, the mammoth steel foundry in Hamilton (about fifty miles from Toronto). I applied for a transfer and later that summer, I started work at the huge Loblaw supermarket at the Jockey Club location on Barton St. in Hamilton. This would be my home for most of the time that I remained in Canada.

One of my first sights was to see a 1957 Chevrolet Impala, parked in the front of the store. It was a give-away in a prize contest. I thought that this was amazing! I could not imagine this happening in England.

The workload was daunting, as this was the second biggest Loblaw supermarket in Ontario, and it was very busy. I was assigned to take care of the huge dairy department and the massive, forty-foot-long, canned food section, and somehow, I managed to "get a system." We used to sell 2,000 litres of milk per day, on the busy days.

You learn how to pick up four litres of milk in one movement, how to pick up four cartons of eggs in one movement, how to load shelves quickly by spinning the cans in your hands to make sure that the English label faces the front, how to face up shelves as you work—all in the need to eliminate, or reduce "wasted motions."

It is amazing now to think that without any compulsion from management there was an unofficial race between all of the full-time staff. It was a matter of pride to see who could do the most work in the least time, and yet, it was all very enjoyable and the ones that worked the hardest and did the most were the ones most likely to be promoted. Once I realized this, I worked harder and was successful in being promoted, eventually to Assistant Manager. In all of this we were supported by our "Saturday Boys". Part time students who worked Thursday, Friday evenings and all day Saturday.

Having already established my dislike of onions and mustard, I now added a new one: *garlic*. All of the staff had sections that they were responsible for. At the same time, we all had to work the cash registers during busy periods. Our store was in the Italian area of Hamilton and for me, there was nothing worse than having customers with heavy "garlic breath" lean into my face and say, "How much is that?" I have not been able to stand garlic ever since.

I had no idea that this fast pace of work would give me such an advantage in later years at Fine Fare.

FRANK FARR

Doreen Abbott

Doreen Abbott was a good-looking, good natured, young girl, easy going, who wished no harm to anybody. A good person.

Doreen did not take to Canada and I did. I quickly made friends and started to take to the Canadian way of life. Doreen just wanted to stay home with her family, and she became very reclusive. Reluctantly, we broke up within a few months of my arrival in Hamilton.

In the meantime, I continued to extend my friendships and my enjoyment of Canadian life: "nickel and dime" poker parties with my friends, hitting the bars in Hamilton, or going on long-weekend fishing trips with my friends from work. I had several casual girlfriends during this time, but nothing of a steady nature.

In February 1959, I decided to return to England. (Immigrants were often a little homesick after the first year in their new country and wanted to go home. They used to call it the $1,000 cure.) This gave me my first experience of New York. I spent a week there, before embarking on the SS Sylvania for Liverpool.

Frank on the SS Sylvania 1959

I did the usual sightseeing things: Statue of Liberty, Empire State Building, Rockefeller Centre, Radio City Music Hall. On my first day in New York, I met a couple of English girls and persuaded one of them to join me in seeing Bobby Darin at the Copa Cabana Nightclub. On the second night, I found the Metropole Bar in Times Square and had the unique experience of seeing several jazz greats on the stage only a few feet from my bar stool. (No cover! No minimum!)

Unfortunately, my return to England was a disappointment. Most of my old friends were in the army; Peter Armitage was in Yemen, serving with the Trucial Oman Scouts. The dance halls didn't seem the same and the job prospects didn't look too good. After four months, I decided to return to Canada.

The manager of the Loblaw Supermarket at the Jockey Club location in Hamilton was Norton Delaney, a man that I admired and maintained a friendly relationship with for many years. I was very lucky that when I returned to Canada from my four months in England, Mr. Delaney offered me my old job back, and I resumed my enjoyable life in Hamilton. I now saw Canada from a new perspective. There was a wonderful feeling of space and growth, and opportunity.

I moved into a shared apartment on Mountain Brow Rd. and I bought my first car, a light-blue 1959 Ford Fairlane 500.

I used to go and park on the edge of the "mountain," looking at the city below and listening to two hours of Sinatra on the radio from 12:00 to 2:00 on Sundays.

I continued to collect books and records and enjoy my love of jazz at jazz festivals in Toronto and The Playboy Jazz Festival in Chicago. I also went to several great concerts at the Burlington Inn: Count Basie, Louis Armstrong, Laverne Baker.

And then I found Buffalo.

I went to a dance hall in Hamilton (unlike in England, the girls would seldom dance with you; it was more like a posing contest). I got speaking to a couple of lads from Newcastle and they invited me to join them for a night out in Buffalo. Off we went, and it was the start of a whole new experience. I continued to go to Buffalo for most weekends for the remaining time that I was in Canada

Frank with his first car, a blue 1959 Ford Fairlane 500 outside Loblaw's in Hamilton, Ontario

Buffalo, New York

Buffalo was an after-hours mecca, ninety minutes' drive from Hamilton, with bars open until three am. There was a large African American population and lots of jazz. Many bars were along Genesee St. The main one that I spent a lot of time in was The Kitty Kat, owned by an older couple and managed by a very tough guy, Johnny Caesar.

I had remained friends with Doreen's younger brother Derek, and he and I embarked on regular trips to Buffalo. We'd drive down on Saturday night and drive back on Sunday night or sometimes Monday or Tuesday morning. It was an exciting time and the experience of a lifetime. Some of it was good and some not so good, but it was always an education.

Here are a couple of memories:

- Leaving work on a Saturday night, but going out for a couple of drinks with friends before heading off to Buffalo later that night. Driving in a freezing blizzard on the deserted Queen Elizabeth Highway. Around 1:00 or 2:00 am in heavy snow, the cap of my radiator blew off. Just steam and no water in the radiator. Not knowing any better, I filled the radiator with snow, which evaporated within a couple of miles. I kept repeating this process (and calling my car a few choice names along the way) until I finally arrived in Buffalo around 7:00 am, convinced that I had frostbite. I made my way to my girlfriend's apartment to be greeted with, "What kept you?"

- Arriving in Buffalo one Saturday night and going to the Kitty Kat, to find one of the seating booths taped off and complete with bullet holes. A mafia hit man (a young, innocent-looking college type) had walked into the bar a couple of nights earlier and casually executed two known gangsters who were sitting at the booth. The hit man quickly left the scene and probably left town never to be heard from again. They believed that he flew in from another city and flew out, once he had completed his task. *And I thought that the mafia only existed in movies.*

It was during these trips to Buffalo that I met my next, more serious girlfriend, Mattie Byers. Mattie was an African-American lady from Buffalo and the barmaid at the Kitty Kat. She looked just like a young version of Sarah Vaughan and she loved jazz.

My time spent visiting Buffalo provided a whole new world of experience for me. This was the real world and I experienced it to the full.

In those days, a twenty-six ounce bottle of most liquors cost $4.50 at the liquor store and in the bar, they sold a one-ounce shot, complete with a mixer, for one dollar. This was highly profitable and the bar owners were happy to sell as many drinks as they could. The bars could serve drinks until 3:00 am.

On one occasion, two or three young men came into the bar late, asked for drinks and then proceeded to buy a drink "all round" for the dozen or so people in the bar. The bartender (my girlfriend) was happy to oblige. No sooner had the drinks been served, than the young men produced their ID as New York State Liquor Authority Agents and advised that the bar would be charged with serving after-hour drinks. A clear case of entrapment.

The bar was forced to close for sixty days (actually padlocked) and the five of us (me, my girlfriend, the manager, and the couple that owned the bar) had the dubious pleasure of getting in the back door and consuming much of the bar's inventory during the sixty days. At the end of this time, we went to the local liquor store, loaded up on new inventory at $4.50 a bottle and started back in business at $1.00 a shot or $26.00 per bottle in sales. An interesting way to make a living.

Frank and friends in Buffalo, NY— at a Johnny Mathis show

Gangsters (the real mafia), the numbers racket, bars, and entertainment, were all a part of life in Buffalo. I saw Johnny Mathis at the main night club in Buffalo, and at this time, there was an amazing merging of the record labels: "race" labels, country, and pop music: Ray Charles, Chubby Checker, Jackie Wilson, Etta James, and many others.

A LIFE IN STAGES

I don't know much about race relations in the US today, but I can honestly say that during the two or three years that I was going to Buffalo, I was often the only white person in a bar or sometimes a dance/concert, and I was never uncomfortable or concerned about my safety. The African-American people that I met and shared time with, treated me with respect at all times. I'm sure that having an African-American girlfriend helped.

At the end of each week-end in Buffalo, I would race back to Hamilton early in the morning, just in time to start work and regale my workmates with the stories of my latest adventure in Buffalo. This earned me the nickname "Buffalo Bill."

Frank and friends at a New York nightclub—1961

Niagara Falls

It is an interesting side-note, that to get to Buffalo, we by-passed Niagara Falls. It's a wonderful sight to see, but once the novelty wore off, just somewhere to pass on the way to Buffalo.

But now, this phase of my life was coming to its end.

I had just furnished my new basement suite in #43 Stoney Creek Rd. with new furniture and a new record player and I had my second car, a gorgeous, beige 1961 Ford Starliner.

Frank with his second car, a 1961 Ford Starliner

Frank in Hamilton with his first boxed set of Louis Armstrong records

FRANK FARR

I was becoming bored, though, and looking for a little more adventure, so I decided to join the American Airforce. They had a recruiting office in Hamilton, and I went there, quite determined to sign-up. I thought that I could sign-up for three years and spend time at Burtonwood in England. When I found out that the minimum was five years, I backed out. Best decision ever. Had I joined, I would have been in Vietnam within a couple of years.

But fate had something else in mind.

Loblaws was owned by Mr. Garfield Weston. He had purchased retail food companies all over the world, and had decided to merge five groups of stores in England into one group, under the banner of Fine Fare. He planned to open 500 new supermarkets during the coming years.

Fine Fare was having difficulty in hiring suitable candidates for store manager positions and above. Garfield Weston had this "brainwave." He would recruit 500 young Canadians to go and work for Fine Fare.

The idea was reported in the press, and encouraged by several of my friends who wanted to go, I applied and was asked to attend an interview in the Loblaw head office at Fleet and Bathurst St. in Toronto. I had been there once before, back in 1957 when I'd first arrived in Canada.

By this time, I was the assistant manager in the huge Loblaw Supermarket in Hamilton, and I was selected as a part of the first fifty young Canadians to join Fine Fare in England.

Mr. Weston organized a send-off dinner at the Royal York Hotel in Toronto with Field Marshall Lord Montgomery as the guest speaker. Lord Montgomery had been Britain's leading soldier of the Second World War, and as deputy commander to General Eisenhower, it was "Monty" who formally accepted the surrender of German forces in Europe. He presented us with a signed copy of his memoir *The Path to Leadership*. Still on my bookshelves today.

Frank and the Loblaw group on the Empress of Canada 1961

A LIFE IN STAGES

Mr. Weston shook our hands and said that he hoped some of us would settle down in England, marry, and go on to be senior managers of his company.

When I write this today, it seems unbelievable in consideration of all that happened.

Only 150 young Canadians actually joined Fine Fare, and I was the only one who remained after the end of our contract, married an English girl, and became the youngest director ever appointed to the board of Fine Fare.

I was twenty-two years old when we left Canada on a cold winter's day in 1961. We boarded the Cunard liner the *Empress of Canada* in Halifax and set sail for Liverpool and a new future.

Somebody at Fine Fare noticed that I came from Leeds, and they assigned me to the large Fine Fare Supermarket nearby in Bradford. This was fortunate, as most of my Canadian colleagues were assigned to London where they spent the next two years partying and having all the fun that they had intended. For me, initially living at home with my mother and brother, I had the opportunity to work hard without too many distractions. I began to apply myself to understanding "Supermarketing" and all that it entailed. I also appreciated that Fine Fare's growth presented a great opportunity.

CHAPTER SIX

❖

Ann and Paula
1962–1964

In February–March 1962, the next phase of my life started. This one was dramatically and everlastingly more important than all the events leading up to it, and all the events that followed.

I worked at the Bradford supermarket and then went to the Shipley branch to help them get ready for opening. (The celebrities who opened the store were Elsie Tanner and Len Fairclough from the new hit TV show "Coronation Street."). Shipley Market Square was packed for this event.

Following the Shipley opening, the company opened a new supermarket in Fleetwood near Blackpool, and it was a bit of a disaster. The store opening was so busy that the shelves were stripped and the store was overwhelmed. The Fine Fare regional manager asked if I, along with others, would go and get the store remerchandised and ready for business ASAP. I agreed, but only on the condition that it had to be clear to all concerned that I was in charge. You can only have one boss when there is a need to get people to work together to tackle a big challenge. Things worked out well (after a couple of all-night shifts and a lot of work) and I returned to Bradford.

Following the Fleetwood experience, the Lancashire management asked me to relocate to the Southport branch and lead a group of several trainees in that region. I agreed and together we rented a large house opposite the local hospital.

Within a couple of weeks, they ran into some problems with the manager of one of their supermarkets. This was in Maghull, approximately half-way between Liverpool and Southport. The local supervisor, Vernon Hough, asked me if I would take over this supermarket on an interim basis. I agreed, and on a very rainy morning, I caught the train from Southport to Maghull, got off the train, and asked for directions to

Ann—Southport, 1962

47

Deyes Lane. It was about two miles away, and off I went, trudging through the rain to this unknown store that would change my life forever.

I had to wait in the shop doorway, until somebody arrived with the keys. In the doorway was a young girl (aged seventeen) who was just starting work at the store that day. Her name was Ann Pope. This was the same Ann Pope that I referenced in an earlier chapter. The same Ann Pope who had been infatuated with the early Elvis of 1957, at the time that I originally set sail for Canada.

Ann and Frank 1962

Back in Southport, I had done my usual and found a basement jazz bar on Lord Street. I had gotten into the habit of joining my friends there for Sunday afternoon jazz sessions. One Sunday, Ann came to the jazz club with one of her friends. Her friend was attracted to one of the Canadians that were part of our group.

I asked Ann for a dance and it soon became clear that we were attracted to each other. We began dating, but her older sister Pauline was not too happy with this. I was almost six years older than Ann and the manager of the store where she worked. However, it made no difference and within a couple of months we were inseparable.

I still had not met Ann's parents, when we had a close call while having a drink in the local Maghull pub (The Hare & Hounds). The barmaid, who knew Ann, told her that her dad had just arrived for his daily pint. Ann quickly disappeared into the washroom, until the barmaid told her that the coast was clear. I had sat at the table all this time, nursing two drinks, although I believe that Ann was only drinking a Babycham. We decided that she would invite me home to meet the Pope family.

George and Esther Pope had grown up in Liverpool and raised their family in a typical small home on Nesfield Street. It wasn't too far from the famous grounds of the two local football clubs, Liverpool United (Anfield) and Everton (Goodison Park).

In 1955, they had taken the big step of purchasing their own home and moving out of Liverpool to Maghull, a few miles from the Aintree Racecourse, where the famous Grand National horse race is held each year.

I met the family, George, Esther, Pauline, Ann, Stanley, and Leslie: "The Popes." They seemed to me to be the perfect family (the best family in Maghull!) I had grown up in a single-parent home with no father, and there was a bigger age difference between me and my siblings than there was between Ann and her family. They really did seem like the perfect family.

A LIFE IN STAGES

George and Esther Pope

Ann—age 5

Leslie Pope and Ann—in Maghull England early '80s

Glynnis, Rachael, Kevin, Christopher, Daniel, Stanley Pope, and Ann— in Canada early '70s

    I immediately liked George and Esther, and we remained good friends for the rest of their lives. George was the best example of a good English working man, a decent man with clear values. Esther was a delight. She had that rare ability to laugh at herself and to make everybody around her laugh. I didn't realize then that I would come to treasure the times that we would spend together over the next forty-five years, travelling the world, laughing at every turn, and always enjoying each other's company. I thank Ann for allowing me into the everlasting pleasure of George and Esther's company.

    George was an electrician and a foreman at Imperial Chemical Industries (ICI). We had many a good-spirited discussion. I would call him a "communist" and he would call me a "capitalist," and we would debate the function of unions. Somehow, we found common ground and we developed a long-lasting, mutual respect. Esther had many jobs over the years, from making parachutes during the war, to working at Jacob's Biscuit Factory and the Maghull Dairy.

It was good news that I got on well with Ann's parents, as I had already decided that I would try to convince Ann to marry me. She was young, beautiful, and intelligent. She had inherited her father's common sense and as the saying goes, "common sense is not so common." I had sown my wild oats and thought that the time had come to settle down. I knew within a couple of months that Ann was the one for me.

We had met in February of 1962. I asked George's permission to ask Ann to marry me (she agreed) and following a search of the jewellery shops in Liverpool, we found the ring that we wanted and I proposed at the jazz bar on Lord Street in Southport in September of 1962. I had to leave the Liverpool area for work-related issues and was assigned to manage the Fine Fare Supermarket in Beverley, Yorkshire. For the whole of that winter, it was one mad dash. Dash out of the supermarket at 6:00 pm on Saturday, catch the bus to Hull, and then get the Trans-Pennine Express to Liverpool, stay at Ann's home on Saturday night, and then catch the overnight train on Sunday, back to Hull, catch the bus to Beverley and dash to the store in time to open at 9:00 am on Monday morning. We were sitting in a coffee shop close to Lime Street train station, in Liverpool, when we heard the first record of a new and upcoming group, "Love Me Do" by The Beatles.

Ann and Frank—St. Andrew's Church, Maghull

We were married in St Andrew's Church in Maghull on Saturday March 30th, 1963—Grand National Day!

Ann's sister Pauline, her best friend Pamela, her cousin Barbara and my niece, Pauline, were the bridesmaids. My brother Michael was my best man. My mother and my sister Olive came over from Leeds for the wedding, along with my mother's long-time friend Kay DaCosta. We held the reception in the Lydiate Village Hall, with seventy-plus guests. Vernon Hough and some of my Fine Fare colleagues arrived unexpectedly at the reception.

On the night of our wedding, we stayed at Ann's aunt's home (Aunty Katie) and on the day following the wedding, we set off for our new home in the flat that we'd rented in The Mews, adjacent to the famous Beverley Bar. George and Esther came out to see us in a week's time, bringing all the wedding presents that we had left behind in Maghull. In 2020, fifty-eight years later and on the other side of the world, we still have a few of those wedding gifts.

Within one year, we moved from Beverley to Guisborough and back to Leeds.

A LIFE IN STAGES

Frank and his best man—Michael Farr

St. Andrew's Church—Pauline Pope, Pauline Dickinson, Frank, Ann, Michael Farr, Barbara Jones, Pamela Wright, George Pope, Esther Pope, Olive Farr

Ann and Frank—March 30, 1963. Wedding reception at Lydiate Village Hall

Frank and Ann—at the wedding reception

Ann's Family

Although they were not my direct family, once we were married, I spent more time with my in-laws than I did with my own family. I have nothing but warm memories of all of Ann's family.

Ann's father, George died in 1998, following a short battle with cancer. Her mother, Esther, died in 2009 at the ripe old age of ninety.

Ann leaving Maghull for Beverley

George and Esther Pope

Ann's older sister Pauline was married to Terry Elsby, and they had one son, Alex. Terry has also died, and Alex lives in Liverpool.

In the years between our marriage and 2020, we have also lost Ann's older sister, Pauline (1997), Ann's wonderful "Aunty Katie," George's mother, Emily, and many of Ann's extended family from all parts of Liverpool.

Ann's younger brother Stanley is married to Glynnis and they live in Kelowna in BC's beautiful Okanagan Valley. Their children Christopher, Daniel, Kevin, and Rachel are all dispersed and living as far away as Taiwan.

Ann's other younger brother, Leslie, is married to Elaine and together with their two sons Liam and Kieran they live in Ormskirk, Lancashire, England.

Following our marriage, our lives changed rapidly as my career with Fine Fare escalated and we began a new chapter of our lives.

Before I forget, I should note Ann's continuing passion for her cryptic crosswords. She inherited this from her dad, and I remember buying her first thesaurus. She has now worn through at least two, has a much larger vocabulary than I do, and her last thesaurus is past being dog-eared. She needs a new one!

Ann still has the commemorative five-shilling piece that many children received on the Queen's coronation day over sixty years ago.

However, on February 19th, 1964, the really big event was the birth of our daughter, Paula Ann Farr, in the Leeds Maternity Hospital.

Everybody tells you that the birth of a child will change your life forever. There is no doubt that being parents to Paula has changed and enriched our lives since this day in 1964. There are so many memories of this happy time.

A LIFE IN STAGES

In those days, mothers remained in hospital for up to a week following a baby's birth. Following Paula's birth, I used to leave the supermarket at lunch time and head up to the hospital to visit Ann and Paula. One day, while waiting for a bus, I went down into one of the basement coffee shops to grab a quick drink. While I was there, I went to the washroom and when I came out, I was astonished to see that the manager had closed the shop and locked the door. I was locked inside.

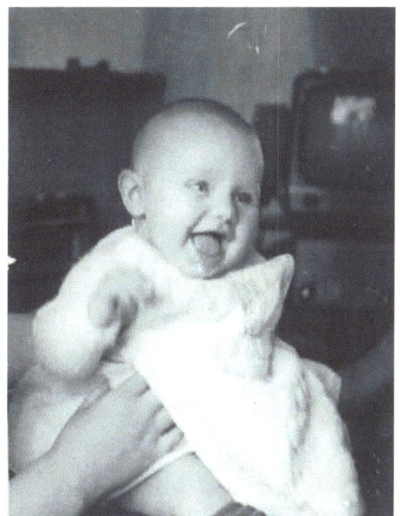

Paula—six months

It took me a little time to realize that my only option was to break out. I had to force open a rear-yard window, climb out, cross the yard, and then climb over a wall. I was convinced that somebody would think that I was breaking in and phone the police. I got away successfully and arrived late at the hospital.

One of the initial conditions of our contract with Fine Fare, was that we would receive a GBP 200 bonus at the end of our two-year contract. I successfully lobbied to get my bonus in advance and we used it to buy new furniture when we set up our first home in Leeds.

In preparation for Ann bringing Paula home, we had purchased a top-of-the-line Hoover Keymatic washer. We were living at #4 Green Lane, Meanwood, in a very nice flat above the doctor's surgery. Well, as luck would have it, the new washing machine overflowed, not once, but twice, through to the floor below and onto the doctor's desk. I remember the poor man phoning me in a fit, on the second time, to let me know that it had happened again. Our frantic efforts (with a hair drier) to dry his carpets out, took a couple of days.

Paula was christened in the local church and most of our relatives were there. Just as the vicar was taking hold of her, Paula kicked out and the phrase, "Who kicked the Vicar?" was coined, I think by Katie. That phrase was repeated many times over the years.

Paula's Christening—Meanwood Church, Leeds

Following Paula's birth, we spent many days and weeks visiting George and Esther in Maghull. These were happy times and a special bond was created between Paula and her grandparents, one that lasted forever.

Following our marriage in 1963 and before we settled in Welwyn Garden City, Hertfordshire in 1968, we moved several times. From Beverley in Yorkshire to Guisborough, to Leeds (Meanwood), to Leamington Spa, back to Leeds (Seacroft), and eventually to Welwyn Garden City.

53

FRANK FARR

This covers the period from Paula's christening through to the time that she started her first school at the age of four and onto our move into our first home purchase (Panshanger) and Paula's start at Panshanger School, aged five.

Ann and Paula (aged two) in Southport

Paula aged three in George and Esther's back garden—Maghull

Paula and Frank in George and Esther's back garden—Maghull

Paula aged three on a day trip to Bridlington, Yorkshire with George and Esther

A LIFE IN STAGES

Paula aged four, Leeds, Yorkshire

First Christmas card from Paula to Frank 1968

Paula at her Uncle Stanley's and Aunt Glynis's wedding—Maghull—1968

CHAPTER SEVEN

The Fine Fare Years—Part One 1961-1970

Personal Growth and Preparation for What was to Come

My Twenties

For most of these years, I was in my mid-twenties. As I look back on this time, I was very hard working, somewhat argumentative, and highly competitive. I always felt that, as far as work was concerned, I could do as well as, if not better than most. I won most of the arguments, but I had yet to learn that there is more than one way to win an argument. Luckily, I had a few close friends and as time moved on, I was fortunate to have Laurie Edwards, Don Neville, Werner de Smidt, and Wallace Monaghan to mentor me and to encourage my professional development.

During the time that I was managing Maghull, there were several changes in the Fine Fare management of that region. The original management from Cooper's of Church Street, Liverpool, was replaced by Fine Fare management with Werner De Smidt as regional director and Mr. Bastiani as regional manager. Vernon Hough stayed on from Cooper's as district supervisor.

Then the control of this group of stores was transferred to the Scott's Bakery Group of Dunning's Bridge Rd. in Aintree.

Here are some of my recollections from my time managing Maghull.

- Mr. Bastiani had a loud and demanding manner. (His bark was worse than his bite) and we worked together for a number of years.

- One of my milestones was sitting with Werner De Smidt in the staff canteen at Maghull, while he extolled the virtues of being a thinking manager. I have always tried, and mostly succeeded, at being a thinking manager. This caused me to embrace the maxim: *"The man who knows 'how' will always have a job. The man who knows 'why' will always be his boss."*

- Liverpool was a hotbed of union activity in those days, and I had a number of run-ins with union representatives, including kicking them out of my store. Scott's management did not approve of my actions.

- Scott's bakery had a habit of dropping excess bakery products off at the store without them having been ordered. I refused to accept responsibility for this, even to the point of leaving the product outside and phoning them to come and pick it up. Scott's management did not approve of that.

In those days it was a big risk to take money to the bank. Robberies were not uncommon, and I used to have a taxi to take me to the bank each day by a different route. Jack Scott came to the store to tell me to stop refusing his bakery deliveries, and while he was there, Mrs. Hargreaves arrived with the taxi. I thought that Jack Scott was going to have a fit. I remember his language: "We don't pay for taxis" (it was seven shillings and sixpence, about $1.50) and he recommended that I get a bike. Apart from being stupid, this was funny, as I had never ridden a bike in my life. I still haven't.

My experience with the Scott brothers was not positive, and I realized that they were not interested in developing us as future managers. The end result was that I contacted Fine Fare Head Office in Welwyn Garden City, Hertfordshire, twenty-five miles north of London, reminded them that I had joined as an executive trainee, and asked to be transferred back to a region that was under Fine Fare's control.

Fine Fare Supermarkets Head Office—Welwyn Garden City

Lesson Learned

I was learning to push back where my own interest was concerned.

My first assignment after leaving Maghull, was to manage the Fine Fare Supermarket in Beverley, Yorkshire. This was where Ann and I established our first home together, at #6 Beverley Mews adjacent to the famous Beverley Bar. Not long after, I was asked to manage the new supermarket in Guisborough.

This proved to be a little embarrassing. Mr. Weston's development program for Fine Fare ran into trouble, and all construction throughout Britain was halted. This included the almost-completed supermarket in Guisborough.

We had just rented a house from a couple of lovely old ladies and to my shame, we did what was known as a "Midnight Flit." We packed all of our belongings into a van and fled for Leeds…without providing any notice.

We moved back in with my mother while we searched the Leeds/Bradford area for a suitable flat, and we eventually settled into the flat on Green Lane.

I was asked to manage the supermarket at Kirkstall Road in Leeds.

I was at this store on Friday November 22nd, 1963, when the assassination of President Kennedy was announced. *Assassination!* The very word seemed so alien, something from the distant past and yet here it was—real. The shock went around the world. It seemed impossible that such a young, vibrant, inspiring leader could die in such an unexpected manner.

When Paula was three months old, I was asked to move on to manage the Fine Fare Supermarket at Crossgates, Leeds. The most remarkable thing about my time at this store was that it opened the opportunity for so many more events that would shape our lives.

It was at this store that I first met Jim Waldron and Steve Murray, who would become life-long friends, along with a small number of their friends, who would work with us or be associated with us over the next few years.

Jim and Steve were working at this store as Saturday boys, and I asked them to help me recruit more of their friends. I can't remember all of their names, but I do remember Paul Bolus and Chris Rawling.

Buying Produce, Increasing Sales and Having Fun

During my time at Kirkstall Rd. and Crossgates, we had some fun with produce. There was a local produce supervisor who bought produce for twenty or so local Fine Fare supermarkets. I was not happy with the job that he was doing and advised him to stop buying for my store. I thought that I could do a better job myself.

I used to go to the Kirkgate Wholesale Market early in the morning and buy the produce for my own store. The normal gross margin on produce was twenty-five percent, and I started to challenge myself to select a seasonal item, lower the margin to ten percent, and target to increase sales on that item by ten times.

I hired my mother to work part-time. She was in her mid-sixties at the time and she had a whale of a time selling our "specials."

Try to imagine a silver-haired lady, standing by this selection of specials: tomatoes, mushrooms, bananas, and sometimes bakery specials, greeting (accosting!) all of the customers who came by. We created a large cardboard "prison" and a sign that read: "Please buy our specials, I have to sell-out before 4:00 pm or the manager (my son) will place me in prison. If I do sell-out, he will double my wages." She always sold out and never had to go to jail.

Unfortunately, one day she slipped and broke a rib and we had to "retire" her. She always looked back on this time with a good laugh.

I continued to buy the store's produce when I moved to Crossgate, and now I included Jim and Steve in the process. We used to meet at the market at 6:00 am. It was hot bacon baps and a fresh mug of tea at Jacomelli's Café and then down to buy the produce. The produce was delivered to the store by 10:00 am and it was usually Steve's job to receive it and make sure that all the fresh produce was on display ASAP.

Olive Farr's house on Norman Street, Kirkstall, Leeds

Also, during my time at this store, Fine Fare launched its first range of "Own Label" products. I had been with Loblaws in Canada when the same thing happened there, and I decided to make as big a deal of it as I could. I ordered large quantities of most of these items and used some of my merchandising knowledge, to create mass displays in every part of the store. This included adding these items as a part of "complementary merchandising" to most of the current specials. By the time that I had finished, the store looked quite different—more colourful, more aggressive, and more sales-oriented.

I believe that I was probably the only store manager in the North of England that took such an approach and my "Own Label" sales were proportionally higher than any of the other supermarkets. And then, one of those unplanned, but impactful events occurred. One that would change the direction of our lives, at least from a professional point of view.

On a Friday afternoon, two Fine Fare executives, J.C. Jones, the outgoing chairman, and Ben Shelley (a Canadian), the incoming chairman, were touring stores in the North of England and turned up at Crossgates. They were quite shocked and impressed with the merchandising approach that we had taken, and during a short conversation, they learned that I had spent almost five years with Loblaws in Canada.

They left to return to Fine Fare's head office in Welwyn Garden City.

On the following Wednesday, Ben Shelley phoned me and asked if I could report to the head office on Thursday. He also asked me to bring my passport!

OMG. What to do? Ann agreed to take Paula to her mother's in Maghull and off I went to Fine Fare's head office. I was asked to join a small group of Fine Fare managers who were going to Canada to assist in the set-up of an aggressive discount operation: "Super City Discount Foods." I had to phone Ann and let her know that I did not know how long this would take. This group included a couple of Fine Fare managers who would later be well-known, George Thyer and Pete Dodsley.

A LIFE IN STAGES

Following our return to England, we joined a similar group that was being set up to convert a number of Fine Fare Supermarkets to a discount operation under the name of "Busy Bee." This operation was led by a man that I only remember as "Nick the Greek." Unfortunately, within a short time I had a major disagreement with "Mr. Nick." (I had worked for ten days straight at Tottenham and when I told Nick that I was going home to my wife and daughter, he was not happy. I explained that I was going home whether he was happy or not, and I would be back in a couple of days.)

I went home and then, instead of heading back to Tottenham, I took a detour to Fine Fare's head office and asked for a meeting with Mr. Laurie Edwards. He was the director of operations for the entire Fine Fare Group. Fortunately for me, he knew of Mr. Nick and did not particularly like him. He asked me if I would go to Birmingham to join Mr. Don Neville and Mr. Doug Robson, who were testing a variety of merchandising/discount options in that region. I remember asking Mr. Edwards about Nick the Greek and he said, "Don't worry about him, we will deal with this." I never heard of Nick the Greek again.

This began a long working relationship between myself, Mr. Edwards, and Mr. Neville.

Shortly after this, Mr. Neville was promoted to Mr. Edward's job and Mr. Edwards assumed the role of managing director, North of England.

Mr. Edwards asked me to take over the management of the larger Fine Fare Supermarket at Leamington Spa and I agreed.

One of the funnier things that I remember from Leamington Spa was that we used to have promotional items in the store, such as gift items that customers could send away for. One time, there was a promotion involving a large, beautiful, golden Teddy Bear, and if I wanted it, I could have it at the end of the promotion.

On the Sunday following the promotion, I took Paula with me and opened the store. Paula watched in surprise as I detached this big Teddy bear from its display and gave it to her. I think that she thought that we were stealing it! Anyway, it was quite the sight to see Paula hugging this new toy all the way home. It was slightly bigger than her. I was at Leamington Spa for about one year, and although I did not know it, there was a little tussle for my services going on in the background.

Don Neville wanted me to join the head office team with responsibility for new store openings, and Laurie Edwards continued to say that he had plans for me in his region. Once I became aware of this situation, I made sure that Don Neville knew that I wanted the head office position. I had developed a flair for merchandising and wanted to learn more. Don Neville was now senior to Mr. Edwards and after a little time, I was offered the job in Fine Fare's head office. My first title was merchandising supervisor.

With the start of my new job, we left Leamington Spa and returned to Leeds. We were fortunate to obtain a new flat, above the shops in the Seacroft Shopping Centre. We remained there until we moved to Welwyn Garden City in 1968.

For the next several years, I reported to Don Neville. He explained to me that the company, under its new chairman (James Gulliver) was going to accelerate its growth again and that one of the difficulties was recruiting staff who were prepared to do the hard work required to get stores opened. The stores had to open to a high standard, and this would also require the store opening team to work long hours, away from home, for extended periods of time.

I could see that this was going to provide me with all of the experience that I was looking for, and I agreed to accept the responsibility for store openings, provided that I could pick my own team. They were more than happy to agree to this, and I was more than happy to be able to renew my relationship with Jim Waldron and Steve Murray.

I met with both of their parents and promised that they would come to no harm and that, in fact, if they were willing to work hard, this would, in turn, become a good opportunity for them. This led to the formation of the Fine Fare merchandising teams.

During the early days, as the merchandising teams were developing. I shared an office in Gatehouse with Ron Allen, and we shared some responsibilities as store inspectors. We used to identify stores with operating difficulties and carry out an inspection to determine the cause and possible remedy for the problem.

One of these stores stands out in my memory. The store in Kirkby, Liverpool was quite busy, but had reported an inventory loss of six percent (the norm was 1.5%), so off I went to Kirkby.

Unannounced, I checked out the store late at night, before my scheduled visit, including checking out the "waste" in the store bins behind the store. Lots to be concerned about there. The next morning, I introduced myself to the store manager, a typical, funny, good-natured Liverpudlian. He seemed to be very popular with the staff and the customers. His opening comment to me was, "Do you want to buy a watch?" He then proceeded to open an office drawer and show me his selection of watches for sale.

I had just explained that I was from head office and had come to investigate his high shortage.

At lunch time, he introduced me to a young lad. "He is in charge of the store for the rest of the day," he announced. "I am going off to the match." He then clarified this, by explaining that he was a strong Liverpool supporter, and that he always took the afternoon off when Liverpool were playing. The assistant store manager and the head butcher were good friends and they were also going with him.

Shortage problem solved! I hope that he had a successful future in the watch business.

One other observation of a similar nature.

In the early days of the supermarket openings, many of the new managers and head butchers had previously managed small stores, and they brought many of their old habits with them. Here are a few:

Butchers regularly did not pay for the meat for their own consumption (and sometimes that of their friends and neighbours).

Store managers regularly did not pay for their own cigarettes and other food items. They also took the money from the coin-operated machines and kiddy-rides that were often in the stores.

They were not really thieves. They just believed that this was one of the perks of the job. I had the most difficulty explaining that super marketing was a professional job and that they could earn more

A LIFE IN STAGES

(and not steal) if they just applied themselves to becoming professional managers and doing a better job at increasing the sales and profits of their stores.

Some made the adjustment well and I was able to encourage their future promotion. Others did not and soon learned that they were not suited for this new type of job.

During this time, my friendship with Jim and Steve increased, as we travelled hundreds of miles together, working many hours, crisscrossing England and Wales, opening and remodelling stores. At this time, we had the use of a small Austin 1100 (CGO 577B). Steve and Jim borrowed this car one weekend and drove off the road into a field on the way to Tadcaster.

I particularly remember Jim and Steve coming over to our Seacroft flat on weekends and playing poker, sometimes for hours on end. They always called Ann "Mrs. Farr," and it took a while for this formality to break down.

Ann made good friends with another lady who moved into the next door flat about the same time that we did. It was also at Seacroft that Paula got her first little bike with training wheels, and she practiced around the apartment block.

Paula and Frank at Seacroft—Christmas 1966

❖

"If you can't say anything positive. It's best to say nothing at all." Doug Robson

"First rule of holes—Stop digging." Anonymous

CHAPTER EIGHT

The Fine Fare Years—Part Two

The Merchandising Teams

Together with Jim and Steve, we worked so hard during these next years. But we gained so much experience and we had so many good times that the memories will last a lifetime.

Don Neville taught me to delegate.

When we only had one team, he told me that the company wanted to open two stores on the same day, one in Sheffield and one in Bristol. I said that this would be difficult, as I could not be in two places at once.

Don's solution was that I split the team in two, with Jim running one and Steve the other. He would provide more people and I would run up and down the highway, making sure that all was well. I explained that when the team opened stores, they were in near-perfect condition and that I could not guarantee this would be the case if we split in two.

With a chuckle, he said, "If there is a minor problem, who is going to complain? You all report to me." With that established, we opened the stores well, and never looked back. On several occasions we opened, or reopened five stores on the same day.

This was my first introduction to Delegation.

Lesson Learned,

"What should you delegate?" The answer is, "Everything, except those things that only you can do, either by expertise or by authority." This became one of my guiding principles for the rest of my career.

Starting with Jim and Steve, over time, we expanded the store opening/merchandising teams to thirty-five people (including some head office support staff). Jim and Steve were always the keys to this. The next two men who joined us were Bill Durant and Geoff Andrews. Among the people who worked with us during this time were Mick Hartley, Steve's younger brother Tony, my brother Michael, Paul Bolus, Chris Rawling, Brian Heilbron, and too many others to remember.

Steve Murray remerchandising the Fine Fare Supermarket in Flint, N. Wales

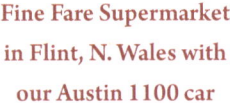

Fine Fare Supermarket in Flint, N. Wales with our Austin 1100 car

I recently exchanged emails with Jim, Steve, and Tony. With further input from Geoff Andrews and Mick Hartley, we identified forty-seven individuals who worked on the merchandising teams during these years.

Jim was assigned to manage the remodel of the Elmo store in Leek, and that was where he met his future wife, the beautiful Angela Walters. Their two children, Nick and Louise, were both born in the Queen Elizabeth II Hospital in Welwyn Garden City.

I should also mention that when we acquired the Elmo chain, they had a merchandising team in place, and I interviewed them to see how they could fit into the Fine Fare structure. Three of them stick in my memory:

John Worthington was the team leader. He became a merchandising team leader with Fine Fare and remained with us until his retirement.

Ted Welburn was the provisions expert on their team. He became an invaluable part of our store-opening operation, and he also remained with us until his retirement.

Richard Bunting was the oddity in this group. His mother knew the managing director at Elmo, and she had secured a position for Richard as a management trainee. I recall that during our interview,

A LIFE IN STAGES

I asked him where he saw his future in retailing. His answer was that within five years, he would like to have my job! Not bad for a young man with no experience.

My response was that I would not always have this job and that it was good to have a healthy ambition. Richard joined us as one of our merchandising team members. He was quite intelligent, but to say that he was a little eccentric would be an understatement. Among the highlights of his time with us were the following:

- In Tredegar in South Wales, he joined in a group of Welsh singers at a wedding. He did not speak a word of Welsh but somehow managed to fake it.

- For a small bet, he drank a full bottle of whiskey in one go. He collapsed and could have killed himself.

- For another bet, he stripped and ran around the fountain on Howardsgate naked.

There were many further examples of Richard's bravado and funny, but eccentric, behaviour.

However, this type of activity led to a bad situation. We used to frequently share the use of our company cars, and Richard crashed Jim Waldron's car. (We quickly established that he was accident prone and did not have a driver's license.) Within a couple of days, the concern from this became more serious. I was advised by Don Neville that Mr. Owen (managing director) and Mr. Gulliver (chairman) had decided that both Richard Bunting and Jim Waldron should be fired.

I was alarmed at the thought of losing Jim, and I also believed that this was unfair. I asked for an urgent meeting with Don Neville and Mr. Owen, knowing that this would be a problem, as Mr. Owen was not really a friend to me or the merchandising teams. I explained my position to them, but Mr. Owen would not agree to change his mind and also explained that I could not intercede with a decision from Mr. Gulliver. Nevertheless, I asked for a meeting with Mr. Gulliver. This was rejected on the grounds that if I was seen to be arguing with Mr. Gulliver, he might fire me. So I proceeded to write a letter to Mr. Gulliver outlining the unfairness in this situation and asserting that Jim was a good and indispensable employee.

Mr. Owen declined to give my letter to Mr. Gulliver, but thankfully, Don Neville agreed to speak to Mr. Gulliver. After few minutes, out came Don Neville with my letter. On it, Mr. Gulliver had written, "Bunting Goes—Waldron Stays." I never did see Richard Bunting again. My guess would be that he either enjoyed good success or total failure in his career.

The merchandising teams worked with me from the start, beginning in 1965 through to the time that I left Fine Fare in 1975. Two other members come to mind.

At some point, Ernie Ripon joined our teams. Ernie worked out of the Fine Fare Distribution Centre at East Kilbride, near Glasgow. One day, we learned that Ernie had won 50,000 GBP in the lottery. Three things came from that:

- Ernie was renting a flat and his landlord was always threatening to kick him out. He bought a new home for himself and his mum.

- Ernie bought a bottle of scotch for each employee at the East Kilbride Distribution Centre. They erected a large banner thanking him.
- Matt McKenzie, the regional director for Scotland, promised that he would always say "please" before ordering Ernie off to work excessive hours on some last-minute project.

One other eccentric, but loveable, character was Alistair MacDonald (Mac). He was the long-time signwriter that we inherited shortly after forming the teams. He was quite the character and he needed special handling. That was initially provided by Michael Merrywether and subsequently Pete Raymond. It was not unusual for Mac and Pete to produce and install up to 500 signs for a store opening. Mac used to enjoy his pint of beer at the end of a long day and often earned "free pints" by doing quick drawings of ladies in the bar.

We all liked Mac and looked out for him on the odd occasions when his combination of drinking while drawing, got a little out of hand.

I should also mention that by the nature of the work, Pete and Mac were always the last to finish. On one occasion when we were working at Redhill, Pete was unable to make a planned visit to a dance at the nurse's residence at St. Peter's Hospital in Chertsey. Feeling sorry for him, Jim and Steve very kindly offered to go in his place. This is where fate determined that Steve would meet the beautiful Irish nurse, Mary Gallagher. Mary had just committed to working in Zambia for a couple of years. Steve and she stayed in touch and following her return to England, they were married in 1971 at St. Theresa's church in Beconsfield. The rest is history and we remain best friends to this day.

A couple of other funny instances come to mind.

During our first remodel of Tolworth (then the biggest supermarket in England), somebody on the merchandising team had the clever idea of placing detergent in the decorative fountain, resulting in great clouds of foam floating down the High Street.

In another instance during the remodelling of Wolverhampton, Mick Hartley dressed up in a bleach bottle costume and proceeded to hide in places around the store, alarming the store clerks and generally causing confusion.

During a ten-year period, together with Jim, Steve, and the rest of the merchandising teams, I believe that we opened over 200 new supermarkets and remodelled many more of the stores in this 550-supermarket group. Many of the stores were remerchandised more than once.

Planning Boards

During this pre-computer period, we established a "planning board" system in our office. The planning boards were eighteen feet long, and four feet deep. They set out the planned activities for the next two years and covered all significant physical activity for 550 supermarkets. These were activities leading up to store openings and remodels as well as any other significant upgrades. For its time, this was quite impressive. Department directors used to stop by to check out what was going on, and even Mr. Gulliver was surprised with the detail of our planning.

I worked closely with Jim and Steve, and we worked hard and for many long hours. We travelled the length and breadth of England, Scotland, and Wales and enjoyed an amazing experience that will probably remain with us for a lifetime.

During this period, James Gulliver decided to reorganize the company's image. This developed into a new "corporate identity" for the entire company and included the refurbishing program. About this time, my title had been changed to merchandising controller and I was also appointed corporate identity coordinator.

This was a fantastic experience for me, as I was learning so much and becoming the acknowledged company expert in these matters.

One of the lessons that I learned during this time was that I began to see gaps or problems with our management procedures and realized that senior managers were often overworked and under pressure. When I started to offer solutions that worked, they were always appreciated.

Some Examples

- I realized that Don Neville was taking work home of an evening. New store orders was the one of the first chores that I offered to take off his hands and he was quite pleased for me to do so, giving me a few tips to get started.

- The next example of this was that I saw him working on new store layouts on weekends or evenings. Again, I offered to deal with this, as I was learning a great deal from having opened so many stores and seeing the mistakes that occurred. He was very pleased to be able to delegate this responsibility to me and this remained one of my prime responsibilities for the remainder of my time with Fine Fare. Having to decide on the layout of so many stores, caused me to develop another habit that has stayed with me over the years: "Give me five options" became a common request. This has evolved into the maxim:

  "A choice of one, is no choice at all."

- This, in turn, led me to think more about the advantages/disadvantages of much of the equipment that we used in our supermarkets. I had a lot of experience working with this equipment and had lots of opinions as to how it could be improved. With Don Neville's support, I gradually assumed more responsibility for equipment selection and approval, working closely with Henry Wyka, the manager of Headway Construction and with Steve Newman, our equipment buyer. I also established a good working relationship with the architect's department and the store construction coordinators. John Talbot was one of these people and somebody with whom I have retained contact. John and his wife Carole visited Vancouver a few years ago and we were able to meet. I have also stayed in touch with Henry Wyka on an annual basis over all these years.

- At a major meeting of all of the company's management, I introduced the company's first "plan-o-grams," one of my proudest Fine Fare moments. This may not seem too significant today, but up until that time, the company did not have any established plans that indicated where every item on the store shelves was to go. It was a real breakthrough for the company, and I was so proud of the work that I and our team had done in developing this invaluable tool. It was also probably the first time that I was required to speak in front of a large audience. Fortunately, I knew my topic well and my presentation was well received by my colleagues.

Bill Durant was the team member who helped me to do a lot of the work on developing these plan-o-grams.

Tony Murray, Steve's brother and one of our merchandising team members, eventually moved to the head office, years after we had left, and had the responsibility for revising the company's plan-o-grams. This time, though, it was done in a more sophisticated manner, supported by computerized data.

Frank and Jim Waldron at the Decimal Supermarket, Olympia, London 1968

There was another project that stands out as a major success at the time.

Britain decided to change to decimal currency during the mid-sixties and Fine Fare was awarded the opportunity to operate a "Decimal Currency Supermarket" in the Olympia Conference Centre in London. I was assigned responsibility for this operation. Customers could purchase genuine new decimal currency and shop within this store. They could keep their change as souvenirs, as the actual launch of decimal currency was six to twelve months in the future.

It was an interesting experience and I won't go into details here. It was a team success and further enhanced our reputation in the company. On a side note, one of the team for this project was also an accomplished hypnotist and at the closing party, we were all intrigued to see a close-up demonstration of multiple hypnosis. Something to be remembered.

A LIFE IN STAGES

Capital Expenditures—FB14C

Like all well-organized companies, Fine Fare had a system of capital budgets and capital spending authorizations. This was a little unwieldly. For example, almost any amount over 100 GBP was a capital expense and every capital request had to be completed with a capital request authorization form FB14C. Following Wallace Monaghan's appointment as managing director, Wallace realized that approving all of these requests was taking up too much of his time and in many cases, he did not know the merits of the request.

He decided to involve me in the process with the instruction that I was to scrutinize all FB14Cs, check into them where necessary, and sign them before they landed on his desk. If I signed them, he would, for the most part, approve them.

I quickly found out that frequently, there were several hundred of these each week and I soon got to the point where my hand would become numb and incapable of completing my signature. My solution was to have a stamp made of my signature. This worked for about two days until I got the phone call. "Mr. Farr, when I say that I want your signature, I do not mean a rubber stamp." It took several explanations and numerous assurances before he would accept my signature stamp. Bill Durant quickly learned how to do the preliminary review and to sort the FB14Cs into some sense of priority. Thank you, Bill Durant (R.I.P.).

There were a number of consequences to this. Frequently the requests came in from executives who were senior to me, and they did not appreciate me holding up some of their pet projects. I had the difficult task of explaining that it was easier to address my concerns, rather than dealing with the managing director, who would not consider an unsigned FB14C.

Through the new store-opening program, and the refurbishing program, our department managed eighty percent+ of the company's physical activities. This allowed us to provide a high degree of co-operation with those executives whose requests were approved. This was a situation that was much appreciated by Mr. Monaghan, as it allowed us to fast-track approved projects, through what had previously been a very bureaucratic process. This sounds like a lot of detail to include here, but at the time it was very important in a group of over 500 supermarkets with five regional managing directors, each with their own needs and priorities. Working with our team, we were able to build a high level of trust and confidence on these issues between these field operations and head office.

These were exciting times at work, and I was gaining the invaluable experience of working with more senior managers.

If I have one regret, it was that in the early years, this required me to work long hours and to be away from home many weeks from Monday to Friday. I have always felt a sense of guilt in how this developed. I was in a unique position to learn so much about the business, but I also knew that this placed an unfair burden on Ann. I always looked forward to returning home on Friday evening and enjoying the weekend with Ann and Paula. My hope was that the future benefits to our lives would make it all worthwhile.

This situation lasted for the first four years. Subsequently, things improved significantly as I adjusted into my growing role at head office and we were able to settle down to a more normal family life in Welwyn Garden City in 1968. However, this still required a lot of evening work, usually at our kitchen table.

Merchandising Team 20yr Reunion— Leeds 1994

Frank, Paul Bolus, Steve Murray, Mick Hartley, Chris Rawling, Geoff Andrews, Pete Raymond, Jim Waldron, Michael Farr, and Peter Armitage

Welwyn Garden City: (WGC)

WGC is an unusual city. Together with Letchworth, it was originally envisioned as a model city to take the overflow population from London. The initial work started in the late 1920s and continued through to the start of the Second World War. After the war, building picked up again and the city took on the shape that it has retained to the present. Using a neo-Georgian style of architecture, the city grew to its planned population of 40,000.

Incidentally, it was unusual for a city of 40,000 people to only have one set of traffic lights. Junctions were controlled via the installation of roundabouts, which were first developed in conjunction with these new model towns.

I pressured the local council on a regular basis and eventually, we were offered the opportunity to rent a house at 111 The Commons. This was one of the earlier homes, close to what would be Paula's first school. The house had a wonderful established garden with willow trees and a small stream at the bottom of the garden. Our first spring and summer there was delightful. The weather was great, and we were able to invite George and Esther down to visit with us, along with Aunty Katie, Leslie, Pauline, and Alex. We enjoyed our first BBQs at this house. This was also the house where we bought our first coloured television, just in time to watch the Mexico City Olympics.

A LIFE IN STAGES

Paula and her cousin Jacqueline 1970

Our first home in Welwyn Garden City, 111 The Commons 1968

Michael Farr, Olive Farr, Olive Dickinson, Albert Dickinson, Mrs. Dickinson, Stanley Dickinson, Harry Kinghorn, Pauline Kinghorn (nee Dickinson), Jacqueline Dickinson, and Paula (bridesmaids)

Following our further persistent lobbying of the council, we managed to get on the waiting list to buy a house in the new development at Panshanger. We were so excited when we were offered the opportunity to buy #8 Westley Wood. Jim and Steve, together with Geoff Andrews, came around and helped us with the cleaning and decorating. This house also became a "home away from home" for many of the merchandising team members during their visits to head office.

Frank and his mother, Olive, at the new home in Panshanger, Welwyn Garden City

The house cost 4,400 British pounds in 1968. We sold it in 1974 for 16,000 pounds and a few years ago, we checked online, and the house was listed at 200,000 pounds. A recent check in 2021 shows these houses are selling for up to 550,000 pounds, an indication of how house prices have risen in the UK.

This really was the icing on the cake—a four-bedroom contemporary house, with its own garage and backing onto a playing field. We were very happy during our six years in this home. All of the neighbours were young couples like ourselves, with young children of Paula's age. We spent a lot of time going from house to house and enjoying each other's company.

Paula proceeded to fill the house/garage with gerbils, a hamster, guinea pigs. It was only a matter of time before we had our first real pet, Paula's lovely little Sheltie, naturally named Lassie.

Paula at Panshanger enjoying her horse book that she still has to this day 1971

Ann at Panshanger 1970

A LIFE IN STAGES

Board games— the beginning of a lifetime hobby of playing games with Ann and Paula

Paula and Frank in the back garden at Panshanger 1972

Ann and Paula in the back garden at Panshanger 1972

Paula—Panshanger School Photo 1972

Paula went to Panshanger School and spent lots of time playing with her friends in the playing field behind our house. Paula's best friends of those days were Joanne Eden, Alison Webster, and Elaine Harrington. Paula and Joanne remain close friends to this day.

It was during our time at Panshanger that Ann and I started to furnish our house with items we still have to this day. We used to go down to London and park my car in the loading dock at our Cooper's Supermarket in Knightsbridge (parking in London was impossible to find and expensive).

Paula and Joanne Eden—reunited again in 2016—St. Albans, Hertfordshire

We would then go off for the rest of the day, dining, going to movies, sightseeing, and window shopping. We soon discovered the "Red Tag" sales days at Harrods and managed to find a few unexpected bargains. We developed a liking for rosewood and we still have the nest of rosewood tables and an attractive, long rosewood coffee table that we found on these "Red Tag" excursions. We also bought a beautiful rosewood dining table from the Welwyn Department Store. During our many moves, we reduced the height of this table and we still have it as a lovely coffee table in our living room.

Early Vacations

During this period, we started to take family vacations. The early ones involved packing everything into the company car and heading off for Wales, Devon, or Cornwall, all beautiful places and lots of fun. Usually we stayed in caravans and often in the rain. Jim and Steve frequently joined us, initially alone and later together with their young families. Usually on these vacations, I had to stay in touch with head office and was still preoccupied with work-related issues.

Jim Waldron and Steve Murray in N. Wales 1968

Steve Murray in our caravan in N. Wales 1968

Steve Murray and Paula, N. Wales

One of the early vacations to N. Wales

A LIFE IN STAGES

Following this, we started taking our first true vacations, completely relaxing and away from a work environment. These vacations were a revelation and I determined that I would always make sure that future vacations would be a complete break from work.

One short, but memorable vacation that we had was Ann, Paula, and I in Paris for our tenth wedding anniversary. Paula was nine and it was so enjoyable to see her sitting in a sidewalk café on the Champs Elysée, wearing sunglasses and drinking Coke. She also had a pony ride along the Champs Elysée, and had her first opportunity to try "*pomme frites*" and a "*jambon* and cheese sandwich." Very sophisticated for a nine-year-old. Not surprisingly, Paula developed a liking for travel and the good life.

The hovercraft ride to and from France was an interesting but bumpy experience.

Ann, Paula, and Frank – leaving for Paris 1973

Paula in Paris on the Champs Elysée 1973

Paula in Paris on the Champs Elysée in 2016

We also had two driving vacations through Europe to northern Italy. The first one was the three of us and my mother. Paula developed a liking for the *"frites"* with salt served by the pool in Jesolo. The hotel had a juke box that played two songs: "Walk on the Wild Side" by Lou Reed and "Bang a Gong" by T-Rex. This trip was so enjoyable that we immediately planned the next vacation, this time with Ann's mum and dad.

Ann and Frank—Jesolo, Italy 1973

This next one was hilarious. By now, I was driving a brown Ford Consul. We double-wrapped our suitcases in black garbage bags, securely fastened them to the roof rack, and hoped they would survive the trip (they did). And off we set. Esther kept us laughing from start to finish, from little hotels in the Dolomite Mountains of northern Italy to Rimini and Venice.

It was a habit in these local hotels to offer samples of the local beverages and we soon learned to look forward to these little treats at the end of each day's drive. We made friends with a huge St. Bernard dog at one of the Dolomite hotels. His name was Harry and I can still see him in my mind. Even when the car broke down and we had to delay our return for a couple of days, Esther could always see the funny side of things and her positive attitude helped make for a very memorable holiday.

These early vacations through France, Luxembourg, Germany, Austria, Switzerland, and Italy were an eye opener. They gave us an appreciation of the beauty of Europe and a sense of history. They were also a foretaste of things to come, as we subsequently enjoyed many vacations around the world.

It was during our time living in Westley Wood that my career with Fine Fare really accelerated. Wallace Monaghan, the managing director of Fine Fare Scotland, was appointed managing director for the whole Fine Fare Group and I now reported to him. We had a very good, but professional, relationship.

One day, he asked me to join him on a two-day visit to Paris. Carrefour had opened their first hypermarket, and it was causing quite a sensation. Mr. Monaghan wanted to see it and thought that I would benefit from being involved.

This store was a revelation. At 16,000 square feet, our store in Tolworth, London was the largest in the UK. This Carrefour store on the outskirts of Paris was 80,000 square feet. We had seen the future. Mr. Monaghan explained to me that if Fine Fare was going to develop such stores, it could take up to five years, and he wanted me to assume some responsibility for the planning of this new growth phase. He wanted me to be a part of The Large Store Development Group.

I returned to Paris within a couple of weeks and spent a whole week measuring and reviewing all that I could about this new type of store.

As result of the report that I produced for Mr. Monaghan, I was given the authority to travel to Europe and visit any new store that I thought might add to our knowledge. My expenses were impossibly tight, but I did visit many stores during the next few years and gained valuable insights as to how these stores were constructed and operated.

Mr. James Gulliver

Around 1965, James Gulliver had been appointed by Mr. Garfield Weston to be the new chairman of Fine Fare. He was a graduate of Harvard Business School and a senior consultant at McKinsey.

Mr. Gulliver subsequently recruited several new and more qualified senior managers, and among them were Michael Bliss and Alistair Grant. I spent some time working with both of them and learned a lot about their approach to management.

Mr. Gulliver was a very strong manager with a terrifying reputation, and I remember several instances where this assumed some importance.

In the early days, he referred to me as Mr. Wheatley and I did not correct him. I thought, one day he may fire Mr. Wheatley (I never did learn who he was) and I would still be okay.

At an early board meeting, (where I was an observer) Mr. Les Major, our director of Meat Operations, was a little late and apologized, explaining that he had been delayed on the phone. Mr. Gulliver quietly but sternly told him, "Next time hang up. My board meetings have priority over your phone calls." This resulted in these very senior executives always being early for board meetings, waiting in the corridor, not wishing to be late.

This type of approach was not always productive. One morning, I was in Liverpool when I received a terse message: "Mr. Gulliver would like you to attend a meeting at Gatehouse at 2:30 pm today." What to do?

I managed to get a flight from Liverpool to Luton and have somebody pick me up and drive me to WGC (twenty minutes early) only to be told Mr. Gulliver had to leave for London. Meeting cancelled until next week.

At another board meeting, Mr. Major (again) became angry, loud, and pounded the table. This was a part of his style. Mr. Gulliver, again quite sternly, told Mr. Major to quiet down. "Nobody raises their voice at my meetings, except me!"

The annual budgeting process was always a stressful time. One year, I had prepared a detailed budget that proposed a fifteen percent increase in the cost of my department. I had done a lot of work on this budget and I was sure of my facts. I supported my proposal with two planning boards that I placed on easels at my end of the boardroom table.

Just as I was about to enter the board meeting, one executive came out, seemingly in shock. His budget proposal had been dismissed and he had been strongly criticized by Mr. Gulliver. He was not a happy man.

My turn was next. Mr. Gulliver took a brief look at my proposed budget and then said, "Obviously you have not heard that I am not prepared to consider any increases in expenses for this next year. Please go away and reduce your budget to ninety-five percent of the current year."

I think that I was supposed to say, "Yes, Mr. Gulliver," and leave. I was too inexperienced to read his mood, so instead I said, "If you will please look at these charts. They represent the work that I understand you want my department to complete next year. This cannot be done for any less than I have requested. Can you please let me know what you would want me to delete from next year's program?"

The director next to me (Les Major, again) kicked me under the table and later told me that he thought that I might be about to be fired. Mr. Gulliver turned to my boss, Mr. Monaghan, and suggested that he should work with me to achieve the required savings and I left the board meeting.

I met Mr. Monaghan the next morning and he told me that Mr. Gulliver was impressed that I was the only one that had done my homework and was prepared to stand up for what I wanted. The outcome was that I prepared a budget equal to the ninety-five percent that the chairman wanted, and early in the next year, I was granted a supplementary budget equal to the amount that I had requested in the first place.

Mr. Gulliver was pleased with my charts, but thought that they were amateur. He told Mr. Monaghan to arrange for me to take a course in statistics, and he sponsored me for membership in The British Institute of Management (BIM).

British Institute of Management Certificate

FRANK FARR

Lesson Learned

Always do your homework. Make sure that you understand your numbers better than anybody else, respectfully stand up for what you believe in, and understand how to make a compromise that allows all parties to get most of what they want.

Through BIM, I had access to their extensive business library and I was able to combine my interest in reading with my interest in business and cover much of the ground that I had missed by not going to university. I think that this became an advantage to me, as I was also more highly motivated and more focused to learn than I would have been at an earlier age

Michael Bliss left Fine Fare to manage a small but aggressive group of supermarkets in the London region and shortly after that, he offered me a job as operations director of this group. It was something that I had to consider, and I felt that I should disclose this to Mr. Monaghan. My thoughts were that, although I was very happy with Fine Fare, I was young and had the responsibility of a family to consider. The opportunity for a promotion, even to a smaller company was something that I had to consider.

The day after I advised Mr. Monaghan, he told me that he had raised the issue with Mr. Gulliver and that Mr. Gulliver had said he wanted me to remain with Fine Fare and that my further promotion within Fine Fare was just a matter of time. That was enough to make me stay. A good decision.

CHAPTER NINE

The Fine Fare Years—Part Three
1970–1975

Directorships and a Conclusion to Fourteen Remarkable Years

My Thirties

During these next few years, I was in my early thirties and I remember waking up to being thirty and having a much more relaxed, but confident approach to work and life in general. I was continuing to enjoy more success at work, I had a great marriage, and Paula was developing into a lovely young girl. I was able to appreciate the support that I had enjoyed from the Simmons in my formative years and to apply some of these learnings with the passage of time.

I was also on top of my work responsibilities, and this allowed me to enjoy our leisure time more fully. We had bought our first home, which we thoroughly enjoyed. We had a small group of friends and we increasingly enjoyed time with our family, particularly with Ann's mum and dad.

Mr. Gulliver proved to be as good as his word and following the opening of Fine Fare's first large store at Kilmarnock, I was advised that I was being promoted to a director's position within the Fine Fare Group. I was thirty-two and the youngest executive ever appointed as a director of this 1,000-store group.

The first large store at Kilmarnock in Scotland, was quickly followed by others at Airdrie, Easterhouses, East Kilbride, and the biggest of them all at the Bridge of Dee in Aberdeen. Ann and Paula came up for the opening of Aberdeen. Paula travelled up and returned by train with my brother Michael. Ann and I enjoyed a nice drive back to Welwyn, passing by Balmoral and the Lake District on the way.

I was very proud to be appointed a director of Fine Fare. However, things are never that simple.

On my appointment as director, I was given the unusual title of "Operations-Director designate—special projects." When I asked what this meant, I got the following explanation: "Mr. Gulliver never demotes directors, he only fires them. By calling you 'designate,' he is putting you on probation, so that he won't have to fire you if you fail."

As far as the "special projects" part is concerned, it really means, "whatever we ask you to do." That part worked out okay, as from then on, I was acting on the direction and authority of the managing director, or the chairman. Not a bad position to be in. I was so pleased with my promotion to director that I forgot to ask about salary. Little mistake with big consequences and a lesson learned.

Right about this time, the government enacted a "Prices and Incomes" Law, and this effectively froze salaries. For the next two years, I accepted ever-increasing responsibilities with no increase in pay. However, I did learn a hell of a lot.

Without going into too many details, here are some of the things that happened.

Shopper's Paradise (1)

On one of my visits to the Birmingham area, I went to check out a new discount supermarket that had opened on the outskirts of Coventry. The store was named Shopper's Paradise. It was very busy, and one notable feature was the popular in-store bakery, selling doughnuts by the thousand (two scoops of jam in every doughnut, thirteen to the dozen). The two young owners were very informal, and I visited this interesting store from time to time.

About a year later, Ann and I were at an industry dinner at the Ritz Hotel in central London and we were seated at the same table as the owners of Shopper's Paradise. During our conversation, they told me that they were planning to sell-out and move to Guernsey.

The end-result of this was that we bought the original Shopper's Paradise and used some of its concepts in developing a much larger chain under the same name.

There were a couple of amusing incidents during this acquisition:

- A short time before the actual take-over, the owners approached me to see if Fine Fare would give them one million pounds of the purchase price in whiskey, to be delivered, in bond, to Guernsey. Ever the entrepreneurs, they planned to open a discount liquor business, catering to the tourists in their new island home. Mr. Monaghan told me to politely say NO! He knew that such a move would upset our relationship with the distillers. This was still a time of producer-controlled retail pricing.

- On the day of the hand-over, Mr. De Smidt and I drove the owners to the Birmingham airport for their flight to Guernsey. They were to receive the purchase funds there the next day. As they departed, they gave us the keys to their car. We had not realized that the car was owned by the company and came with the deal. This car was above my grade, but I think that Werner managed to get it as his new company car.

In 1970, Mr. Gulliver was seconded to work with Mr. Galen Weston in Toronto, as Galen addressed the challenges of rescuing the Weston Family's retail operations in North America. Mr. Gulliver took several of Fine Fare's senior directors to Toronto with him, to provide assistance in the management of the Loblaw store group.

Mr. Neville, Mr. Addington, Mr. Padden, and Mr. Barrett each spent extended periods in Toronto. During this period, Mr. Neville, with Mr. Gulliver's approval, invited me to come over to Toronto and assist in their plans to put in place a refurbishing program similar to the one that I was managing in Fine Fare. I enjoyed two visits to Toronto, and this enabled me to renew my acquaintance with Mr. Galen Weston.

I also learned a very valuable lesson. I had dinner one night with Mr. Neville and Mr. Gulliver and I asked Mr. Gulliver how on earth he could spend all this time in Toronto while still having responsibility for Fine Fare, which was itself undergoing some challenges. Mr. Monaghan had assumed the responsibility for the operation of Fine Fare in Mr. Gulliver's absence.

Mr. Gulliver gave me some profound advice. He said that he was in weekly contact with Mr. Monaghan, but he was also provided with key-line performance charts on a regular basis. With these, he could monitor the company's performance by studying the variances of these key lines.

I adopted this advice and I have used it ever since, in monitoring all of my responsibilities both at 7-Eleven and at the various companies that I have consulted with over the years.

Lessons Learned

*Key Line Trend Reports are the most simple and efficient
tool for measuring company performance.*

Once I returned to the UK following my second visit to Toronto. Mr. Monaghan advised me that he would not be able to spare me for any more of these projects. He wanted me to stay home.

In fairly quick time, several other things happened.

Mr. Gulliver returned from Canada and left Fine Fare, to start up his own enterprise (Oriol Foods) taking Alistair Grant with him. Wallace Monaghan was appointed chairman of Fine Fare.

At this time, I inherited a "special phone," which had been installed by Mr. Gulliver. This was a direct line *from* the chairman (not *to* the chairman). If this phone rings, drop everything else and answer it! Shortly after Wallace Monaghan became chairman, he removed these phones. He told me that he had hated them from day one.

Just before he removed them, I had an interesting experience. One of the senior project managers in the architect's department, phoned me in a panic. He had just returned from a visit to new stores under construction, and found that one of the stores was going to be 10,000 GBP over budget. He was concerned that he might get fired. He wanted my advice on what to do and his first thought was to move the cost to some other store, or to spread this extra cost to several different stores to minimize the problem.

I told him that he should not even consider this, and that if he did, Mr. Monaghan would be so annoyed that he probably would fire him. I offered to meet with him immediately to help find a solution. At the same time, I asked him to write a factual report without covering up the problem. He was a good employee and I would support him at the next board meeting.

I immediately received a call (on the special phone) from Mr. Monaghan to come to his office. He explained that he had wanted to speak to me, and he had picked up the phone and inadvertently overheard my comments to the project manager. He congratulated me on the advice that I had given and told me that I had probably saved the project manager's job. He was also impressed that the project manager had turned to me for advice, rather than go to his own boss.

Shopper's Paradise (2)

One day, Wallace Monaghan asked me to join him to visit our supermarket at Hanley in the midlands. Hanley was a larger-than-average supermarket but was losing money. A local discount competitor had offered to buy it and Mr. Monaghan, who had never visited this store, wanted to check it out before making a decision. His main concern was "How can a small local competitor make a go of this location and we cannot?"

On the way there and back, we discussed discount operations. I had been involved in a number of previous discount experiments: Super City Discount Foods in Canada, Busy Bee in Fine Fare, and discount merchandising with Don Neville and Doug Robson. Mr. Monaghan had also tried his own experiment, "Man with the Axe" in Scotland. I had developed strong opinions as to why these "in-house" discount operations had failed and why some independents succeed.

Within a couple of weeks, Mr. Monaghan decided not to sell Hanley and to start a new discount operation modelled after the operation of Shopper's Paradise, the large discount supermarket that we had recently acquired. He appointed me as Director of Discount Operations and assigned John Clegg to assist me as general manager.

Later, the responsibility for Shopper's Paradise was passed on to another director, Brian Bayliss. Shopper's Paradise eventually grew into a group of over a hundred locations.

Shopper's Paradise gave me the opportunity to experiment with a number of merchandising innovations that were not commonly used in supermarkets in the UK:

- **Finspa:** Industrial racking (in bright "Alert Orange") as an alternative to traditional supermarket shelving. Note: The next time I saw this in a supermarket was in the original Save-On-Foods in North Vancouver, many years later.

- **Series 75 Baskets:** Imported from France and used as substitutes for regular shelves. Plus a larger size for use on gondola ends.

- **Pallets and Clairtainers**: Bringing pallets and wire "clairtainers" directly into the Finspa racking to eliminate handling time and cost.

A LIFE IN STAGES

- **Double-size Shopping Carts**: Again, a first in the UK. Imported from "Caddie" in France.

- **Travellators:** At two of our larger discount stores we introduced "travellators," to facilitate multi-level shopping. Note: We had a lot of fun on the night before launching one of these, trying to get these huge shopping carts with special wheels, to fail on the travellator. We were very concerned about the possibility of injuring somebody, although these units had been tried and proven in both Germany and France.

Wallace Monaghan also created a new business development group under the control of my old associate, Werner de Smidt. I was appointed as one of three new business development directors as a part of this new group. The other two were Brian Bayliss and Ray Bray.

So, at this time, I was:

- **Director of Merchandising** (with responsibility for the merchandising teams and store planning.)

- **Director of Fine Fare Discount** (with responsibility for Fine Fare's growing discount operations, Shopper's Paradise)

- **Director of Large Store Development** as a part of Werner de Smidt's Group

And

- **Director of New Business Development**. In this responsibility, I had the support of Gordon Terrell as we ventured into frozen food stores, health and beauty stores, and wine and spirit stores.

These new business development projects were focused on developing a "tail-end" use for smaller supermarkets that were nearing the end of their useful lives.

I worked closely with Werner de Smidt on the development of forecasting models for the performance of these stores, and the growing number of new stores that were being opened within the large store development group.

The necessity of using pro-formas for forecasting purposes and to justify capital expenditures, is something that has stayed with me and I continue to use these tools today.

On reflection, I wonder how I managed to cover such a broad area of responsibilities. But the key was in Don Neville's advice concerning delegation.

Jim Waldron and Steve Murray, supported by Geoff Andrews and Bill Durant, were effectively running the merchandising teams.

John Clegg was running the day-to-day operations of Shopper's Paradise.

Gordon Terrel was running the business development test stores (frozen food, discount health and beauty stores, and wine and spirit stores).

This allowed me to spend up to two weeks each month preparing board reports and attending board meetings. Both Mr. Gulliver and then Mr. Monaghan were tough managers, demanding high-quality reports and discussion. There were no short cuts to getting these reports completed. A lot of it was produced at our kitchen table of an evening.

These were interesting years and I was being exposed to so much experience and to the thinking practices of many different managers. Again, I did not realize that this was preparing me for the challenges to come.

All of this was wonderful, but change was on the horizon.

Regrettably, it was time for me to leave.

Wallace Monaghan was an excellent general manager and I really did enjoy a good working relationship with him. We used to enjoy tea in his office on a Saturday morning to discuss a variety of topics. He was a typical taciturn Scotsman. He never called me by my first name and seldom gave praise. One day, he explained that although he did not agree with giving praise, I should know that he trusted me, and that he would rate my performance as nine out of ten. *Very gratifying.*

However, once he became chairman, he had to make several decisions relating to the future management structure of the company. One of these decisions was to ask me to leave the business development group under Werner de Smidt and join a new group that he was putting together under a newly recruited senior director, Terry Bennison.

This was a major disappointment to me.

I already knew Terry Bennison from his previous company, and his bad reputation preceded him. I was not happy with this prospect and explained why. However, out of loyalty to Mr. Monaghan, I agreed to report to Mr. Bennison, and we were asked to take a weekend, travel to the continent, and work out our differences. During this trip, I told Mr. Bennison that his reputation was such that I would have difficulty placing my trust in him, but I would give it a try. I also told him that I would review my position in six months to see how things were working out.

After six months, I gave the whole situation considered thought and determined that Mr. Bennison and I could no longer work together (his values were the opposite of mine). However, I did not want to add to Mr. Monaghan's challenges. It was time to leave.

I handed in my resignation to Mr. Monaghan on a Saturday morning. This was the only time, he ever called me by my first name *"Frank, you are a blithering idiot."* I told him that my mind was made up, and he told me that he would expect me to work out my statutory three-months' notice period. I agreed.

On the Monday, I contacted Alistair Grant, who was with James Gulliver's new company, Oriol Foods (subsequently Argyle Foods). Alistair asked me not to approach other companies until he had an opportunity to speak with Mr. Gulliver.

On Wednesday, Alistair phoned me to say that they would offer me a senior position with at least the same salary and benefits that I had enjoyed at Fine Fare. On the following Monday, I met with

A LIFE IN STAGES

Alistair and Mr. Gulliver (call me James!) and they offered me the position of Managing Director of Oriol Foods. I accepted and returned to Fine Fare to work out my notice.

It was a long three months. During this time, Ann and I toured parts of Lancashire and Cheshire, trying to decide where we would live. I also arranged to have an ear operation as I was beginning to lose the hearing in my left ear.

It was not to be.

Towards the end of my notice period, Wallace Monaghan was speaking with Mr. Galen Weston in Toronto and happened to mention that I was leaving to join Mr. Gulliver. Mr. Weston told Mr. Monaghan to arrange for me to visit him in Toronto within the next couple of days. What do you do when one of the richest men in the world says that he would like to talk to you? I went and this led to my relocating back to Canada in January 1975.

I was very fortunate that this occurred before my scheduled surgery. If the surgery had gone ahead, I would not have been able to fly for at least six months and my life would have been changed forever. I have managed to get through the balance of my life without this surgery.

This brings the Fine Fare part of my story to a close, but without repeating much of what I have said about this time, I must pay respect to the five men that played such a huge part in my development as a professional manager during these years.

I had learned how to be an effective supervisor and a leader, while appreciating the value of teamwork. Jim Waldron, Steve Murray, and I made a great team.

I had learned how to establish objectives, measure results, and not be easily deterred.

I had evolved into "Firm, Factual, Friendly Frank."

R.I.P. Laurie Edwards, Don Neville, Werner de Smidt, Wallace Monaghan, and James Gulliver.

Had I decided to stay with Oriol Foods, I would probably have been appointed managing director of Safeway UK, as this company was acquired within two years, by James Gulliver and Alistair Grant through Argyll Foods, the successor company to Oriol Foods.

Both James Gulliver and Alistair Grant (Sir Alistair Grant) became very active in Scottish affairs, but both died at a relatively young age.

I view my time at Fine Fare as my formative years, as it relates to my growth and understanding of management. My successive promotions at Fine Fare and my experience working with many senior managers, gave me the confidence to take on the next series of challenges that were coming my way.

One of the ways in which I benefited, was that Mr. Gulliver had arranged for Fine Fare to purchase a large country house outside of Welwyn Garden City (Barneswood) and to redevelop it as a residential training centre. One of my roles was to provide merchandising training for executive trainees at Barneswood. This also provided me with the opportunity to attend any other courses that were being provided by other experts. I took full advantage of this opportunity and continued to learn more and more about my chosen profession.

FRANK FARR

Fine Fare Collage 1961–1975

A LIFE IN STAGES

**Farewell to Fine Fare—
Barnswood, December 1974**

Esther, Paula, Ann, Frank—Leaving for Canada Party—December 1974

"Delegation—what to delegate? Everything, except those things that only you can do, either by skill or responsibility." Don Neville

"Give me some options. A choice of one is no choice at all." Frank Farr

In business "That which gets measured, gets done" James Gulliver

CHAPTER TEN

Canada Again—The Tamblyn Years 1975–1978

My meeting with Mr. Weston in Toronto was short. He outlined that he was going to replace/hire more than a hundred senior managers in North America during the next few years and asked me if I would be interested in joining his new team as vice-president of development for the Loblaw Group. Our meeting was interrupted by the news that his latest supermarket in Ireland had just been bombed by the IRA, and he rushed off to get more details. I had visited that supermarket a few weeks previously.

In many ways this was a dream come true, as I had left Loblaw's as an assistant supermarket manager thirteen years previous. However, I decided to stick to my guns and go back to the job that was waiting for me at Oriol Foods. Following Mr. Weston's departure, I was left to deal with his two right-hand men, Dick Currie and Dave Nichol. I spent the rest of the week with them.

I was faced with the choice of accepting a high profile but specialized position with this giant corporation, or being a general manager, running a smaller but promising company, back in the UK. I was also concerned that Ann would not easily settle into living in Toronto with its bad winters.

Dave Nicol sensed that he was losing me and suggested that I go out to Vancouver to meet Ray Addington. Ray had been a co-director of Fine Fare and had now settled in Vancouver as president of Kelly Douglas, the company that ran the Weston organization's retail businesses in Western Canada. I agreed to go, and my companion on the flight was Serge Darkazanli.

Serge Darkazanli was a somewhat charismatic character, clearly very smart and ambitious. He was relocating to Vancouver to run the Kelly Douglas pharmacy chain, Isaacs' Pharmacy, and to convert it to the Tamblyn Brand as a part of the national chain owned by Loblaws. Ray and Serge offered me the position of senior vice-president of Tamblyn (West) with the understanding that Serge would move on within a couple of years and that I would then take over and run this 150-store chain of drug stores. I accepted, subject to Ann and Paula agreeing to move to Canada.

I was so impressed with Vancouver and I thought that, as a professional manager, I could adjust to the pharmacy business and do a good job. I also visited some homes for sale in the British Properties area of West Vancouver and decided that if we could afford to live in this beautiful part of the world, we should take the risk.

The next couple of months were hectic. I returned to Vancouver with Ann and Paula on what was their first flight. They also fell in love with this wonderful place, and we arranged to purchase the house in the British Properties that I had seen on my earlier visit. During this week, we stayed at the Bayshore Hotel, next to Stanley Park. This was quite a highlight for the three of us. The Bayshore was then the premier hotel in Vancouver; we were on the waterfront and adjacent to Stanley Park. This was our first experience of Vancouver, and we were hooked.

We sold our home in Welwyn Garden City, obtained permission to immigrate to Canada and flew into our new home during the first week of January 1975. We could stand on our outside deck and see for miles over the city of Vancouver to Mount Baker in the US, over the Georgia Strait to Vancouver Island, and back to the North Shore Mountains.

We arrived just in time for a major snow fall. This was the most snow that we had ever experienced as a family. And the first time that Ann and Paula had seen real snow—feet of it! My mother, who had never flown before, also joined us for the first three months, as I was sure that I would need to travel during my adjustment to my new job.

A week after we arrived, we went to the airport to pick up our dog, Lassie.

Lassie at Seymour Mountain

The first year was a remarkable experience for Ann, Paula, and me. We enjoyed getting to know the Vancouver region and so many of its attractions, places that were new and exciting to see for the first time: Stanley Park, Ambleside Park, Granville Market, Queen Elizabeth Park, and the Conservatory, Horseshoe Bay and the BC Ferries, Grouse Mountain, the local ski hills, and the new development at Whistler. Quite frankly, it was a lot to take in and it usually took our breath away. We felt so fortunate to have arrived in a place of such natural beauty.

The most welcome adjustment from our lifestyle in England was the abundance of wildlife and the closeness to nature. We quickly became used to our first friendly visitors, a family of raccoons with little "bandit" faces, who would come to our kitchen window and beg for food. (We soon learned that this was not advised.) It was also a nice surprise to see the pair of eagles that flew by every morning and returned again in the evening, followed by the frequent appearances of a huge blue heron.

Our biggest surprise (and scare), was to see an adult black bear sitting on a rock, not ten feet from our back door. It took several days and a visit from the conservation officer before we felt that it was safe to venture into the back garden.

From a nature perspective, it was interesting to speculate that we were living on the outer limits of human development, and in theory, we could have walked out of our back door and continued to the North Pole without necessarily coming to another city. Quite the difference from life in Welwyn Garden City.

The home that we purchased was 1120 Hillside Road, in the middle of the Properties. It was a half- acre, full-view property, with a split-level, colonial style home of 2,100 square feet. We loved our new home, which we thought of as the height of luxury.

Ann and Paula began adjusting to the West Coast lifestyle. Ann's main adjustment was learning to drive and adjusting to the shopping, most of which seemed an improvement on what we had left behind. Paula had to adjust to a new school. We were surprised to find that the curriculum was a full year behind the one that she'd had in England. The social adjustment for Paula was the most difficult. Ten years old and no new friends, except for her pet sheltie Lassie. At one point we were wondering if we had done the right thing and whether we should consider returning to England.

However, once Paula made new friends, things settled down and all was well. Paula's first friends were Jill Rosebourne and Tracey Cox, with whom she is still friends today. She made many other friends during those her early school days at Westcott and later Sentinel School.

The British Properties is a residential development, nestled in the North Shore Mountains of West Vancouver, with panoramic views out over the city and for fifty miles south to Mt. Baker and the USA, and fifty miles west to the southern tip of Vancouver Island.

The area was bought by the British Guinness family in the 1930s and expanded following the opening of the Lion's Gate Bridge (also paid for by the Guinness family to encourage the development of their North Shore property). The "Properties" was, at that time, regarded as one of the prime residential areas in Canada.

George, Ann, Esther, and Lassie at 1120 Hillside Road, West Vancouver

Before leaving England, we had a going-away dinner at the Hilton Hotel at Heathrow Airport, with Jim and Angela Waldron, and Steve and Mary Murray. It was a tearful goodbye, and we promised to stay in touch and hoped to revisit England at some time in the future.

But here again fate intervened.

As soon as I started work in Vancouver, I realized that, faced with the plan to convert the Isaacs' stores to Tamblyn Drugmarts, I would need to hire and train a store opening and remodelling team. But where to find the right people and how long would it take to hire and train them?

Inspiration!

On a Friday evening, about two weeks after our arrival in Vancouver, I phoned Jim, just before he was going out to the Welwyn Arms Pub to meet Steve. I knew that he and Steve both had passports and that they had some vacation time due, so I invited them to come to Vancouver with a view to joining me on this new adventure with Tamblyn.

Within a week, they were in Vancouver for an introductory visit, enjoying a record snowfall up in the Properties.

I was very thankful that they accepted my offer. They returned to England, gave their notice to Fine Fare, and arrived in Vancouver during the first week of May with their families, five months after our arrival. Their first stop in Vancouver was The Tropicana Hotel in the downtown area and then they moved to new homes in North Vancouver, Burnaby, and subsequently to their current homes in North Delta.

Jim Waldron, Lassie, Louise Waldron, Frank, Olive, Nick Waldron, and Ann—at the Hillside House 1975

I have commented at the beginning of these stories that it is amazing to see the impact that we all have on other people's lives. Often this has resulted from an unexpected phone call, or today an e-mail or a text.

A LIFE IN STAGES

It is interesting to stop at this point and think about the consequences of that one phone call between Wallace Monaghan and Galen Weston in November of 1974 and that one phone call two months later between me and Jim in January of 1975.

In the years following the arrival of Jim and Angela, and Steve and Mary and their families in Canada, three of Steve's brothers, together with their families, joined our happy group in Canada: Andrew, Tony and Liz, and Martin and Sandra.

Jim and Angela had two children, Nick and Louise.

Nick is married to Linda.

Louise is married to Chris and they have a son, Jake

Steve and Mary had four children, Andrew, Charlotte, Sinead, and Joanne

Andrew has a son Liam and a partner, Sandy

Charlotte is married to Jorge Marrujo and they have three children, Tomas, James, and Mateo.

Sinead is married to Denis Ryan and they have two children, Aine and Declan.

Joanne is married to Kevin Devine and they have two children, Kate and Lucy.

Tony and Liz have two children, Helen and Josephine

Josephine has a partner, Jason, and they have one daughter, Gemma

Andrew was married to Wendy and they had one son, Riley

Martin and Sandra had two children, Alison and Tyler

Alison has a partner and she has two children, Charlie and Ben.

It has been a genuine pleasure to see how these families have grown and developed. Collectively, they are a lovely group of people and the kids are amazing.

Forty people living in Canada, and raising their families in British Columbia. All resulting from a couple of unplanned phone calls back in 1974-5. WOW!

Steve and Mary Murray with Andrew, Charlotte, Sinead and Jo July 2020

Jim Waldron and Rebecca Fry, Steve and Mary Murray with the extended Murray family—at Andy Murray's fiftieth birthday July 2020

My company car in my new position was a silver Chevrolet Impala and this provided us with the opportunity to enjoy our first vacations in Canada, touring Vancouver Island, up through the beautiful Okanagan valley, and on to the Rockies: Banff, Lake Louise, and Jasper, together with Paula and Ann's parents.

Ann and I, together with Jim and Angela and Steve and Mary, also enjoyed our fun time at Fast Eddy's, a night club in North Vancouver. We actually experienced our first earthquake there one night, and we had trouble deciding if it really was an earthquake or the alcohol. (It was an earthquake.)

Ann, Frank, Angela and Jim Waldron and Mary and Steve Murray – Fast Eddie's Nightclub in North Vancouver 1976

Frank and Ann—Fast Eddie's

A LIFE IN STAGES

The housing situation fascinated us, with such an incredible range of houses for sale. We visited many open houses and fell in love with and eventually purchased our second house on Chartwell Place, still in the British Properties. This was a 3,600 square foot house and it was a considerable step up from the house on Hillside Rd. I remember that this home had a fish-shaped bar on the lower level and a built-in aquarium in the wall, behind the bar.

It was during this time that we also enjoyed many fishing trips on the west coast.

And so, the Tamblyn experience began, starting in 1975 and lasting through to 1978.

We had 150 drugstores located from Victoria on Vancouver Island to Thunder Bay in Northern Ontario. The eastern wing of the company (operated out of Toronto) had approximately 250 locations in Ontario. The company had a mixed record of profitability and the job for Serge and me was to turn the western group around.

Frank and Ann at the Chartwell Place home 1977

During our work on rebranding the stores from Isaacs to Tamblyn, we had some interesting experiences. One of the best was our opportunity to spend time in the Okanagan. Working from a base in Vernon, we enjoyed a lot of fun times.

We also discovered the challenges of the Canadian winter at -44 degrees (with the windchill factor) in Calgary and many other very cold experiences.

George Pope and Nick Waldron— fishing with Ted Peck

There are three follow-ups to this drug store part of the story:

Kelly Douglas owned the Nabob Coffee Company, Western Canada's leading coffee manufacturer. In 1976, Serge convinced Loblaws that Nabob had peaked and now would be a good time to sell. A sale was arranged to a Swiss company, Jacobs, and Serge developed a plan to use the money to buy London Drugs. London Drugs, at that time, was a small, but successful chain of five or six large drug stores in Vancouver.

Although the chain had been founded in 1945 by Sam Bass, it was now owned by The Daylin Corporation of LA. Daylin ran into some financial difficulties, and it put London Drugs up for sale. Serge thought that we could buy it with the proceeds from the sale of Nabob. Serge and I made several visits to London Drugs' head office and Serge became good friends with Sam Bass. I didn't.

99

FRANK FARR

In quick order, we learned that Loblaws had found a more important use for the money (Dick Currie wanted it for National Tea). Murray Koffler, the founder of Shopper's Drug Mart, believed that he had an agreement to buy London Drugs and flew his team into Vancouver to close the deal. However, he had missed out by one day. Tong Louie, who owned IGA in Western Canada, had closed on the deal the day before. The Louie family went on to develop London Drugs into the dominant large drug store format in Western Canada with eighty-two stores as of 2019.

Working with Serge was an interesting experience. He was a very bright, hard-working executive and I cannot fault him on his business prowess. But life is not all business and on a personal basis, I could no longer work with/for him. Serge was clever, but he had an unusual management style that was difficult to handle.

There are a couple of memories from my time, working with Serge.

Serge had worked at McKinsey with Dave Nicol and Dick Currie, and he had an extremely efficient way of making presentations (the McKinsey way). I admired this method (Forced Choices), and I have used it to great advantage during the remainder of my career.

My final breaking point with Serge came following a meeting of the Kelly Douglas board in Vancouver. I attended a dinner at Ray Addington's home. Galen Weston was there, and he greeted me with his usual "Frank Farr, how are you?" He proceeded to add his congratulations on my new position as president of Tamblyn's. Although this was anticipated, I was not aware that the decision had been made. Mr. Weston told me that they had discussed this at that day's board meeting. Serge was moving over to Kelly Douglas and I would take over at Tamblyn as planned.

Serge was not around for the next couple of weeks and when he returned, I learned a couple of disturbing facts. On the one hand, he had been in England meeting Wallace Monaghan and visiting my old offices in Welwyn Garden City. He had never mentioned this to me, and I was quite offended. He also told me that although he was going over to Kelly Douglas as Ray Addington's deputy, he intended to remain as president of Tamblyn and to maintain an office in both premises.

We had succeeded in our work with Tamblyn, but were always a long, long, way behind the market leader, Shopper's Drug Mart. During the next year, it became clear that despite the fact that we had turned the company around, it would not play a role in the future of Kelly Douglas and an agreement was reached to sell the company to Boots, the chemists from England.

I had previous experience dealing with Boots in England. They had co-developed a property with Fine Fare at London Rd. in Brighton, and I had acted as the liaison on this project. Boots dominated the pharmacy business in the UK where there is a large Boots store in every city and town in the country. They were keenly interested in expanding to North America. I got on very well with the two Boots executives assigned to run Boots Canada and they offered me the position of director of development for North America, based in Toronto. Together with Jim Waldron, I checked out several homes in the Toronto region, but my heart was not in it.

There were several reasons:

A LIFE IN STAGES

- I did not want to relocate to Toronto and I did not think that Ann and Paula would be happy with such a move.

- Boots had a traditional, old-school management system, and I did not know how they would adapt to the competitive environment of North America.

- I was not confident that they would provide the many millions of dollars that it would take to develop a strong market share in these new markets.

- I was already in touch with The Southland Corporation (7-Eleven) and my initial talks were encouraging.

Technically, I worked for Boots for two months to oversee the transition from Tamblyn to Boots.

I had decided that it was again, time to leave, and I finalized my agreement to join The Southland Corporation, as the division manager for Southland Canada, Inc. This was the best business decision that I ever made. It changed our lives forever and for the better.

I left Kelly Douglas in June of 1978 and joined Southland Canada on July 1st, 1978.

Boots eventually abandoned this initial expansion into North America. It remains the dominant pharmacy retailer in the UK, but in 2014, Boots became a subsidiary of Boots-Walgreen with its head office in the USA.

Loblaws sold its Canadian Drug Store operation (Tamblyn) to Boots in 1978. Boots subsequently sold its Canadian operation to Shopper's Drug Mart in 1980, and finally, Loblaws bought Shoppers Drug Mart in a mammoth 12.4 billion-dollar deal in 2013.

Ray Addington died in 2008. I went to his "celebration of life" and met Serge Darkazanli there. He had retired from Kelly Douglas and by another twist of fate, his son had married Ray Addington's daughter Annabel, and so these two families had a more permanent bond.

Some remaining thoughts from my time in the pharmacy business:

Pharmacists were good people, who wanted to play a role in their communities as a part of the health triangle of doctors, dentists, and pharmacists. However, they were generally not good businesspeople.

The pharmacy business was very seasonal, with most stores making their profit during the final quarter of the year. The inventory turns were very slow, as low as four turns per year on franchise cosmetics and pharmaceutical inventory.

Frank at Tamblyn's Head Office 1977

The experience did end up being very valuable, as two of my future assignments were with pharmacy companies in Armenia and Georgia.

I missed my time in food retailing, where inventory turns much faster, profitability was more evenly spread, and the pace of decision making is more rapid. This was immediately apparent once I returned to the food business with 7-Eleven in July of 1978.

❖

"You fail to understand the nature of our relationship." Serge Darkazanli

This was one of Serge's most forceful quotes, when he wanted to assert his dominance over subordinates. It is the type of statement that should be reserved for difficult circumstances. I have only had to use it twice, but each time it had the desired effect.

CHAPTER ELEVEN

The Weston Family

My departure from Tamblyn's (Kelly Douglas) was also the end of my relationship with the Weston family and the enormous influence that they had on my life up to this date.

Garfield Weston

In earlier chapters, I have mentioned how Mr. Garfield Weston's decision to hire young Canadians to join his companies in England had led to my move back home and my subsequent career with Fine Fare. I was the only one of this group of Canadians who lived up to his expectations. Without the actions of Mr. Garfield Weston in 1961, I never would have met Ann, and Paula would not have been born.

During my years with Fine Fare, I met Mr. Weston on three other occasions, all related to projects that I was responsible for.

Fine Fare owned two prestige Cooper's Supermarkets in London. One was on Knightsbridge and one was on Edgeware Road. On one occasion, Mr. Weston visited the Edgeware Rd. store, along with Hugo Mann. Mr. Mann was the founder and owner of Deutscher Supermarkets in Germany. Allegedly, Mr. Mann pointed out that the Cooper's store was somewhat outdated and offered to refurbish it along the lines of his recently opened Deutscher Supermarket in Bonn, Germany.

This caused some consternation in the Fine Fare head office, where the chairman, Mr. James Gulliver, decided that it would be inappropriate to have a German supermarket company remodel one of our premier locations. By this time, I was the Director of Merchandising for Fine Fare, with the responsibility for the planning and opening of new stores. I was assigned the responsibility to remodel and reopen the Cooper's store on Edgeware Rd. My mandate was that cost was not a concern, and that the final result should compare favourably with the Deutscher Supermarket in Bonn. Fortunately, I had already seen this store.

We did complete the extensive remodel of the Edgeware Rd. store and I was very proud at the re-opening to learn that Mr. Weston was pleased with the final result. It was agreed that we would apply the same remedy to its sister store in Knightsbridge. The re-opening of the Knightsbridge store was marked by the presence of Garfield Weston's 2nd eldest son, Gary Weston.

The two other times that I met Mr. Garfield Weston were at The Decimal Supermarket in London, and at the opening of Britain's largest supermarket in Aberdeen. He did not realize that I had been one of that first group that he had invited to join Fine Fare back in 1961.

As suggested by Mr. Weston, I had settled in the UK, married an English girl and gone on to be a director of several companies within the Fine Fare Group.

Mr. Garfield Weston died in Toronto in 1978 at the age of eighty.

Because the Aberdeen store was the largest supermarket in Britain, we had much discussion in search of an appropriate name for the new store. It was originally named Fine Fare—Coopers.

We considered many alternatives. Mammoth, Giant, and Mega were among the names considered. We had hired a local bus company to transport local shoppers to and from the store and shortly after the store opened, we saw the double decker bus coming into the parking lot with the wording "Superstore" on the front. The locals had decided on the name and we (Wallace Monaghan; Werner de Smidt, managing director of Fine Fare Scotland; and I) agreed that this was appropriate. This was the first time that I am aware of that the name "Superstore" was used, and I have recently verified this recollection with my good friend Werner de Smidt (now ninety-three years of age and living in Huntingdon). Fine Fare adopted the "Superstore" name for all of the large stores that followed, and this name was subsequently adopted by the Canadian Supermarket operations and perpetuated as "The Real Canadian Superstore."

Gary Weston

I only met him on three occasions.

Following the retirement of Mr. Garfield Weston, Gary, his second eldest son, assumed responsibility for the company's UK operations, Associated British Foods (ABF). Gary's primary background had been in running the family's bakery and retail operations in Australia and South Africa.

I first met him when he came to Fine Fare's head office to meet and greet the directors of Fine Fare.

The second time that I met him was at the reopening of the Knightsbridge Coopers store. My only recollection of this was that, on the night before the opening, as I was prowling the store to make sure that everything was as perfect as it could be, Gary's young son, George, found a price marker and enjoyed himself running up and down some of the aisles marking and mismarking as many items , as he could. I had to assign somebody to follow him and clean up as he went along his mischievous way. I was not very happy with him. Following the passing of Gary, that young lad, George Weston, now runs the ABF conglomerate. This includes the very successful Primark chain.

The third time that I met Gary was at the ABF head office in central London. At the time, one of my responsibilities was to manage Fine Fare's relationships with franchise operations that operated specialty sections within our superstore group. It had been agreed that the regional bakeries, a part of ABF, would operate the in-store bakeries in the Fine Fare Superstores. I visited ABF Headquarters to finalize store plans and other operating issues with my colleagues at ABF and on one of these visits, I was again introduced to Mr. Gary Weston.

Mr. Gary Weston died in London in 2002. Aged 74.

Galen Weston

Galen Weston is the youngest son of Garfield Weston. He is two years younger than I am. During my early years with Fine Fare, Galen was living and working in Ireland, running a small supermarket company called Power Supermarkets. (This was the name of a rival company in Canada.) He would from time to time visit the Fine Fare stores in the UK.

During my early years at Fine Fare, I was occasionally between assignments, and at these times, I would volunteer to complete re-merchandising projects in various locations within the Fine Fare Regions. On one of these occasions, I was working at some of the supermarkets in the Hull region and Galen Weston came into the store that I was working on. He mentioned that he had visited several stores in the area that had recently been remerchandised (by me) and wanted to talk with me. This was the first of several discussions that Galen had with me over the next few years.

At Galen's request, I did visit a few of his stores in Ireland, including the Penney's department store in Dublin and also the latest new Irish supermarket under construction.

Around 1970–1972 the Weston family had to make some difficult choices regarding the future of their flagship Loblaw company in Canada. Although Loblaw was a Canadian operation, it was the controlling company for the family's retail operations in North America and these totalled more than 2,000 supermarkets under a variety of brands, primarily National Tea of Chicago.

The company had a high level of long-term debt that it was having difficulty financing from internally generated funds. It was time for Loblaw's to sink or swim. The decision was made that the family would inject the required funds and that Galen would return to Canada to lead the rescue of this family jewel.

Galen's decision to return to Canada was also influenced by his high profile in Ireland, at a time when violence by the IRA was on the rise. There had been an unsuccessful kidnap attempt on Galen and a more successful kidnapping and ransom of one of his key managers. His ability to live a normal life at his home outside of Dublin was no longer possible.

Galen returned to Canada and to help him in his transition, Mr. Gulliver and several senior Fine Fare directors joined Loblaws on an interim basis. Don Neville asked me to join them in Toronto to set up the remodelling operation that was a part of the relaunch plans for the Loblaw and National Tea Brands.

During the visit to Canada to work with Don Neville, I had my first opportunity to meet Don Watt, Dave Nicol, and Dick Currie. These three men had a profound and long-lasting impact on Galen's challenge to turn around the Weston family's fortunes in North America.

Dave Nicol had been Galen's college roommate. He was recruited from McKinsey to work alongside Galen around 1972. Dave was an outstanding communicator, promoter, and marketer. He was the original "President" of President's Choice.

Dick Currie had also been with McKinsey and was recommended by Dave Nicol as the outstanding manager that he proved to be. He was the tough-minded manager who was needed to bring order and efficiency to a huge group of disconnected businesses.

Don Watt was the design genius behind the advertising firm of Break, Pane and Watt. Galen encouraged Don to strike out on his own, and he became one of the leading retail designers in North America. So much of what we see as the face of Weston's retailing operations, owes a great deal to Don's designs. I had the pleasure of a very enjoyable dinner in Don's home during this visit (Canada goose and wild rice).

I was offered the position of vice president of store development for the Loblaw companies. I was very flattered but had several reservations:

1. I did not think that Ann would be happy living in Toronto

2. I was being asked to reprise my specialist experience in Fine Fare, as compared with the opportunity of general management, running a company in the UK.

3. I also had a vague unease regarding the future chemistry between myself and Dave Nicol.

I did, however, accept the position of senior vice-president of Tamblyn (West) due to the fact that we fell in love with Vancouver and decided to make our future home there.

Galen was involved in three ways:

1. He arranged for a letter to be provided to the Canadian High Commissioner in London, requesting an expedited approval of our immigration request.

2. Despite being ill with a strong cold, he phoned me from his home in Toronto on the day that we arrived (at the Bayshore Hotel in Vancouver) to wish me well and to tell me to give him a call, should I encounter any concerns. (Later, I did come close to taking him up on this, but thought better of it.)

3. The dinner at Ray Addington's home in Vancouver, in 1978 was my final meeting with Galen, and I am left with the memory of a good man who saw some potential in me, thought well of me, and provided us the opportunity for a fresh start in wonderful Vancouver.

I am thankful to both Mr. Garfield Weston, for his decision to invite me to return to England in 1961 and my successful eighteen-year career with the Weston companies and to Mr. Galen Weston, for his consideration and support leading up to his invitation in 1974 to return to Canada and join his North American management team.

This opened the door for all that followed, including my career with 7-Eleven and also the great good fortune to enjoy our life in Vancouver and to see the impact that all of this has had on Jim Waldron, Steve Murray, and their extended families, as they joined me for much of this adventure.

As I think of this part of my story, I am reminded of two facts that are entwined in the themes of my life:

1. Although we do not always realize it, we are all impacted by the lives of those with whom we come in contact, often in ways that are not clear at the time.

2. While luck plays a part in all our lives, there is also a saying that "Good luck is where preparation meets opportunity." I think that in 1978, I was prepared for the opportunities that followed.

❖

"What are you doing that is new, different, innovative, or controversial?"
Galen Weston/Frank Farr

CHAPTER TWELVE

The 7-Eleven Years – Part One 1978-1990

A New Direction—A New Life

My Forties

I was just short of my fortieth birthday when I joined 7-Eleven and the decade of my forties was an amazing time of growth. They say that nothing succeeds like success and for me this proved to be true. The remarkable success that we were able to achieve for 7-Eleven in Canada, allowed me to grow both personally and professionally. I genuinely believed that no task was too big and that I could succeed with whatever life might bring. Apart from work, our vacations were a revelation. Seeing and experiencing so many parts of the world was eye opening. These were the best of times, and Ann, Paula, and I made the most of them.

The Beginning

In 1978, I was still working with the Weston Organization as the senior vice-president for Tamblyn Drugmarts (West) but change was inevitable.

The Weston organization had agreed to sell the chain to Boots of England and I was faced with several choices:

- Remain with the Weston Group in some unspecified capacity

- Join Boots as vice-president of North American development
- Return to England as managing director of Oriol Foods (Argyle Foods)

Each of these choices presented some upside opportunities and a lot of unknowns.

Out of the blue, I was contacted by Dez Hubbell. Dez had been the cosmetics coordinator for Tamblyn, but had moved on, and was now working for a head-hunting firm based in Toronto. She had learned that The Southland Corporation of Dallas, Texas, was looking for a new division manager, for its fledgling Canadian 7-Eleven operation, based out of Calgary. I had no particular interest in this position, but Dez wanted to use my name as a way of introducing herself to Southland. I agreed.

The Southland Corporation had been founded in 1927 in Dallas by Joe C. Thompson. The original stores traded under the name of U-Totem with a totem pole for its logo. As the store hours were gradually extended from 7:00 am to 11:00 pm the 7-Eleven name was adopted in 1946.

In the US, the company's name was The Southland Corporation, and it was the operator of the 7-Eleven convenience stores, Oak Farm Dairies, Chief Auto Parts, and many other businesses. In Canada, the company's name was Southland Canada, Inc. operating as 7-Eleven. I will refer to the US company as The Southland Corporation and to the Canadian company as 7-Eleven Canada.

I was contacted by Southland and asked to come down to their Dallas office. I knew of Southland. (In those days, if you wanted to know anything about the supermarket industry in the US, you studied Safeway and at the same time The Southland Corporation,

was famous for its development of convenience stores.) Out of respect for the company, and with the thought of getting an unexpected visit to Dallas, I agreed to go. I assumed that I would meet with one of their senior executives, have a polite discussion, and that would be the end of it.

That's not quite the way that it worked out. I travelled down on a Friday evening to be met by their HR manager, who took me to my hotel and arranged to pick me up at 8:30 on the Saturday morning. In the morning, we went to the head office and he proceeded to tell me that they wanted me to take "The Long Test." I was surprised by this, but I thought, *It's their dime, let's go ahead.*

The long test was designed to identify the capability and aptitude for the specific position/ job being considered and for suitability for promotion to a higher-level position.

What they called the long test, was a five-hour-long series of test papers. I filled them in diligently and they took each paper away to be scored by Dave Finley, the VP of human resources. He was in touch with Dick Dole and Jodie Thompson, who were both executive vice presidents of Southland. They were out at Jodie's ranch and were prepared to come back into town, if the test results were encouraging. Apparently, they were, as Dick and Jodie, in jeans and jean jackets, arranged to meet me for dinner.

I had done my homework and I had lots of questions for them. This surprised them for two reasons: 1) They thought that I had applied for the job, and 2) Southland was so successful that they were not used to being "grilled" by a prospective employee.

A LIFE IN STAGES

They offered me the job of running the company's operations in Canada and we agreed to continue the dialogue after I returned to Vancouver. I was very impressed with what I learned of the company, but more so by the attitude and approach to business that I saw in these two young executives. (They were both about the same age as me, thirty-nine at the time.)

During the next several weeks, we had many conversations. They used to call me at 6:00 am (8:00 am Dallas time). Finally, I decided not to join them, and advised Jodie of this on one of our morning calls. Later that morning, Dick phoned me, apologized for calling me at work ,and made the following point: "We are a great company and people seldom refuse to join us. We must have got our lines crossed in our discussions."

He was right. I had gotten hung up on three issues and I explained them to Dick:

- I was concerned about selling our home

- The job offer came with a big bonus opportunity, but I was wary of such offers, given my recent experiences with Serge Darkazanli

- They were not offering a company car

Dick asked me to phone him again the next morning. I did and his response was:

- We want you to be in Calgary. We will assume the responsibility of selling your home

- We will guarantee your bonus

- You can have any car that you think is appropriate.

Not just because of these concessions, but because of the manner in which they were made, I decided to accept their offer. This also required a leap of faith from both Ann and Paula. They were happy in Vancouver and had no knowledge of Calgary.

I remember Dick saying, "Give your wife a big hug. You just made a very good decision." He was right again. It was the best business decision that I ever made and the beginning of a twenty-year career with an amazing company.

I had not appreciated the Texans' feelings about cars. They had no company cars, but did provide an adequate allowance, assuming that a car was so individual that nobody would want to have a standard, company-issued one. They agreed to provide me with a car, but as soon as I understood their thinking, I changed the company car that they provided for their generous car allowance and bought my first Cadillac.

My twenty years with 7-Eleven is best broken into two distinct phases: 1978–1990 and 1990–1998.

FRANK FARR

Phase One: 1978–1990 The Glory Days

On joining the company, I spent my first week in Dallas, meeting with the chairman, John Thompson; the president, Jere Thompson; and most of the department heads. On the Friday, Dick and Jodie took me for dinner and at the end of the dinner, Dick asked Jodie, "Did you tell him?"

Jodie reached inside his jacket pocket and pulled out an envelope. In it was a very generous cheque. For more than my annual salary and far more than I had expected. He said 'We told you that we would guarantee your first year's bonus. Here it is." (Remember, this was in 1978.)

I was surprised and said, "But I have not earned anything yet."

Dick replied, "You will."

Frank at the 7-Eleven Head Office in Calgary in 1978

I returned to Canada determined to give this company my all and to justify the trust that they had placed in me. I believe that I lived up to their expectations.

When I met John Thompson, John's comments to me were along the following lines: "I hope that you will find your home with us. We are the best example of working capitalism that you will find. You can fulfil all of your ambitions within Southland. If you take care of our business, we will take care of you." He also said, "Business does not go in straight lines. You will have your good months and bad. If you have a bad month, you will not hear from me, but remember that our staff are our most valuable asset. If you mistreat our staff, I will fire you. Do not forget that."

Words to live by and I tried to live by them for all of my time at 7-Eleven.

Note

At the time that I left Kelly Douglas, I had one final meeting with Ray Addington. He suggested that I should speak to his vice-president of distribution, as he was aware that they were suppliers to 7-Eleven. Interestingly the VP of distribution's only comment was, "Yes we supply 7-Eleven, they are one of our nuisance accounts."

I had just agreed to join 7-Eleven with the mandate to grow the company as fast as I could. Within two months, I arranged to relieve them of their nuisance account by transferring our business from Kelly Douglas to Wallace & Carey and we went on to become the sixth largest food retailer in British Columbia

A LIFE IN STAGES

I returned to Vancouver and we prepared to sell our house and get ready for our move to Calgary.

The house sale was interesting. Southland appointed a Vancouver lawyer, David Gillanders, to handle the sale. The basic proposition was that he would get three estimates for the value of our home. Southland would guarantee us the middle price, and if they got anything higher, they would split the upside with me 50/50. Surprisingly, the house sold quickly, for higher than the middle price, and true to their word, they split the upside with me. David Gillanders became a friend over many years, both professionally and personally. Eventually, we arranged for him to be appointed as a director of Southland Canada.

Following a gorgeous trip over the Rockies, we arrived in Calgary on July 1st, 1978. We had agreed to rent a home, and this gave us another unexpected experience. We did not know that there was a large Mormon population in Calgary, and we had rented the home from a Mormon family. It is a Mormon tradition to store a year's supply of food, and the basement was like a grocery store, with row upon row of preserved foods, and the garden was full of fresh vegetables. The owners were typically generous and invited us to use any of their food that we wished. We were quite surprised. We subsequently purchased a home on Parkside Drive in SE Calgary.

On joining the company, I was advised that they had recently made several appointments in Canada, but I should not feel bound by these decisions and could change them if I felt it appropriate.

Jimmie Musselwhite receiving the Steve Pond award from Frank

The successes that stood out were, Jimmie Musselwhite, Merchandising Manager; Steve Pond, Zone Manager; Mike Sugden, Calgary (1) District Manager; and Terry Cashin, Calgary (2) District Manager. The rest of the changes were okay, except that I did have to ask two of the other district managers to leave the company after a couple of years.

Steve Pond was a good friend, unfortunately, he died of a heart attack within my first year with the company. Jimmie, and Mike remained friends for all my years with 7-Eleven.

Some funny instances from our first year in Calgary.

- We had a large group of visitors from the US and we spent several days touring stores. At the end of this visit, we arranged for a dinner in Calgary at Hy's Steakhouse. There were about twenty of us enjoying dinner and occupying the centre of the restaurant, when one of my US colleagues drew my attention to three young ladies sitting in an elevated booth, as they were looking our way.

Paula—Grade 9 in Calgary

Here, to my surprise, were Paula, Jill Rosebourne, and Corrine Carpenter. Paula's two friends were visiting from Vancouver. Jill's father, Don Rosebourne, was Hy Eisenstat's partner and of course, Jill was welcome to eat at any of her dad's restaurants. Here were the three of them, sitting at the best table in the restaurant, enjoying the best food and drink (Paula was fourteen at the time!) Quite the sight. I was so proud to say to the group, "That's my daughter."

- The Calgary Stampede was an unbelievable event. Regular business in Calgary comes to a stop, as everybody goes to the stampede. At 7-Eleven, we were no exception. I arranged for the company to construct a mini 7-Eleven within the Stampede grounds. We just sold "Slurpees" and sold 10,000 within ten days.

Mini 7-Eleven at the Calgary Stampede 1978

- Stampede breakfasts at the leading hotels were another feature, starting at 7:30 am and going until noon. They were regular breakfasts, except the only beverage was "vodka and orange" with live entertainment from rotating bands. Home to sleep for a couple of hours and then off to the chuckwagon races and the rodeo. Non-stop for ten days. Unbelievable!

Jimmie Musselwhite, Grant Richards, and John Timms—7-Eleven Breakfast 1978

- Steve Pond took me to his favourite bar, Lonnie's, to show me where a famous "attack donkey" had bitten into the front of the bar. He also introduced me to his friend Fred Meester. Fred soon joined 7-Eleven and spent many years with us working in Calgary, Winnipeg, Toronto, and Vancouver.

A LIFE IN STAGES

Wallace & Carey—Frank Carey

Shortly after I joined 7-Eleven in Calgary, I had my first meeting with Frank and Larry Carey. Wallace & Carey were our suppliers in Alberta, and Frank was busy assuming the management of the company from his father. There was an interesting comparison with Kelly Douglas. They had explained to me that 7-Eleven was a "nuisance" account. Frank Carey told me that we were Wallace & Carey's most important customer and they were pledged to work with and support us in our growth plans.

Withing a few short weeks, I asked Frank to take over the supply of our British Columbia stores and once that was completed, I asked him to take over the supply of our Saskatchewan and Manitoba stores. A year later, I also asked them to take over the supply of our Ontario stores. They did all of this successfully and efficiently.

Frank Carey and I became friends and that friendship lasted for over forty years until Frank's unexpected passing in 2019.

Frank was a remarkable man, a man of his word, a man anchored in firm values and supported by a wonderful family. I had many enjoyable times with him: Stampede parties at the original family home in North Calgary, many golf weekends to fabulous resorts, and great times at the magnificent new home that he and Anita built on the northern outskirts of Calgary. On the grounds of this home, Frank built a "professional quality" executive golf course, and I had the pleasure of playing there on many occasions. Frank also joined Steve Krumholz, Steve LeRoy, Jim Waldron, and me, on a very enjoyable visit to the 7-Eleven operation in England and Denmark.

We last met in Vancouver, only a few weeks prior to his passing. He was proud of his accomplishment in transferring the control of the company to his son Patrick, who will now lead the company through its third generation.

7-Eleven U.S. vs. Canada

During my time in Calgary, I realized that many of the US managers had limited knowledge of Canada and often arrived in Canada without the appreciation that, not only were we a different country; we were also a separate company. They confused our national holiday on July 1st with their national holiday on July 4th and could not understand why our offices were not open on July 1st.

I did several things to try to address this:

I placed a large Canadian flag in the lobby of all of our Canadian district offices.

For Canada Day, I sent miniature (desk-sized) Canadian flags to all of the directors and department heads in Dallas, and also sent each of them a tie emblazoned with a maple leaf.

I stopped the production, in Canada, of our financial statements in US dollars.

They quickly understood the point that I was making, and Jere Thompson reciprocated by making sure that the Canadian flag was flown at the Dallas head office when I was attending meetings.

Relocation from Calgary to Vancouver

Despite the good times, our move to Calgary was a mixed blessing. The people were friendly, and the work was enjoyable. We bought a home, but quickly became aware that Calgary was in the middle of a boom and that most of my subordinates were renting homes, as house prices were even higher than in Vancouver.

Ann and Paula also had a difficult time adjusting to the move from Vancouver to Calgary.

The biggest problem came during that first winter. It was a particularly cold one, and this caused problems for both Ann and Paula. The mixture of snow and ice made it difficult for Ann to drive and the Calgary school system was such that Paula had to travel several miles to school, often in a freezing-cold bus that had been parked outside for the night, in minus twenty to thirty-degree temperatures. At times, the situation was very difficult. At the end of the school day, the bus would drop Paula off about a mile from our house and she had to walk home in windy, sub-zero temperatures.

One day, I came home from work to find Ann and Paula in tears. Ann was busy trying to warm Paula's frozen jeans in front of the fire.

I made an instant decision. We would return to Vancouver, and I promised them that they would not spend another winter in Calgary. The crying stopped. The smiles came out, and I knew that I had made the right decision.

Now what to do???

Within a few weeks, I was in Dallas, to make the following argument:

- From a personal perspective: I loved the company and I loved my job, but my family was not settling in Calgary and we would be returning to Vancouver. I would be happy to remain with the company, if necessary, in a lesser position, but we were going back to Vancouver.

- From a business perspective: We already had forty stores in the Calgary District and that was unlikely to grow to more than sixty. We only had fourteen stores in the Vancouver Region, but the growth potential was unlimited. The Vancouver Region included twelve different municipalities with different bylaws, and this could best be managed from Vancouver.

- Many of our head-office employees were from Vancouver. They could not afford to buy homes in Calgary, and we were at risk of losing them back to Vancouver.

I remember Dick and Jodie listening to me and Jodie said, "I don't blame you for not settling in Calgary; it reminds me of Fort Worth."

Dick simply said, "Okay, you can move the office from Calgary to Vancouver."

I was very pleased at this decision. Yet another example of quick decisions by these two Texans.

Once I was back in Calgary, I asked our construction manager, Fred Morris, to take a look at potential office space in Vancouver. I knew that Burnaby was central to the Lower Mainland and I had a certain type of office building in mind. I was quite surprised when he called me to say that the very building that I had directed him to was available to lease.

I flew out to Vancouver that same day, saw the building, and approved a lease. We moved into our new offices within sixty days—late 1979. On my first day in the new office, I phoned Dick Dole to tell him. He was pleasantly shocked. He had assumed that I would complete the move sometime within the next year!

7-Eleven management team at the first Vancouver head office, on Canada Way in Burnaby 1979

Ann, Olive Farr, Olive Dickinson (Frank's sister), and Suzanne Dickinson (Frank's niece) – visiting from England—photo taken at the 7-Eleven head office on Canada Way, Burnaby

We found a great new home, back in the British Properties on Cammeray Road. Over time we moved to 2311 Westhill Drive and then, higher up the hill at 2398 Westhill Drive. It was a splendid full-view home of a little over 5,200 square feet with a cantilevered pool overlooking the city. This was to be our home for the next twelve years.

FRANK FARR

Frank, Paula, Ann at Paula's high school graduation 1982

Frank, Jim Waldron, and Steve Murray at the Cammeray house

2311 Westhill Drive, West Vancouver

2398 Westhill Drive, West Vancouver

Ann and Frank at the Horseshoe Bay Keg, West Vancouver

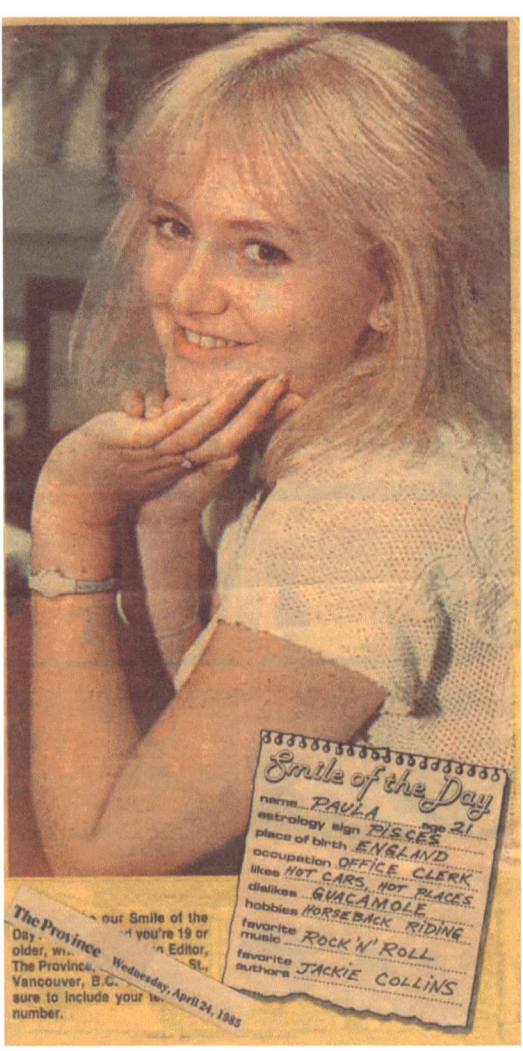

Paula "Smile of the Day" photo in The Province newspaper—photos taken at the 7-Eleven head office in Burnaby in 1985

A LIFE IN STAGES

Some recollections along the way:

In 1982, following her graduation from Sentinel High School, Paula joined me at 7-Eleven, spending most of her time working on a variety of assignments in the development department, before her appointment as my executive assistant in 1996.

Fishing and Golf Trips

When I joined the company, 7-Eleven had a habit of taking its key managers on an annual fishing trip to Scott Lake in the Northwest Territories.

There were usually about twelve of us in a lone camp, on a lake a hundred miles long and frozen for nine or ten months of the year. Just lake trout and northern pike. They were good times and usually a couple of senior managers from Dallas would join us.

It was quite the experience and I remember it vividly. There we were, out on the lake early in the morning, catching lake trout and pan-frying them over a small campfire. It doesn't get any tastier than that. A genuine Canadian experience. We were a long way from Leeds!

There was one famous incident when Dave Boyer, dressed in a gorilla outfit, and acting like a deranged bear, scared the living daylight out of a couple of our staff, including John Timms, our human resources manager.

Fishing Camp at Scott Lake—Northwest Territories 1980

119

Following the move to Vancouver, these trips changed to salmon fishing on the coast. These were rough and ready affairs, basically in fishing camps. As we were growing and adding more female staff, it seemed a little out of place for a guys' only trip. We wanted to change things so that we could share this benefit with our female department managers. This was the start of our annual visits to Phoenix.

The next few years were busy and exciting. Dick had told me that they wanted to grow in Canada and there was no limit to the capital available for new store growth. It was okay to open as many stores as I could, provided that they were profitable. Based on our experience, we were confident that, if we paid proper attention to site selection, the stores would be successful.

When I joined, we had one real estate manager, Len Teskey, and one construction manager, Fred Morris.

The staff did not believe me when I told them that we were going to hire a lot more people in this department. When I joined 7-Eleven and moved to Calgary, Jim Waldron and Steve Murray had remained in Vancouver, working with Boots during the takeover of the Tamblyn stores. As soon as we were settled back in Vancouver, I offered Jim and Steve positions within the 7-Eleven development department. They accepted and under their leadership, we built this group to over twenty employees.

Apart from all the work, the culture shock was the most surprising and enjoyable. Adrian Evans was my predecessor in Canada. He was promoted to regional manager and was my boss, when I took over. He was an absolute pleasure to work with. He was based in Chicago, with five divisions reporting to him: me, Gerny Bellof, Charles Beck, and two others. We were all doing well, and we had some amazingly good times. There were business meetings in Chicago, budget meetings in Phoenix, and vacation breaks in Cuernavaca and Acapulco with our wives. They really were remarkable times.

During this time, we increasingly developed our relationship with the major oil companies. The senior representative for Esso recommended that we should hire one of his employees to assist us in the more professional management of locations that we were leasing from them. His name was Roger Storms.

Adrian Evans and the division managers in Cuernavaca, Mexico

Roger became one of the defining figures in our growth and profitability over the next twenty years. While his manner could seem to be a little "rough and ready" at times, I found him to be very thoughtful…a good example of the thinking manager. Roger worked very closely with me, as we discussed the options and opportunities to build our relationship with the oil companies and gain access to real estate that would otherwise be too expensive for us to obtain.

He also understood that each oil company had its own culture and ways of looking at business. With his encouragement, we hired Peter Flach from Texaco, Bill Runciman from Imperial Oil, Simon Evans from Chevron, Gord Groff from Esso, and Laurence Richler from Imperial Oil. In total this gave us over seventy-plus years of experienced oil company executives and we benefited from their experience.

During my time with 7-Eleven, with Roger's leadership, we grew 7-Eleven Canada from ten gas station operations to over 365, in partnership with Imperial Oil (ESSO), Petro-Canada, Texaco, Shell, and Chevron. It was a remarkable achievement, not equalled anywhere in the Southland Corporation and it would not have been possible without the insight and vision of Roger Storms.

When I first joined 7-Eleven, my area of responsibility did not include Ontario. Following my first visit there, I decided that the area was not being well managed (by the 7-Eleven group in Philadelphia), and I agreed with Dick Dole that we would take these stores over. This presented quite a challenge. In addition to the three-hour time difference with Vancouver, Toronto is over 3,000 kilometres from Vancouver, and I knew that the culture was very different from the West.

Peter Flach

Roger had organized a meeting with Texaco in Toronto, and in advance of the meeting, he advised me that one of the Texaco team executives might be a problem. He asked a lot of challenging questions and therefore, I should be well prepared.

The executive that he identified was Peter Flach, and Roger was correct. Not only was Peter tough but he was also smart. Following the meeting, I arranged to meet with him and within a short time, I asked him to join us at 7-Eleven to manage our operations in Ontario. He agreed.

Peter Flach became a good friend in 7-Eleven. He managed our operations in Ontario for the rest of his years with 7-Eleven. Peter eventually left to manage the Becker's 700-store group in Ontario, and subsequently as president of the Ontario Brewers Association (a billion-dollar retailer). He and I have retained a close friendship following our retirement from fulltime work.

During these years, 7-Eleven Canada was growing by leaps and bounds: 100 stores, 200 stores, 300 stores, 400 stores, 450-plus stores. We were building a Canadian success story.

When we opened our 300th store in Canada. Dick Dole presented me with my 7-Eleven company ring. This ring is inscribed *"Opus Praeclarum"* and contains three diamonds to commemorate our achievement. The closest interpretation of this is "For Outstanding Service."

Within a year of receiving this ring, I lost it in the snow on a very cold day in Winnipeg (my fingers shrunk with the cold), and I never thought that I would see it again. I offered a $500 reward to anybody who could find and return it, and after some vigorous searching, it was located in a snowbank outside the second store that we had visited on that day. I still treasure this ring and by the way, Jim Waldron still has his 7-Eleven company ring, awarded some years later.

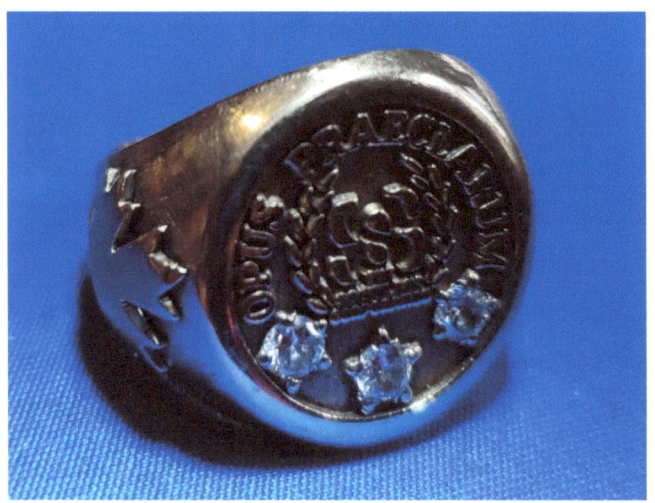

Frank's 7-Eleven ring, celebrating 300 stores in Canada

We were always encouraged in this growth by the key managers in Dallas, and for much of this period of growth, the new Canadian stores were the most profitable new stores in Southland. This was despite the fact that we could not sell beer, wine, or liquor in Canada. One of the other highlights of this time was the annual "sales meetings" that Jimmie used to organize across the company. They were great meetings and it seemed that they provided that extra energy that was needed to achieve the results that we were seeking.

7-Eleven Air Force

Frank and Jim Waldron at the opening of the Skydome Stadium in Toronto, Ontario in 1989

When I joined 7-Eleven, the company had two small corporate jets (Sabreliners). Over the next few years, they bought two replacement jets (Gulfstream 11), and then they inherited two more, as a part of their acquisition of certain assets of Braniff Airlines. This acquisition also included the FX Base at Love Field in Dallas.

As usual, the company always did things in a first class, business-like fashion. The 7-Eleven Love Field operation quickly won numerous awards across the US. Within some guidelines, we could arrange to use these airplanes and on several occasions, we used them to facilitate cross-Canada sales meetings:

Toronto–Winnipeg–Edmonton–Calgary–Vancouver. We could attend five sales meetings in five days. On one particularly cold visit to Winnipeg, the plane's doors froze. This was corrected, but the pilots were not too keen to fly into Winnipeg again during winter.

On a number of other occasions, we were able to fly between Vancouver and Dallas, usually with stops in Chicago or Denver as we dropped off or picked up other Southland executives.

The company apartments in Dallas

The company maintained two remarkable apartments in Dallas. These apartments were mainly for the use of visiting executives of Southland International Franchisees (primarily the Japanese). The apartments were extravagantly furnished, complete with very expensive art. If they were not occupied by guests, they were available to senior executives of the company, and I certainly enjoyed the times that I was able to use one of them. One time was with Ann as we drove down from Dallas to Austin and San Antonio.

Jimmie Musselwhite

We used to joke that Jimmie must have been born in a 7-Eleven, as his loyalty to the company was unquestionable. Jimmie was from the southern US and had worked in Memphis, Tennessee before transferring to Vancouver. After we launched "Big Gulp," it was unusual to see Jimmie without his Big Gulp in hand at every meeting. On one occasion, Jodie Thompson, who always appreciated Jimmie, took him off to Austin, Texas on the company jet and had his bootmaker make a pair of custom boots for Jimmie. I am sure that Jimmie still has them.

Jimmie was the marketing manager during most of these years. During this time, he had the support of Harry O'Grady and Jim Humphrey, as we achieved some of our landmark successes. Jim Humphrey's creative, energetic approach to our work, combined with his ability to think "outside of the box" provided a fun element that added to our success.

In the early days, our biggest advantage was the fact that we were open twenty-four hours and that our sandwich kitchens (commissaries) were able to provide our stores with a never-ending selection of sandwiches and other freshly made items. (Subway had not yet started to make an impact.) From this base, we were able to drive our sales in "Slurpee" and "Big Gulp" to ever-increasing levels. We continued to develop new initiatives.

ATMs

We were the first retail chain to introduce ATMs into a large number of stores. Jim Humphrey came up with "Get your bread where you get your bread." Corny, but it worked.

Rent a Movie

By an odd coincidence, I met two entrepreneurs who had just started a "Rent a Movie" (video cassette) business and following some discussion, we agreed to place their program in selected 7-Eleven stores. This business grew to such an extent that within two years we were achieving over $12 million a year in movie-rental income. This type of success did not escape the attention of our parent company, and they came to a similar agreement with these two Canadian businessmen. The business grew at a fantastic pace throughout North America.

I am not sure what the final arrangement was in the US, but we managed to exit this very profitable business just before the rental movie business totally collapsed. Timing is everything.

Post Offices

We were the first retail chain to add franchised post offices to our stores. This followed an unexpected meeting between me and Frank Smith. He had been one of the fifty first young Canadians to join Fine Fare back in 1961 and now he was the manager of franchising for Canada Post.

Chester Fried Chicken and Pizza Hut

We had considerable success selling chicken and pizza in our stores with some stores achieving quite remarkable sales. Chuck Hutchinson and the growing team of food service staff that we were developing at this time, deserve most of the credit for this initiative.

3 D Glasses

We had one, short lived, but remarkable, success with 3D glasses. When the first 3D movie on TV was announced, we bought 20,000 pairs of 3D glasses at fifty cents each and sold them for one dollar. We were one of the few stores selling them, and people were lined up out of the stores. We quickly sold out.

7-Eleven then arranged to buy the rights for the next 3D blockbuster to be shown on TV, and we controlled the scheduling. We arranged for the film to be shown in BC on a Tuesday, Alberta on a Wednesday, Saskatchewan and Manitoba on a Thursday, and Ontario on a Friday. We bought 200,000 pairs for twenty-five cents each and sold them in the three western provinces for a dollar. Our competition (Mac's) also bought a large number.

We flooded the stores in BC so that we would not lose a sale. As soon as the movie was shown, we transferred all of the stock to Alberta and flooded those stores. As soon as the movie was shown there, we transferred all of the stock to Saskatchewan/Manitoba and flooded those stores. As soon as the movie was shown there, we transferred all of the stock to Ontario, but we lowered the price to fifty cents.

We sold out of all of our stock, but Mac's were left with large quantities that they had bought for fifty cents and were trying to sell for a dollar. I'm not sure if Mac's ever understood what happened, but I'm sure that this contributed to the high level of dislike between the two companies *(Remember when I came back from my first visit to Dallas, back in 1978, determined to beat 7-Eleven's competition.)*

BC Place and G.M. Place

During the early years, I used to visit Dallas on a regular basis and one of the highlights was to be invited to see the Dallas Cowboys games in The Texas Stadium. The private suites were a luxury and a cultural experience. Oak Farm Dairies had their own suite and so did the Thompson family and 7-Eleven. It was quite the experience going from suite to suite, enjoying the game and mingling with the visiting celebrities.

In 1983, partly as a preparation for Expo in 1986, Vancouver opened its own 60,000 seat covered arena, BC Place. Southland Canada was on a roll, so I carefully asked Dick and Jodie if I could secure one of the luxury suites for 7-Eleven Canada. To my delight, they said yes. Another example of quick decision making by these two Texans.

We enjoyed the use of this facility from 1983 until my retirement in 1998 (Suite #6). We had some wonderful times there and for the last several years, Paula was in charge of our social committee, along with Charlotte Murray and Pauline Moore. This included the management of our suites. I think that this was one of her most enjoyable responsibilities. We saw many sporting events with both soccer and North American football. We had access to the suite for two hours before an event and for one hour following the event, just enough time for a friendly poker game! I had the privilege of presenting the World Cup of Soccer to the New York team (it included Pele) following their defeat of the Vancouver team, which included five former ex-Leeds United players. The noise of the crowd at mid-field was deafening.

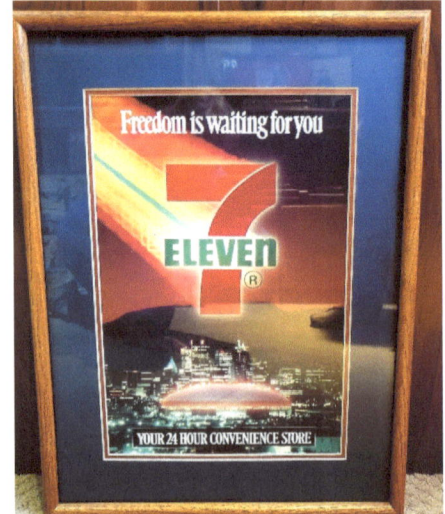

We also enjoyed many concerts from this suite. I think that David Bowie may have been the first but there were many more: Garth Brooks, The Three Tenors, Simon and Garfunkle, Waylon and Willie, Rod Stewart, Michael Jackson, U2, and many more over the years! Always an enjoyable night out.

In 1995, GM Place opened in Vancouver, although this was much smaller than BC Place (35,000 seats) it promised to be a great venue with a new NBA basketball team and of course the Vancouver Canucks. I did not feel that we should have two such suites, but arranged to share a suite with Benson & Hedges. We enjoyed the use of this facility up until the time of my retirement in 1998.

Expo 86

Frank and Grace McCarthy announcing 7-Eleven's involvement in Expo 86

Vancouver had the pleasure of hosting the World Expo in 1986. This was also a remarkable experience that put Vancouver on the "world map" more than ever before. Expo ran from April to October and for almost all of that time, we had great weather. This brought the crowds out in unexpected numbers. 7-Eleven became one of the founding members of "The Canadian Club" in the centre of the Expo grounds. This was a wonderful retreat from the crowds with a great bar and a wonderful restaurant. We spent lots of time there, entertaining a constant stream of 7-Eleven visitors from all parts of the US. On one memorable evening, we had John Thompson, Jere Thompson, Dick Dole, and Grace McCarthy, the deputy premier of BC who joined us for a cruise around Vancouver Harbour and dinner at the Canadian Club. Grace was the key figure in arranging for Vancouver to host Expo. Jere Thompson struck up a good relationship with Grace and her husband Ray.

A LIFE IN STAGES

Public Relations

Back in Calgary in 1978, I had realized that 7-Eleven would benefit from an aggressive public relations strategy. I continued this policy through our time in Vancouver. Just prior to Expo, our public relations consultant made me aware that the provincial government was soliciting corporations to pay for various infrastructure elements.

In the US, Southland had become a big sponsor of the US Cycling Team in preparation for the LA Olympics scheduled for 1984, and our consultant wondered if we would be interested in sponsoring a cycle trail to be built in Vancouver from the waterfront to New Westminster under/adjacent to the new Sky Train route. The cost was $600,000. I was not sure.

I phoned Jere Thompson to ask his opinion, as this was a lot of money. His reply was "Frank, we trust you to make the right decisions for 7-Eleven Canada. Just let me know if you decide not to do it."

I decided to go ahead. This was the start of a long friendship with Grace McCarthy.

It was proposed that we would provide a team of bike riders to celebrate the opening of the 7-Eleven Bicycle Trail. However, I cannot ride a bike. I managed to get out of that one by asking Jere Thompson to do the honours. He agreed and on the day, he and Grace led a group of 7-Eleven employees and some of their children, including Charlotte Murray, on a ride along the bike trail.

7-Eleven Cycling Team—Gastown, Vancouver Grand Prix with Frank and Jimmie Musselwhite top right

Although all of this sounds like "party time," we need to remember that during these years, we were all working very hard. "Work hard, play hard!" For two years in a row, we opened fifty stores (an average of one per week), and I had to approve each location.

This sounds unrealistic, but I used to physically check up to 400 potential sites each year. We had a system that provided me with a detailed information book. This allowed me to check six to ten sites per day. When we were on the road, we used to spread the trips between visiting existing stores and looking at potential new stores. Until we reached 350 operating stores in Canada, I managed to visit every store at least once each year.

Frank and Grace McCarthy—Bicycle Trail Dedication 1986

FRANK FARR

Part of our development process was what became known as "The Major Market Study," which involved the pre-evaluation of as many potential locations in a given market as possible. Paula had joined 7-Eleven in 1982, following her graduation from Sentinel High School and continued her education at college (BCIT) to obtain her Business Management Systems Certificate. Paula worked in the construction, real estate and development departments and worked on the major market study for a few years. I was always worried to see her take off for long trips on her own to different parts of the country. But she always came back safe and made a big contribution to our ability to grow as successfully as we did.

BC Business Top 100 Companies

Our New Office

We had moved into our first office in Vancouver during 1979 and the ten-year lease was due to expire in 1989. I knew that two other divisions of 7-Eleven were building their own offices, so I enquired with Dick, Jodie, and Jere to see if they preferred me to renew our lease, or if they'd consider building our own office. As usual, the reply was, "You are running Canada, considering property values, what do you recommend? I said that we should build and own our own office. They agreed.

Frank in the new 7-Eleven head office on Willingdon Green, Burnaby

I remember that when I submitted the capital expense proposal, Jere said, "Okay but don't come back to the well." We put a firm control in place and with the good management of Jim and Steve, we came in on time and under budget.

During the building of the office, John and Jere visited Vancouver, and I assumed that they would want to see the new office under construction. We did pull up close to the building site, but they declined to check out the building. John's comment was, "Take us to see stores, that's where we make our money."

Four related points.

- The division manager of the Capital Division (Washington DC) did not manage his office building budget well and lost his job.

- We spent $5.2 million on the office (including $500,000 for office furniture) The actual land cost was $711,000 and although there were only three floors, we had the buttons in the elevator changed to "Ground Floor" and floors 7 and 11.

A LIFE IN STAGES

- During the LBO, when Southland was looking for money, I offered to buy the building myself and lease it back to the company, but this proposal did not go forward, due to the various bank covenants.

- When the company decided to sell the office in 2008, it sold for $10 million. The office had proved to be a good investment.

As a home for all of us, the office was a great success and we had many memorable events there.

Designing and building our own office provided the opportunity for several firsts. The building included an exercise area, showers, and changing rooms. The roof had space for seating and BBQs. We used to have a BBQ on the roof deck following successful board meetings. We created a staff cafeteria (Creekside Café) with outside seating alongside the creek. This was the site of many celebrations: Christmas open houses, birthday parties, etc. One of our staff was married in the Creekside Cafe and we actually had the final party there for both Paula and me when we left the company in 1998.

We also leased property close to the office, for British Columbia's first corporate day care centre. Free to employees.

We had many enjoyable Christmas parties away from the office. Two that I recall were at the Hotel Vancouver and another one was at Westwood Plateau Golf Course.

**Another 7-Eleven Christmas Party
at the Hotel Vancouver**

**Ann and Frank at the 7-Eleven
Christmas Party, Hotel Vancouver**

**Development Department Group
at the Hotel Vancouver**

FRANK FARR

7-Eleven Bonusses, Contests, and Incentives

It had been 7-Eleven's long-term policy to award generous bonusses, always tied to performance.

The company's attitude to this had been developed in the 1930s, when the founder, Joe C Thompson, used to holiday with his family in Jasper Park in Canada. They shared vacations there with other distinguished US businessmen and had many an interesting discussion during the evenings. One of the conclusions that they arrived at was that to be effective, a bonus plan should be: 1) Attainable and 2) Capable of changing your lifestyle.

Here are a couple of examples of how this worked in practice.

In the year that I joined the company, 1978, Jimmie Musselwhite, our merchandising manager won a Chevrolet Corvette. I believe that it changed his lifestyle. In one of our other incentive competitions, Southland offered a prize of $100,000 to the winning store supervisor in North America. This prize was won by one of our supervisors in Vancouver. It certainly changed her lifestyle. She was living at home and bought a new house for herself and her parents. Canadians often won these North American Incentive competitions.

Also in 1978, 7-Eleven Canada did so well that everybody who was entitled to a bonus received a double bonus. This was something that happened from time to time during my twenty years with the company.

One benefit, which I was not aware of when I joined, was that my position qualified me to receive an annual free gift of stock in the company as well as a quantity of stock-options based on annual results. The benefits package for people in my position was improved on a regular basis, as Dave Finley, vice-president of human resources, identified additional opportunities, with the full support of John Thompson. We referred to these benefits as Golden Handcuffs. This concept continued for the life of 7-Eleven during the time that the Thompsons controlled the company. (It stopped immediately following the Japanese takeover.)

People often use the words bonus and incentive as if they are interchangeable. At 7-Eleven we took the position that bonusses were strategic and tied to the bottom-line performance of the company. Incentives were tactical and usually targeted at short-term objectives.

A LIFE IN STAGES

Frank and Ann—attending a food industry dinner

Paula—special event at the 7-Eleven Head Office

Frank and Paula—The Granville Island Keg

❖

"Give your head a shake. Get rid of them ghosts and willibuggers running around in your head." Adrian Evans

❖

*"How are things going?
Well if it gets any better, I won't be able to stand it." Adrian Evans*

❖

"I've not had such fun since the hogs ate my little brother." Jimmie Musselwhite

CHAPTER THIRTEEN

7-Eleven Travel and Vacations

"Spoiler Alert!" *This section is long, if you don't like reading about other people's travel and vacations, you might want to give this chapter a miss.*

They say that travel broadens the mind and this was certainly the case with us. We learned much of local customs from Jesus in Cuernavaca, our tour guide in Bali, and Big Chi in Beijing.

Coming from the north of England as I did, the wonders of the Grand Canyon and the Great Wall of China were beyond belief. The opportunity to see so many places and cultures, certainly opened our eyes and minds to the much bigger world than we had experienced in our earlier years. Ann, Paula, and I had a lot to learn and we took every opportunity to do so. We worked hard and we played hard. This period, when I was in my forties and early fifties was the height of our traveling times. It was an amazing combination of family vacations and 7-Eleven-related travel opportunities. Some of them were once-in-a-lifetime experiences, never to be repeated.

During the early years, Ann and I had joined Adrian Evans' group on planning/budgeting trips to Phoenix. Over time, I substituted our Canadian management team's fishing trip for golfing trips to Phoenix. We stayed at The Pointe at Squaw Peak, The Pointe at South Mountain, and The Pointe at Tapitao. I believe that they were some of the most enjoyable events that our team ever had.

Ann and Frank flying to another vacation destination

Ann and I also used these trips to Phoenix to head off on side trips around the south west US. We had a lot of fun finding little bars and honky-tonk dance halls in a number of towns in Arizona, New Mexico and West Texas. Thinking of those stops in Tucson, Santa Fe, and El Paso brings back many good memories.

133

Yellowstone National Park

Our first mini-adventure was not long after we headed south. I had recently been to Texas where drinking and driving was still a way of life. We had a cooler of beer in the van and it was a hot day. I passed a "cold one" to George and had one myself.

Before long, I was surprised to find a police car waving us off into a lay-by and then realized that there was also a police car behind us. A trucker had seen me having a beer and phoned in to the local police. I had honestly not given any thought to this and spent the next little while explaining that we were tourists and did not appreciate the local law. The policeman patiently explained that he could put me in jail for drinking and driving.

With a promise that I would not think of doing this again, he waved us on and wished us a great vacation!

Reno, Crater Lake, and The Grand Canyon

Paula and her best friend Jill Rosebourne, together with Esther and George, joined us for this trip. We must have arrived at the Grand Canyon on a quiet day, because we were able to rent two rooms in the Canyon Lodge, including a rooftop deck overlooking the Grand Canyon. These rooms were usually booked up to a year in advance. We bought some food from the local store and had a BBQ on the deck, enjoying the sunset while overlooking one of the natural wonders of the world. The next morning, we were up early to see the sunrise on this breath-taking scene.

Quite the experience. Never to be forgotten.

Las Vegas/Palm Springs

During this time with 7-Eleven, we had plenty of opportunities to visit Las Vegas and enjoy many lasting memories.

The first instances were when we were invited to spend weekends in Las Vegas courtesy of a local Vancouver radio station. Jim and Angela also joined us on a few of these trips.

Jim and Angela Waldron and Ann and Frank in Vegas

Cherie and Gurny Bellof, Ann, Frank, and Paula in Vegas

The real adventures started when we visited this amazing city with 7-Eleven, as a part of the Jerry Lewis Telethon in support of the Muscular Dystrophy Association. (MDA). It was a pleasant surprise to meet Jerry in person and to realize that apart from his fame as a comedian, he was a very serious and astute businessman. He took his responsibilities with MDA very seriously and the annual MDA Las Vegas events became one of the highlights of the year.

Frank and Jerry Lewis in Las Vegas at the Jerry Lewis MDA Telethon

At that time, 7-Eleven had approximately a hundred stores in Las Vegas and these were managed by a zone manager. On our frequent visits to LV, we could check out the acts, phone the 7-Eleven office, and obtain "free" passes to almost any show. These were "pass-line" privileges that enabled us to pass the line of hundreds waiting to see the shows, go to the head of the line, and only have to pay the doorman a modest tip ($25) to get our choice of seats. I remember doing this along with Jim and Angela, Gerny and his wife Cherie, and also George and Esther.

Among the entertainers that we saw were Englebert Humperdinck (Angela's favourite), Dianna Ross, Kenny Rodgers, Siegfried and Roy, and The Everly Brothers. However, there was no doubt that the best show that we saw in LV was Sammy Davis Jr. This was his opening show following a long absence from Vegas and the theatre was packed. This was by far the best live performance that we have ever seen.

Paula and Frank walking the strip in Las Vegas

Ann in Palm Springs

One of our most enjoyable trips with 7-Eleven was to Palm Springs with the Coca Cola Group. Coca Cola really knew how to put on a star-studded event. OJ Simpson acted as the host and it was fun relaxing in the hot tub with Donna Summer, James Woods, Robert Wagner, and Jill Ireland. Our dinner table hosts were George Segal and Jerry Van Dyke.

Jamaica—Bahamas

During these early 7-Eleven years, Ann and I also had the enjoyment of joining in some vendor trips to Jamaica and The Bahamas. These were our first visits to the Caribbean and our lasting impressions were of fabulous beaches and lobster BBQs.

A LIFE IN STAGES

Hawaii

Early on in the 7-Eleven years, we learned that we had stores in Hawaii and that the district office had an upstairs apartment that was available for rent at a nominal cost. We booked it and together with George and Esther, headed off for our first visit to this paradise in the Pacific.

Quite the experience. The office staff greeted us with leis at the airport. They had also organized a dinner cruise and before long we were enjoying quite a party, before heading ashore for a visit to a pub and a game of darts. The staff at this office made us feel very welcome and made a big difference to our first visit to this wonderful place. We drove up and down the island, seeing all of the sights and on one memorable day, we were caught in a tropical deluge. We were truly soaked before we could get back into our car and I'll never forget the look on George's face as he took his shirt off to wring it out at the next stop.

We decided that this was the best spot to enjoy vacations and for the next several years Ann, Paula, and I went to Hawaii for our annual vacations. On a couple of later visits, we were able to stay at the company's new condo in Honolulu.

Frank in Oahu

As well as Oahu, we also spent some time on Maui with George and Esther. (I "liberated" my first pineapple from one of the fields along the road (it was delicious!) and enjoyed our first drive along the road to Hana. We enjoyed our time at Kihei and Lahaina with its giant banyan tree.

We also did the drive up to the Mt. Haleakala Volcano to see the sunset.

A visit to Pearl Harbour and the USS *Arizona* was a memorable experience and the war cemetery in Honolulu with the mosaic of the World War Two battles in the Pacific was also very moving.

These were great vacations. Ann and Paula enjoyed shopping for souvenirs in the

Paula and Frank on a catamaran, Waikiki Beach

International Market Place. Although Waikiki Beach is the most picturesque and the most famous, we enjoyed the Ala Moana Beach. We stayed in many nice hotels in Hawaii, but we also found a small motel close to the beach in Honolulu, The Breakers.

FRANK FARR

On one infamous day there, Ann and Paula went shopping and I decided to stay by the pool and at the poolside bar. Several very strong Mai-Tais later, Ann and Paula returned, to find me comatose on the bed in our room. I did not wake up until the next morning. I think that we stayed at The Breakers twice more, once with Jim, Angela, and family and once with both Jim and Steve's families.

Mary, Andy, Charlotte, Sinead Murray, Angela, Louise Waldron, Jo, Steve Murray, and Jim Waldron—The Breakers Motel, Waikiki Beach

Frank, Ann, Nick, Jim, Louise, and Angela Waldron in Waikiki

Ann and Paula in Oahu

On one other memorable trip through Honolulu, we met a young man who later insisted on giving us not one, but two ukuleles. I just checked the hall cupboard and we still have them in March of 2020. We had lots of fun on our many visits to this wonderful tropical paradise.

A LIFE IN STAGES

The "Regional Steves" at a
7-Eleven meeting in Oahu

Texas—San Antonio—The Alamo—New Orleans

I had regular trips to Dallas and saw something of Texas. At the same time, 7-Eleven arranged for several meetings in New Orleans. I could not wait to see more of this interesting and different part of the US.

Ann and I had a wonderful holiday, flying into Dallas and then driving down to Austin and San Antonio, before driving across Texas and down through Louisiana to New Orleans.

San Antonio, with its River Walk and The Alamo, was a fabulous place to visit and enjoy. We drank so much in the bars along the Riverwalk that I am surprised that I did not fall in. What a great time!

We then drove through rural East Texas (I liberated cotton balls from the fields), and then we headed down towards New Orleans. We had our first taste of fried catfish in a small hotel in Natchitoches, Louisiana.

New Orleans is Magical

New Orleans is different from anywhere else in the US. A mixed heritage of French, Creole and American cultures, it's unique and we loved it. We stayed at The Royal Sonesta Hotel on Bourbon St. and spent our days and nights roaming the French Quarter and enjoying the sights and sounds of this unique treasure. We could not wait to get back.

We drove back to San Antonio via Houston and the only memory that I have of this, is driving though Houston in a torrential rainstorm so strong that we had to pull over until it passed.

Ann and Frank aboard The Natchez on
the Mississippi River, New Orleans

There are two more trips like this that I remember.

A couple of years later, we took George and Esther and flew into San Antonio. We did the bars on the Riverwalk (Esther and I had a lot of fun dancing in Dirty Dick's, where the bartender, Cliff Hang (!) remembered my drink (Canadian Club and Coke) from our visit of two years earlier.

Esther and Frank dancing at Dirty Dick's, San Antonio, Texas

We then drove south and across the Gulf of Mexico to Galveston and on to New Orleans. I can't remember the exact reaction from George and Esther, but I do remember George sitting down on the steps of one of the bars, looking on in amazement at the crowds on Bourbon St. We arranged to stay at an attractive boutique hotel, The Cornstalk. This hotel was famous for having been highlighted in the Elvis Presley movie, *King Creole*. We had a fun-filled few days there.

On another occasion, this time with 7-Eleven, we had the company of Jim and Angela as we made our way from bar to bar in the French Quarter. One of the interesting features of this town is that you can drink in the street. Two of the most popular drinks are "hurricanes" and "tornados." Jim still has a packet of Pat O'Brian's Hurricane Mix on his bar. We drank ours many years ago.

As I write this in 2020, I am looking at two blue-hued prints of New Orleans on my office walls and thinking of the good times that we had in this wonderful city.

Windstar

In 1986, we, along with several of our senior managers, won a 7-Eleven incentive competition to go on the maiden voyage of the *Windstar*, a 660-foot boutique sailing ship with just seventy-five cabins. Delicious food and very personalized service. This cruise was in the Caribbean, starting and ending in Puerto Rico. We visited Antigua, St. Kitts, St. Lucia, St. Martin, and Dominica. This again was one of the ongoing rewards for taking care of Southland's business—another "once in a lifetime" experience, courtesy of our great company. During a stop at St. Kitts, I managed to locate Dr. Rufus King. He had been a governor of my school at Kneesworth Hall and had retired to his original home. We had a long and interesting conversation. However, he was nearing his end, and passed away within a couple of weeks of my visit.

A LIFE IN STAGES

Southeast US—Charleston—Florida—Key West

I am not sure of the order of these trips but my first visit to Florida was with Jimmie Musselwhite to the Superbowl in Miami, courtesy of Pepsi-Canada. I visited Florida on three more occasions to see the Superbowl in Tampa and in Miami again.

Following one of these trips, Ann was with me and we stayed in Tampa (played Trivia in the hotel lobby) and then drove across the Everglades to Key Largo and down to Key West. We only stayed in Key West for one night at a hotel on Duval St. This was another fun trip and we resolved to do it again at the first opportunity.

On another Pepsi trip, we stayed in Orlando and Paula joined us for this one. We visited Disneyworld and Ft. Lauderdale.

On another occasion, eager to get back to Key West, we flew into Ft. Lauderdale, stayed a couple of nights, and then drove down the Keys to Key West. Paula joined us for this trip, and we had quite the adventure.

Hotel accommodation is limited and expensive in Key West. Jim Humphrey had mentioned to me that one place to stay was known as "The Truman Annex." I found it and it was perfect. Once the summer residence of President Truman, this property is now the location of many vacation homes and many of them were available for rent. Perfect for us.

Frank, Ann, and Paula in Fort Lauderdale, Florida

We settled into a nice condo with our private pool in this gated property, quietly off to one side of Duval St. Duval St. is like a miniature version of Bourbon St. in New Orleans. There are bars, cafes, and a fun, music-filled atmosphere with many remembrances of the time that Ernest Hemingway lived there. We had a good time. In one bar, a young American serviceman approached me in a very deferential way to ask if he could dance with Paula. I said, "You will have to ask her." He did and she said yes. They danced the night away. We all had a great time and we immediately added Key West to San Antonio, New Orleans, and Sonoma on our list of favourite places to visit in the US.

We think that it was following our visit to the Atlanta Olympics in 1996, that Ann and I decided to take a drive down the east coast. We wanted to see the Old South. We drove from Atlanta out to the coast, stayed in Charleston and Savannah, and continued to Ft. Lauderdale. Both Charleston and Savannah were interesting reminders of what the Old South must have been.

FRANK FARR

Mexico: The 7-Eleven visits

About this time, we had our first taste of Mexico. The Thompson family's summer home was in Cuernavaca in the mountains south of Mexico City and they made this home available to their senior managers. This home had four bedrooms on either side of a swimming pool and the whole property had views of the famous volcano Mt. Popocatepetl in the distance. It really was quite special.

One odd thing. We were requested to leave our laundry on the bathroom floor and the staff would take it away, wash and iron it, and leave it outside our room later in the day. Jerry Lewis had stayed there a few weeks earlier and the staff were surprised when he did not pick up his fresh laundry. Apparently, his manager told them that Mr. Lewis only wears socks and underwear once and then he discards them. I think that the staff quite enjoyed this daily supply of free clothing.

I also remember the impressive statue of Emiliano Zapata in the centre of the city, on his horse pointing his machete in the direction of Mexico City. This was the area of the country from where he had led his march on Mexico City during the Mexican Revolution of 1910–1920. The other and more senior revolutionary, Pancho Villa, had approached Mexico City from the north. It was thought-provoking to see this statue and realize that many of the older folk in the town would have lived through those dangerous days.

Statue of Emiliano Zapata in the centre of Cuernavaca

Within a few years, Braniff Airlines went bankrupt and Southland purchased some of their assets. The primary asset was the aircraft base in Love Field and two aircraft. However, Braniff had also leased two beautiful homes in Acapulco, and Southland assumed the leases. There were two homes, built into the cliffs overlooking Acapulco with cantilevered pools on the view side. One of these homes was featured in the movie *"10"* featuring Dudley Moore and Bo Derek.

As per usual, these were made available for senior Southland staff. It was during our visit there that I caught the large sailfish that we had mounted in our home for many years.

Gerny Bellof, Frank, Ann, Karen Evans, Cherie Bellof, Charles and Pam Beck in Acapulco, Mexico

A LIFE IN STAGES

Olympics and the Super Bowl

Los Angeles Olympics 1984

Southland paid for the Olympic Cycling Velodrome in Los Angeles and for the Practice Velodrome in Colorado Springs. This led the company into a strong sponsorship relationship with the L.A. Olympics. Southland chartered the *Pacific Princess*, the original *Love Boat* and used it as a floating hotel for Southland people to stay in during the Olympic events. Ann and I went, along with all of our management team. It was quite the experience and for one night we left LA and sailed around Catalina Island, so that they could open the casino on board ship. Bob Hope was the primary entertainer for this event.

Ann and Frank on board the Pacific Princess (the original Love Boat), at the Los Angeles Olympics 1984

Roger and Ruth Storms, Steve Murray, Diana Evans, Ann, Simon Evans, Angela and Jim Waldron, and Mary Murray on board the Pacific Princess 1984

Calgary Olympics 1988

Our next Olympic Experience was when Tony Eames, President of Coca Cola Canada, invited us to the Winter Olympics in Calgary in 1988. Although this was closer to home, it was still quite the experience. Coca Cola had commissioned David Foster to compose the anthem for these events and he and his wife were guests with us at Tony's dinner table. David Foster's wife at the time was Ginger Thompson, the long-time girlfriend of the late Elvis Presley. After she had given me a warm welcome kiss, I realized that I had just "Kissed the lips that have kissed Elvis." At parties for the next several years, I tried to sell kisses as "Elvis kisses twice removed," but after a few years and no takers, I gave up.

FRANK FARR

Seoul Olympics 1988 (Asia #1)

Following this great event in Calgary, Tony also invited us to the Summer Olympics in Seoul, Korea. Again, this was another amazing experience. We were there for the men's soccer finals, and for the Closing Ceremonies. On the way back we stopped off in Tokyo as the guests of Coca-Cola Japan.

This was the peak of the time for "knock-off" brand merchandise and we enjoyed bargain shopping at the Itaewon street market in Seoul. Watches and clothing were the main attractions. I bought a pair of "FILA" runners. They may have been knock-offs, but they were well made. I wore them until a year ago, when Ann made me throw them away, as they were literally falling apart after twenty years.

Barcelona Olympics 1992

These were the fourth Olympics that we attended and probably the best experience of all, as we combined this with a side visit to Seville for the World Expo. Coca Cola had rented a new cruise ship, the *Crystal Harmony,* as their hotel for the Olympics and the whole affair was amazing from start to finish. Apart from the Olympic events, we had a wonderful time in Barcelona, wandering along La Strada, dining in fine restaurants, and learning first-hand about the amazing Antoni Gaudi. The buildings and parks designed by him were a treat to see, and of course the famous church, La Sagrada Familia was bewilderingly spectacular.

After the Closing Ceremony, we left for Seville and the World Expo. WOW! Apart from another very hot day in Beijing, the time that we spent in Seville was one of the hottest days that we have ever experienced. It was forty-nine degrees on the day that we arrived, and it had gone over fifty degrees on the day before. We arrived in the heat of the day and there was a small tour bus waiting for us. The bus had been waiting in the full sunshine! Twelve people boarded the bus and the first two begged to be let off within a short distance. Others followed, until only Ann and I were left on board. Somehow, we were okay.

Two things helped during the following days.

Many of the walkways on the Expo grounds had been provided with mist sprays that really worked, bringing the temperature down to a manageable level. And there was a lot to drink. In Canada, if you order a black Russian, you usually get one shot each of vodka and Kahlua. A small drink. In Seville they were not measuring any of the drinks and Ann had her share (and more) of very large black Russians.

Ann has reminded me that in Seville, I had to dash off to a local store to buy a pair of dress shoes, as I was going back via Leeds to attend the wedding of Michael (my younger brother) and Elaine.

A LIFE IN STAGES

Atlanta Olympics 1996

And finally, Tony and Robin invited us to the Summer Olympics in Atlanta in 1996. Atlanta is also the home of Coca Cola, so they were determined to put on a good show. Two of the things that stand out in my memory are:

The very enjoyable time that we had with Tony and Robin at the equestrian events.

And a couple of enjoyable dinners that we had in the Russian restaurant on the top floor of our hotel. There was Tony and Robin from Coca Cola; Ann and I from 7-Eleven; Jim Treliving, the founder of Boston Pizza and his wife Blodwyn; and Ron Joyce, the founder of Tim Hortons and his girlfriend Sandy Beauchamp. We consumed lots of vodka and at the same time, we exchanged many business stories.

Super Bowl

Because Coca-Cola is heavily involved in the Olympics, Pepsi-Cola stays away, and in turn, they are major sponsors of The Super Bowl, Americana at its best.

I am not sure of the dates, but starting with one Superbowl in Tampa that I attended with Jimmie Musselwhite, I had the opportunity to attend several Superbowl events in Miami, Ft. Lauderdale, Tampa again, and one at the Rose Bowl in LA. These were fun-filled events.

Ann joined me for one of these events and we had the pleasure of seeing Whitney Houston perform at the half-time show. She was at her peak at this time and the show was something special.

Japan—China—Thailand—Hong Kong (Asia 2): With 7-Eleven

Our visit to the Seoul Olympics was our first experience of Asia and this only aroused our interest in seeing more. We did not have long to wait. During the next several years, we had several more visits to Asia. Each one is hard to describe. The Orient is unique, and complex, with so many layers that it is all but impossible to comprehend.

In the fall of 1985, 7-Eleven announced a major incentive trip to Europe: London, Paris, Rome, etc. Unfortunately, a week or two before we were due to leave, terrorists hijacked the cruise ship *Achille Lauro* and threw a wheelchair-bound American tourist overboard. It was decided to cancel our trip as an unnecessary risk.

Within a month, Dick Dole had scheduled a replacement trip to the Orient, for early in 1986. Initially, we were disappointed. We knew Europe and what to expect, we were not familiar with any details of the Orient from a tourist perspective. We were in for the surprise of our lives.

Dick Dole liked to do things first class, and this was his opportunity.

We flew first class on Thai Airlines from Los Angeles. There were fourteen couples plus Dick and Gerny Bellof. I remember us sitting on the floor of the front cabin on this jumbo jet, playing Trivia Pursuit.

We stayed in Tokyo overnight on our way to Beijing. Narita Airport was under expansion at the time and the local farming community was protesting. As a result, the airport was under a security blanket. When the Japanese do something like this, they can overdo it. There were armoured police everywhere, water cannons, explosive-sniffing dogs, bus inspections, etc. It was like being in the middle of a war zone.

On the flight from Tokyo to Beijing, we were given the usual tourist speech of the day. "This is a communist country—you cannot take in any magazines, tapes, records, etc. and while there, you must not discuss politics, religion, etc. with any of the locals." We were a little apprehensive and did not know what to expect.

Beijing was a revelation. The security at the airport was almost non-existent and later we realized that Japan had every reason to be concerned about protests in a free and democratic society. On the other hand, the Chinese were not really concerned about any public protests, or irregular activities in a highly controlled authoritarian society. This took a little getting used to

The Hilton Great Wall

We stayed at the Hilton "Great Wall" Hotel, one of the only Western-style hotels in Beijing at this time. Each morning at 9:00 precisely, our tour bus would leave for our sightseeing trip of the day. We saw as much as was possible in five days. Every sight seemed more amazing than the last.

One of the features of this hotel was that all of the staff had been seconded from a local commune. Their salary went to the commune and the staff were not too inclined to provide good service.

Tiananmen Square

This square can hold a million people and includes Mao Tse Tung's mausoleum. The square was a place where families would gather to fly kites and just socialize. The sight of thirty white-skinned Americans (including one very tall black couple) was more than their curiosity could handle and they crowded around us, very closely. We asked our guide why, and she explained several things:

- They are still not used to seeing Westerners
- They are fascinated by your colourful clothes. (At this time, most Chinese were still wearing their Mao suits.)
- They are fascinated by the ladies' make-up and they want to get close enough to observe.

- Their nickname for us was "big noses" and they were also curious about our tall black couple.

- They were not rude, just curious.

In the spring of 1986 China was still in its early stage of emerging from a rigidly controlled economy. The most impressive thing for us was obtaining a sense of China's immense history and to see so many happy, smiling faces.

The Forbidden City (The Imperial Palace)

This is an unbelievably massive palace covering over 180 acres and including over ninety palaces. A curious place. There's a huge portrait of Mao at the entrance and then several courtyards surrounded by many "halls." The Hall of Supreme Harmony, The Hall of Heavenly Purity, The Hall of Earthly Tranquillity, The Hall of Union and Peace, and on and on.

The reason that it is known as the Forbidden City was that for centuries, commoners were not allowed to enter and in fact, were only now allowed to see inside. Therefore, there could be no buildings of any height within the city of Beijing. (This has long since changed.)

The Summer Palace

This was outside of the city and where the rulers would go in summer to escape the heat and problems of the city. This was an unusual place, where we had the pleasure of dining at The Fanshang Restaurant on a "Royal Menu" from over a hundred years ago.

Ann and Frank at the Fanshang Restaurant/Summer Palace, Beijing

Ming Tombs

On our way to the Great Wall, we had the opportunity to visit the Ming Tombs. This is an area, where thirteen emperors of China are buried

The Great Wall

We had the usual trip out to the Badaling section of the Great Wall. This was quite the surprise. This Great Wall has to be seen to be believed. It was built in sections over a period of 2,000 years and at its peak was 4,000 kilometres long.

The section at Badaling is fully restored and Ann and I still have our certificates: ("I have mounted The Great Wall,") dated April 9th, 1986. This certificate is a part of the collage of photos, mementoes, etc. from this trip, and I still have it on my office wall thirty four years later.

China was desperate for foreign currency and provided you were paying in US dollars; you could do just about anything. As a prelude to actually going to the Great Wall, we were treated to a helicopter flight over the wall and the surrounding area. This was in a military helicopter (no luxuries). But it was nonetheless an unusual experience.

Diaoyutai State Gardens (WOW!)

I have no idea what it cost, but we were treated to a night out at the Diaoyutai State Gardens. We were actually booked to stay there, but got bumped by an international government delegation.

This is hard to describe, but you have to imagine dusty Beijing, just emerging from its dismal winter weather. We are driven up to the gates of this very private place. Armed soldiers at the gate, and then inside!

There are beautiful villas, set back in luxurious landscaped gardens, Peacocks on the lawns. Illuminated waterfalls and ponds. Absolutely splendid. These are the villas used to accommodate visiting heads of state, in the very best conditions that China could provide. President Nixon and Kissinger had stayed there, as well as other heads of state over the years and here we were.

We had an amazing meal. Dick Dole had the honour of smashing the clay off one of the baked entrees. As we finished eating, the music and entertainment began.

Dinner at the Diaoyutai State Gardens 1986

First, we had a State brass band, playing all the American favourites that they had learned to play for visiting dignitaries, mainly Sousa marches.

Next, we had the Beijing Circus, providing jugglers, dancers, dragons, and other amazing entertainers.

Finally, we had the Beijing Philharmonic Orchestra playing a selection of Western classical music.

Absolutely mesmerizing.

A LIFE IN STAGES

The Fortune Commune

One of our trips was out to a local commune, the Fortune Commune. Its function was to grow vegetables for the city.

On approaching the commune, we had to stop as a local work team was digging a ditch across the road. Mr. Sing and Mr. Sung (our minders) asked the work team to fill the ditch back up, so that our bus could cross. They politely followed instructions and repeated the process on our way out.

We inspected some greenhouses and were surprised to find that each one had a little old lady, who actually lived in the greenhouse to make sure that everything was working okay.

The commune had its own rudimentary hospital, school, and day-care. The children were wonderful, happy and well looked after. Some of these facilities and the children are on my collage.

Spinach!

When we were there, we noticed hundreds of trucks delivering vegetables into the city. We asked why this was happening. The answer was *spinach*. Apparently, potatoes were the only vegetable available during the winter and as soon as the conditions allowed, alternative vegetables were provided. We were witnessing the season's first shipments of very welcome spinach from the surrounding communes.

Morning Exercises—Bicycles—Street Cleaners

On some mornings, we were up early and ventured out for a short walk. Three things captured our attention.

In every park or clear space, there were dozens and dozens of people practicing their morning Tai Chi exercises, in groups or individually.

At first, the morning is quiet and then slowly the sound starts and grows louder and suddenly, we are surrounded by thousands of people going to work on their bikes. What an incredible sight. Singles, doubles, families, all on bikes crossing each other's paths without accident. The sound and sight of this was astounding. I am sure that this has changed a lot, as more people can now afford cars.

On looking down the streets, we could see a small cloud of dust that seemed to be moving. This turned out to be a team of streetsweepers from one of the communes. Their job was to sweep a small section of the main streets (using old fashioned brooms) and then wait for the ride back to the commune, only to repeat the exercise again the following morning.

FRANK FARR

The Friendship Store. Shopping?

Shopping in Beijing at this time was unusual. Imagine thirty American tourists looking for somewhere to shop. We did not see any shops on our sightseeing tours, but we were asked to be patient, as Thursday was the day to visit "The Friendship Store." This was an allegedly famous store that was available to foreigners and diplomats to purchase imported food, clothes, etc.

What a let-down. The Friendship Store was a five-story building in the centre of Beijing with food in a supermarket on the basement floor. The best way that I can describe this store is to think of a small-town department store of the late '40s or early '50s.

On all of the upper floors, merchandise was displayed in cabinets behind counters and the staff did not seem particularly interested in taking items out of the display cases to show us. As a group, we did not buy anything. The supermarket downstairs was not much better, I remember the refrigerated cases as being rusty and not well maintained. All considered, not very appealing to thirty shopping-starved Americans. (Thankfully, better was in store.)

Maxim's

On our last evening in Beijing, we were treated to an evening at the Beijing version of Maxim's, the famous Paris nightclub. Unfortunately, this also did not live up to its billing and we headed back to the hotel at around 9:00 pm.

Old Beijing—The Hutong Houses

We were also able to visit some of the few remaining "Hutong" Houses. These were clusters of houses built down the lanes and surrounding a common kitchen, etc. Although they were poor, they looked quite charming. We entered several and noted that each one had a coloured TV. This might have been set up as a show. Almost all of these Hutongs are being replaced as Beijing builds ring roads and new, modern buildings.

Naturally, we had all been impressed with the amazing sights in Beijing and the region but seeing a country that was just emerging from decades of isolation was an eye opener. Yet another reminder of how fortunate we were to live in a democracy, where we take our freedoms for granted.

On the next day, we left for Thailand. OMG!

Bangkok

We arrived in Bangkok late at night and having just left the relative quiet of Beijing, we were shocked. Bangkok was "jumping" at midnight.

Having just experienced one type of culture shock, we were unprepared for this next shock to our system. There are almost too many things to remember.

The Mandarin Oriental

At this time, the Mandarin Oriental was rated as the best business hotel in the world. It lived up to its reputation.

The next morning, we were off to our first tour of this amazing city, including The Royal Palace and The Golden Temple. It was hot and Dick Dole quickly arranged for "cold beverages" to be supplied to our bus.

The Government Jewellery Shop

On our way back to the hotel, we experienced one of the unique features of Bangkok, "The Jewellery Shop." Again you have to imagine this group of shopping-starved Americans, along with their wives, heading into a jewellery shop. Firstly, the customers are plied with free drinks, then the sales assistants, working in teams, show you all of their fabulous jewellery. If you seem attracted to a ring, they will quickly show you matching necklaces, earrings, bracelets, etc. and vice versa.

I don't know, but my guess is that the Americans spent $20,000—$30,000 dollars in about an hour.

I found the atmosphere and drinks a little overwhelming and agreed with Ann that we would return the next day, Sunday morning, when it would be a little quieter. We did and Ann is still the proud owner of some very nice jewellery from Bangkok.

Street Markets

After our experiences in Seoul at the Itaewon Street Market, our next such experiences were in Bangkok. The most famous of these is "Patpong." Interestingly, this short street has a 7-Eleven at each end. The street is short but wide, allowing for the street market in the middle of the road and the bars and restaurants on either side. We enjoyed this experience and made sure to note this Bangkok landmark for future visits.

Tuk-Tuks

There is some form of this in many Asian cities, but the Tuk-Tuks in Bangkok were amazingly cheap and effective for getting around. That is if you can manage to get them to take you where you want to go, rather than their favourite shop, bar, or whatever along the way. We did enjoy some races around the city on both this trip and future trips that we made.

FRANK FARR

River Trips, Floating Market, Elephant Rides, etc.

We also enjoyed the opportunity to ride on the "Long Tail" boats, up the huge Chao Phraya River in Bangkok as well as visiting the Floating Market, the elephant rides, and other assorted tourist traps. All the things that are usual for this type of trip.

After several days in Bangkok, the group left for Hong Kong.

Hong Kong

In Hong Kong, we had yet another opportunity to stay at one of the world-famous hotels in the Orient, the Peninsula Hotel. On our first night in Hong Kong, we had dinner in Gaddi's Restaurant in this hotel. I still have the menu on a shelf in my office.

We also had an amazing dinner at the Regent Hotel, and this was probably the highest level of service that we had in any of these legendary oriental hotels. I have never experienced a level of service as high as this in any hotels in the West.

Ann and Frank at the Regent Hotel, Hong Kong

One of the features of Hong Kong is their twenty-four-hour tailoring service and I, along with many of the group, arranged to go to one of these famous tailors, get measured, and have custom-made suits, blazers, and shirts, delivered to our rooms later the same day. All at very reasonable prices.

I can't remember how the final night went, but I do remember that the affair was attended by an honour guard of Gurkhas. Not sure how this was arranged.

As I mentioned at the start of this trip, in the true Thompson/Southland tradition, Dick Dole wanted to provide us with the best, and on this trip, he outdid himself. As a souvenir, he arranged for us to get dressing gowns in red and blue Thai silk embroidered with our names. We still have them thirty-four years later. A gift to be treasured.

We found our initial exposure to the Orient to be so attractive that we vowed to go back again as soon as we could, and we did on more than one occasion.

A LIFE IN STAGES

Collage of the 7-Eleven trip to Asia

FRANK FARR

Hong Kong—Bangkok—Pattaya (Asia 3)

Hong Kong

For our next vacation, Paula joined us, first to Hong Kong and then to Thailand. We stayed at the Hyatt Hotel in Hong Kong and set about exploring this amazing Oriental/British City. Paula quickly figured out the underground system and this was a big help in getting around. In these days, there were endless bargains to be had, mainly at the numerous street markets. There really were many irresistible bargains.

Paula in Hong Kong Airport

Bangkok

We left for Bangkok and this was a different experience than the last one. We stayed at the Mandarin Oriental again and set off to enjoy the city. We covered all of the amazing sights from our first trip and our pleasure was to see Paula experiencing these exciting places for the first time in her life. We shopped at the markets and again enjoyed Patpong.

Floating Market in Bangkok, Thailand

A LIFE IN STAGES

Pattaya:

We left Bangkok and headed south to the resort town of Pattaya. This was an unusual experience. Although to enjoy this loud, bawdy resort requires an open and tolerant mind, it really is a fun place.

The one story that sticks in my mind is that "the US regularly sends its aircraft carriers there for R&R. There'll be 6,000 sailors in port and there's a girl waiting for each one of them. Pattaya has bars and bar girls galore.

The general impression is that the girls only receive accommodation and food from the bar owners, and then work for tips. If they receive one dollar tip every time they serve a drink, it must add up. When you sit at the bar, the barmaid will serve your drink and then stay and play bar games as long as you are there, always hoping for that extra tip and waiting for the US Fleet to arrive every six weeks.

They call Thailand "The land of Smiles" and there is no doubt that the people are very friendly. We stayed at a very modern hotel on a hill outside of the town.

One day as we were getting ready to head into town, we were advised to be prepared to get "WET" and place our wallets, cameras, and other items in plastic bags. Today was the main day of the annual "Songkran" (Water) Festival and as the name implies, this involved lots of water.

The Royal Cliff Beach Resort, Pattaya, Thailand

As we stepped out of our taxi in the centre of the town, two young boys ran out to greet us, dumping glasses of water on all three of us. For the next couple of hours, we watched the crowds and the parade pass by. The young men on the floats had oil drums filled with water and they used ladles to drench the crowd on the sidewalk. The young men on the sidewalk had hoses connected to taps and they in turn drenched the people on the parade.

This sounds crazy and it was, but it was also fun. I think that all three of us got buckets of water over our heads at one time or another. We were covered in white paste, which is also a part of the ritual. At noon, a loud blast on horns signalled the end of the water festivities and we found a bar for some shelter and to dry off.

155

The young woman in the bar took one look at us, started to laugh and gave Ann and Paula wipes to clean the paste off. We had a good chat with her that was interesting. She came from one of the inland villages and she had trained as a teacher. However, she could not get a job as a teacher and the only work that she could get was in the bars. She had saved up to pay the fees and bribes required to obtain a passport. She showed this to us and declared that she always had it with her, ready to use at a day's notice, if she met Mr. Right.

At the Songkran Water Festival in Pattaya, Thailand

She was hoping to meet a Canadian, because "unlike the Americans, if a Canadian tells you that he loves you, he means it," and she was hoping to meet her Mr. Right and go to live in Canada. I believe that her story was the same as so many others at that time.

Pattaya is home to two long-time groups of transvestites. They operate two well-known show lounges and we enjoyed our visits to one of these. They seem to enjoy a special status in Pattaya as they are well liked and contribute to the local culture. On one of our early evenings, we innocently went into the open fronted bar to see the stage show, which was funny, bawdy, and very entertaining. Outside of the bar, these young men would sit on their motor scooters, posing in their low cut, long dresses with the skirts split all the way up to their thighs. Paula was with us for all of this., but we never felt uncomfortable or threatened. Pattaya was a fun experience.

Ann and Paula, bar hopping in Pattaya, Thailand

Paula downtown Pattaya, Thailand

A LIFE IN STAGES

We could not wait to go back again, and we found the perfect excuse as George and Esther were celebrating their fiftieth wedding anniversary.

We took a long time to plan our next trip and we did not tell George and Esther the details until the last minute.

Hong Kong—Beijing—Bangkok—Phuket (Asia 4)

We loved George and Esther, and we were determined to make this the trip of a lifetime for them. Once George realized where we were going, he started checking the maps and wondering what we were all going to see. Ann and I decided that they should join us in seeing the best that we had seen on our previous trips and off we went.

We had the time of our lives.

We started in Hong Kong and stayed at the Shangri La Hotel. We explored the city and its sights and street markets. We went to the top of the mountain and we spent time at the Stanley Market. I still have the carving of a fisherman that I bought at this market. Paula remembered the subway system and again, this helped us get around. We enjoyed going on the famous Hong Kong Harbour Ferry and we were astounded and a little fearful of the fresh food in the open markets.

Paula and Frank at the Shangri La Hotel in Hong Kong

On one evening we did find ourselves in what may be the only Irish Pub in Hong Kong. It's always surprising that people will travel the world and then find somewhere—something familiar to enjoy.

On one of our last days there, it was hot and humid, and we found ourselves at a gigantic water park on the outskirts of the city. Esther loved this water park.

Hong Kong is an amazing place and we always enjoyed ourselves during our visits to one of the world's most unusual cities. We left there and headed for Beijing. WOW, WOW and WOW again!

Beijing

To say that Beijing had changed is an understatement. We stayed at the Palace Hotel. In four or five years, Beijing had gone from The Great Wall Hilton being the best (but poor) hotel in town, to having a selection of five-star hotels to choose from.

We had arranged for our own tour guide. We learned to call him "Big Chi." He was knowledgeable and fun. It was interesting to learn that his wife also worked for the government tour company. They both worked six days per week and did not always have the same day off. Big Chi loved to fish and on his days off, he would go to a stocked lake, drink beer, and fish with his friends. We had a good time with him.

We had arrived at the end of April and yet it was incredibly hot. The only other time that we have been this hot was during our visit to Seville for the Expo. We did all of the usual tourist things and it was such a pleasure to see George and Esther climb The Great Wall—something that they would never have imagined. Esther was never overly tactful, and it was funny to hear her in Tiananmen Square patiently asking Big Chi, "Is this where the tanks ran over the student demonstrator?" There was no way, that our tour guide, an employee of the government tourism agency, could reply to that one.

George and Esther on the Great Wall

Tiananmen Square, Imperial Palace

Shopping

On our original visit to Beijing, I noted that the only place to shop was "The Friendship Store."

This was no longer the case. Along the roads leading to Tiananmen Square there were modern department stores and boutiques galore. What a change. We found a really interesting indoor market that had lots of bargains. Paula and Ann purchased attractive flower-patterned linen jackets for a fraction of what we would have paid back in Vancouver if such clothes had been available. We also purchased a lovely blue and white traditional patterned dish. I just checked and we still have it. So many mementos from all of these wonderful places.

Big Chi took great pleasure in advising us that Beijing had just completed its first "Ring Road" and that two more were planned for the next few years.

I think that the rest of the world has watched in awe as China has changed in the most unbelievable ways, more so than any country in the history of the world and we have been present to witness it. During our first visit in 1986, the physical changes were just starting to show. Most people were still wearing Mao suits and foreigners were still an oddity. Within four years, everything was changing at an incredible rate and this change has continued to accelerate.

It was Winston Churchill who said, "Beware of waking the sleeping giant." Well, the giant is awake. Millions of people have been lifted out of centuries of poverty and the world will never be the same again.

Then we left Beijing for Thailand.

Thailand

Our first stop was Bangkok and again we stayed at the Mandarin Oriental, which was just as good as it was the first time. The young man who had "managed" the elevator on our 7-Eleven trip several years earlier was still there, earning his tips by being unfailingly polite to all of the ladies. I think that George and Esther were astounded by the Gold Temple and the Royal Palace. We had some hilarious rides around the city on the Tuk-Tuks.

Frank, Ann, Esther and George at the Golden Temples in Bangkok, Thailand

We had a long day out at the markets and as usual ended up at Patpong street market. Ann, Paula, and Esther wanted to do some more shopping and I picked out a good bar that George and I would enjoy.

It was one of the bars that also has a Thai boxing ring in the bar and George enjoyed his first experience of a Thai boxing match up close. We were in the bar for a while and noticed that many of the "ladies" at the bar were actually men. We mentioned this discreetly to Ann and Paula when they joined us. Paula then pointed this out to Esther. Esther in her typical, innocent way proceeded to point to these "girls" individually and quite clearly. "You mean she's a man?" and "Is she a man?" We all looked the other way and changed the subject. Fun Times in Bangkok!

We left Bangkok for Phuket.

Phuket

This was a lot of fun. Very much like Pattaya but more attractive, as it is an island with nice beaches. Once again, the girls were shopping, and George and I found a bar. We had been there for a while when George turned to me and said, "I think that this is a knocking shop." That's English slang for a pick-up bar and George had noticed the older European tourists and the young Thai girls coming and going. I told him he was correct.

Soon, Ann, Paula, and Esther were back to report that where we were was quiet, compared with the street and the bars around the corner. They were right. The next street over was one big party. We saw bar after bar on a short street, each one competing for the customers' business. Each one with more outrageous behaviour than the last

I can still see this street in my mind. Once seen, never forgotten!

We were still bitten by the "oriental bug" and we had one more adventure lined up.

Hong Kong—Bali—Singapore—Penang (Asia 5)

For this trip it was just the three of us, Ann, Paula, and me.

Hong Kong

Using Hong Kong as a base, we headed there again, did all of the usual things again and still found more to see and enjoy in this lively, vibrant city (shortly to be returned to China and Chinese rule). Because of the impending change, it seemed that the British elements of Hong Kong stood out more than ever. The British had done a fantastic job of allowing Hong Kong to grow and prosper during the century and a half that it was under British rule. It will be interesting to see what the Chinese make of it and how long they will tolerate Western style democracy now that they have it back.

It is now July 2020 and new, draconian laws prohibiting protest or dissent have just come into place in Hong Kong, along with a police crackdown and numerous arrests. The UK has announced that it will facilitate citizenship to large numbers of Hong Kong residents as a result of this latest crackdown.

Bali

From Hong Kong, we headed to Bali. We flew on Garuda Airlines and all that I can remember is having a bumpy ride and terrible food.

Despite its reputation, Bali was a mixed experience; the first two days were dreadful, and the last few days were very good.

For the first two days, we stayed at a very nice hotel close to Kuta Beach. The only thing was that we could not venture into the water, as there was an infestation of stinging jelly fish. We were restricted to the hotel pool and that was very plain. When we ventured for a walk on the Kuta Beach, we were continually pestered by hawkers, who didn't want to take no for an answer. I did buy an imitation "blowgun" complete with darts. It is still on my desk not ten feet away.

A LIFE IN STAGES

We also took a taxi into the centre of the capital. Denpasar. It was a dreadful place! The sun sets early and then you see that the entire town is enveloped in a horrible smog of gasoline fumes from all of the badly maintained vehicles. This was not our idea of the paradise that we expected Bali to be.

In desperation, I went miles to a couple of travel agencies to see if I could get an earlier flight out to our next destination, Penang, Malaysia. I tried very hard but with no luck. This turned out to be good, as we had a much more enjoyable end to our week in Bali.

We hired a young man to be our tour guide and take us up into the highlands of central Bali. The three days that we spent with this young man were very interesting and a lot of fun.

Our young guide gave us some local "colour."

- In Bali, there are three castes: lower class, middle class and upper class. Each one speaks in their own dialect and you must learn all three, so that you can converse correctly with each person, in the way that they expect.

- In Bali, there are three types of marriage, planned between families, forced by family members, and elopement between couples. There is a whole range of traditions associated with these customs.

- In Bali, children are responsible for the proper burial of their parents. If they cannot afford it, the responsibility falls to the grandchildren and so on until a proper burial ceremony has taken place. If this takes a long time the remains are eventually dug up from a temporary grave, for the proper burial in the family plot.

- Our guide could not get over that he had heard that in Western countries, we have shops that just sell dog food! In Bali, the dogs live on whatever scraps they can find. He also confided that dog meat is considered a delicacy to be shared at "men only" parties. The dog meat is rich in iron and that is good for the men.

- Although Bali is an island, seafood is not popular with the local population. They regard it as possibly contaminated and the fishermen are regarded as the lowest of the classes.

We had a good time touring the interior of Bali with this interesting young man. We enjoyed his company and learned a lot about Bali. He had a curiosity about the outside world and had difficulty understanding how Paula could possibly have her own home. After a week in Bali, we headed off to Singapore.

Singapore

Here we were again in one of the legendary oriental cities, but this one is different. Hong Kong is very oriental, but Singapore is truly modern and very Westernized. The main street, Orchard Street, could be in any major Western city and the whole place is modern, efficient, and clean. We saw the first of many 7-Eleven stores to come, while we were touring this city.

This city of 5.6 million with a mixture of Chinese, Malay, and Indian population has a long history under British rule. It was captured by the Japanese during the Second World War and endured several years of great suffering. After the war, and following its separation from Malaysia, this city state was governed in a beneficial but autocratic way by President Lee Kuan Yew. He did an amazing job. Singapore is probably the most successful city of its type in the world. Lee's son, Lee Hsien Loong, has ruled Singapore following his father's retirement. He has continued to do an amazing job but has recently announced his pending retirement. They will be lucky to find someone to follow in his footsteps.

The harbour was the busiest that I have ever seen. Hundreds of ships of every size and nationality, working their way through the straits of Singapore.

This was an amazing city. It is a testament to how a city state can be successfully run by a benevolent dictatorship, for the benefit of all of its people.

It was during our visit to Singapore that I had my first serious problems with stomach and back pain. These problems were eventually resolved, but during this trip, I frequently had to stop and rest.

Penang

An island state in the country of Malaysia, Penang, sometimes known as "The Jewel of The Orient," is another of those legendary British outposts. It is separated from the mainland by the Malacca Straits. Still with many reminders of its colonial times, its capital is Georgetown.

We enjoyed our time there, as a welcome change from the miserable time that we'd had just had on Kuta Beach in Bali.

Some of the things that were very enjoyable on most of our visits to Asia were the seafood markets. In many of them, you can select your seafood of choice and take it home, or alternatively, they will cook it for you on the spot: steamed, boiled, fried or however you would like it. Often, Ann and Paula would go shopping and I would identify a convenient bar to meet when shopping was done. In some cases, this was next to one of these seafood markets and I would indulge myself in more than one helping of giant prawns, deep fried, or steamed to perfection, and washed down with a cold beer. It doesn't get any better than that and I think that of all the times that I did this, the best was in Penang. Three helpings of giant deep-fried prawns and at least three cold beers. Fabulous.

We had three more days in Hong Kong before returning to Vancouver. This was our last trip to the Orient as a family and I am sure that these memories will be with us for the rest of our days.

A LIFE IN STAGES

The Glory Days

I called this period The Glory Days and they really were. They covered a period of twelve years from 1978 through to 1990. The Southland Corporation enjoyed ever-increasing growth in sales and profits. Its management team in North America, was becoming more sophisticated and the level of confidence in the future was unlimited. The popular slogan of the day was "The future's so bright, we've got to wear shades."

However, bearing in mind John Thompson's words that business does not go in straight lines, events began to take shape that would change the future of 7-Eleven forever in ways that were unimaginable in the glory days.

In writing this, I can't help but record the difference in culture between my enjoyable eighteen years at Fine Fare/Tamblyn, and my twenty, sometimes crazy years at 7-Eleven.

At Fine Fare/Tamblyn, although the atmosphere was friendly, parties and social events were a rarity. They were usually limited to one formal senior executive dinner and dance per year. Golf was frowned upon.

At 7-Eleven we practiced what we preached. "Work Hard. Play Hard. Have Fun."

The parties, social events, travel rewards, and other functions were many and often. Bonusses, incentives, raising money for MDA. and all of the fun activities that went along with them, were an accepted way of life. Golf was celebrated.

The culture of a company starts at the top, and it is notable that for the most part Fine Fare was managed by frugal, cost-conscious Scotsmen. 7-Eleven. on the other hand, was managed by hard working, but generous, outgoing Texans.

❖

"International organizations should think globally and act locally." Tony Eames

"Travel changes you. As you move through this life and this world you change things slightly, you leave marks behind, however small. And in return, life—and travel—leave marks on you." – Anthony Bourdain

CHAPTER FOURTEEN

The 7-Eleven Years Part Two 1990–1998

My Fifties

I was in my fifties and still fit, healthy, and confident. These were good years and really a continuation of the good times of my forties. Although there is no doubt that I had to develop a more mature approach, as the events of this decade evolved. It was during these years that I bought my first Rolls Royce. I had gone down to the Jaguar dealership in Vancouver, with the idea of buying a Jaguar, and stopped by the Rolls Royce/Bentley showroom to check out a Bentley Turbo. This was out of my price range, but I ended up with a Georgian Silver 1986 Rolls Royce Silver Spirit.

7-Eleven Head Office on Willingdon Green, Burnaby with Frank's 1986 Rolls Royce Silver Spirit

I can't quite explain why a Rolls Royce is such a special car, although I do remember that the only one that I saw in my childhood was the lord mayor of Leeds' car with the license plate MUM1. And now I have had the pleasure of owning three of them starting in 1994.

I don't think that they are any more technically advanced than the last Cadillac that I had, and the audio quality is not the best, but I suppose it's just the sheer elegance of the unique design. There is definitely something special in smoothly cruising down the highway, with power to spare, surrounded by the superb quality of the leather, the wood veneers, and the sheepskin carpets. A pure indulgence.

FRANK FARR

The second phase: The LBO and 7-Eleven Japan

It is difficult to put the events of this second phase in perspective without understanding three essential aspects.

1. The Southland Corporation became a victim of its own success.

2. The Thompson family, inexplicitly had not retained ownership of a majority of the company's shares.

3. Timing is everything, and sometimes, timing will work against you, no matter what you do.

Here is the background to the events of this second phase: The dates may be a little out, I believe that the facts are accurate. Unfortunately, the financial details are a somewhat complicated, but I am describing them in the clearest terms I can.

In its growth period of the '70s and '80s, Southland had accumulated about 3,000 gas stations in the US. This made us one of the largest independent gas retailers in the US, but we were dependent on the major oil companies both for price and the availability of supplies.

Dallas and Houston are the centres of the oil business in the US and there are many knowledgeable oil industry executives in the Dallas area. The idea began to form that Southland should consider buying its own refinery, and gradually a team was assembled to search for a possible acquisition. One refinery that might be for sale, was the Cities Service refinery in Lake Charles, Louisiana.

Southland had determined that it could afford to pay up to $750 million for the right acquisition. Cities Service (controlled by the legendary US businessman, Dr. Armand Hammer) had determined that it wanted to sell its refinery, but that it also wanted to sell 1,500 miles of pipeline and storage facilities as well. It wanted $1.5 billion for these total assets.

At that point, a deal looked unlikely. However, Southland retained the very distinguished Mr. Robert Straus, to act as a broker and put a deal together. Mr. Straus was reported as saying "We have a willing buyer and a willing seller. We have the makings of a deal." Mr. Straus, respectfully, arranged for Dr. Hammer to withdraw personally from the negotiations and over a period of several weeks, a deal was completed.

I do not know what the final price was, but Southland came away as the new owners of a 300,000 barrel-a-day, state-of-the-art refinery, bigger than any refinery in operation in Canada at the time. There were 1,500 miles of pipeline, a number of storage facilities, and several hundred City Service gas stations.

The company promptly set about selling the pipeline and storage facilities. Along with the gas stations, Southland acquired several senior to middle-level managers. One of the middle-level managers was a young manager named Jim Keyes.

I was one of the Southland executives flown down to the refinery at Lake Charles, to learn about the mechanical and financial aspects of refining. The big deal was that the refinery was in the process of installing a hydrocracker (a 200 million-dollar investment). The company was very proud of its new acquisition and its future in the oil business was assured.

Unfortunately, this is where the complications started.

Southland was a highly profitable dairy producer and food retailer. Because its profits were not volatile, the stock traded at approximately sixteen times earnings.

The major oil companies are oil refiners and distributors. Because their earnings were volatile, they traded at approximately twelve times earnings.

The stock market was undecided on how to value the new Southland, and for a while the value of the stock dropped to a multiple closer to twelve times earnings. This resulted in Southland being undervalued, opening the window for the vulture investors, and leaving Southland vulnerable.

Carl Icahn and Sam Belzberg

Carl Icahn is a US-based billionaire and a legendary corporate raider. He decided that Southland was an attractive target for his activities. He was joined in this venture by Sam Belzberg. Based in Vancouver.

One day, when John Thompson was in Paris, he received a call from Mr. Icahn. The call was to inform John that Icahn's company had purchased five percent of Southland's shares and that, as required by law, he was advising John that he intended to buy more. As a follow-up to this, he wanted to have a seat on the board of Southland and to elect several other board members. According to John Thompson, he told Icahn to "go to hell."

The Thompson family only owned twenty-seven percent of the shares in Southland and were therefore vulnerable to a hostile take-over.

John, Jere, and Jodie engaged lawyers and other independent financial advisors, to advise Southland on how to fend off this unwelcome take-over.

One of their key financial advisors was Michael Milken and his advice was for the Thompsons to stage a reverse take-over, using the company's assets as financial leverage to take the company private, in what was known as a leveraged buy-out (LBO) This meant buying back all of the stock that they did not already own. This type of leveraged buy-out was not uncommon for the time. Some of them were successful, some were not. Unfortunately, the Southland LBO was ultimately unsuccessful, but this was primarily due to timing.

Michael Milken was one of the many people who were subsequently convicted of financial crimes during this period. He served some time in jail and was released after a couple of years, due to declining health. (He was suffering from cancer.) He subsequently recovered, has done a lot of good in his later life, and was pardoned by President Trump in February 2020.

Cityplace

Prior to the LBO, the Thompsons had been quietly assembling property adjacent to the head office on Haskell Avenue in North Dallas. Once they had assembled the 150 acres that they required, they announced the development of Cityplace as the future headquarters of the Southland Corporation.

Cityplace was a visionary development (by architects based in Montreal). It comprised two, forty-two story connected towers to be built on either side of the North-Central Freeway. It was to be a landmark development for Dallas, with very little surface parking and very impressive landscaping. The two towers were to be clad in an unusual shade of "pink" marble. The whole thing was quite inspiring. From the windows of the eleventh-floor lounge in our existing building, we were able to watch the first tower rise and be completed. Moving into this new office was a remarkable event. The offices and meeting rooms were very impressive and the forty-second-floor lounge was a wonderful replacement for the eleventh-floor lounge in the original head office.

Unfortunately, the LBO and the events that followed, brought the development of Cityplace to a halt. The second tower was never completed. (The pink-marble cladding was stored in a warehouse in Dallas.) The vultures descended, and one of the other legendary Texan families bought the remaining real estate at a big discount. I always thought that this aspect of the LBO was particularly devastating for Jere Thompson, as he had played the lead role for the family, in relation to Cityplace.

All of this and the events that followed, can fairly be described as characteristic of the "Greed Economy" that consumed business, during the late '80s and early '90s. Carl Icahn's opportunistic attack on The Southland Corporation, was one of the examples of the "Corporate Raider" mentality that became rampant during this era. This group of vultures, who seldom built companies, disrupted reputable, well-run companies, often with disastrous results, as their targets became laden with too much debt, and many lives and careers were ruined in the process. (There were many other similar examples. The Nabisco Affair, was one of the more infamous LBOs of the time).

The Leveraged Buy-out (LBO) and Bad Timing

The Thompsons engaged independent council to place a fair value on Southland and the company was valued at $5.2 billion. This meant that the stock, which had dropped to around $45 was going to be bought back at approximately $78. This included buying stock back from me and all of the other senior managers, who had been granted stock gifts or stock options over the years.

We used some of this money to pay off our final mortgage and I should note that from a personal perspective, this was the point when I finally realized that I had achieved my long-standing objective of securing the financial security of my family. I had to stop and reflect that I had fulfilled that promise that I had made to myself back in the late 1940s following the death of my father. A major turning point.

Earnings Before Interest, Taxation, Depreciation, and Amortisation: (EBITDA)

During this time, we all became very familiar with this accounting term. It became the term of measurement for Southland's financial performance and the basis on which we were paid and earned our bonuses. I changed the license plate on my car to "EBITDA" to provide me with a daily reminder of my working priorities. I retained this licence plate for several years, until my retirement from 7-Eleven Canada.

Working with Milken and others, the Thompson family started the process of putting together the necessary financing. Financing of this type is completed in "tranches" or segments, with different financial institutions being involved in each tranche. The first tranches are the biggest ones, provided by the bigger banks at lower interest rates, because they have priority in repayment. The subsequent tranches are provided by smaller banks at higher interest rates with a lower priority of repayment.

All was going according to plan, until "Black Monday" in October of 1987. The stock market crashed. Interest rates skyrocketed and unfortunately for the Thompsons, all of the financial tranches were not in place. These numbers seem a little unrealistic to most of us, but there were two final tranches to be put in place: one of $200 million and one of $150 million. Due to the market crash, these two tranches were priced at sixteen percent and eighteen percent interest.

These rates were unheard of, but John and the family had to choose between paying these high rates, or cancelling the deal. This would have required the payment of substantial cancellation fees and still leaving their company vulnerable to Carl Icahn and Sam Belzberg. The Thompsons decided to complete the LBO.

Carl Icahn and Sam Belzberg made a fortune by selling the stock that they had bought at the beginning of this process. My understanding at the time, was that Sam Belzberg made many millions profit on his shares. At a dinner in Vancouver, Sam Belzberg approached me to say that he thought that the Thompsons were having some difficulty with the LBO and I should let John Thompson know that he would be willing to help. I phoned John the next day and John's response was "Sam Belzberg can go to hell."

Reorganization

Following the LBO, the Thompsons set about reorganizing the company to meet the challenges ahead. A task force was assembled in Dallas and the entire organization was examined and restructured. I was flattered to be told that my position in Canada was secure, and that once they had completed the reorganization of the US, they would share the results with me and ask me to undertake a similar review of Southland Canada.

One of the key decisions in the US was to break the company down into smaller business units (more divisions) from ten to eighteen. My boss, Adrian Evans, was transferred to the corporate head office to head up construction and I found myself with a new regional manager, Steve Krumholz. It was quickly apparent that Steve and his colleagues were a different breed of managers, bright, hard-working, and determined to meet the company's objectives.

We were more committed to the company's success than ever, as we had all been "gifted" significant stock-options in the new company.

Following the model of the US, and in consideration of our geographical size, I reorganized Southland Canada into three mini-divisions. Peter Flach was appointed division manager for Ontario, Roger Storms was appointed division manager for the Prairies, and Jimmie Musselwhite was appointed division manager for British Columbia. These positions also qualified for stock options in the new company. The three positions reported to me and my title was changed to vice-president—general manager for Southland Canada.

This situation seemed to work for the next several years, although it was obvious that the strain of meeting the high interest payments was having an impact on the parent company's cash flow.

All through this period, the stores continued to be profitable. There was never a time when the company did not make an operating profit.

Successively, we learned that the company was selling off non-core assets to enable it to meet its debt obligations. This included selling the refinery to Venezuelan interests in return for long-term supply agreements, Oak Farm Dairies, and the Chief Auto Parts Group. I think that the seriousness of the problem finally hit home when Southland sold Oak Farm Dairies; this was the company's biggest non 7-Eleven asset, and this clearly affected the Thompson family's confidence in meeting the financial obligations of the LBO. This was also my first realization of the myth of "your friendly banker."

The banks will always demand their pound of flesh, come what may.

While all of this was going on south of the border, 7-Eleven Canada was doing very well. Steve's region was also doing quite well, and he and I worked together in a positive relationship to improve 7-Eleven Canada's profitability. As a part of this, we cut back on the three-division status, as we chose not to incur the cost of three separate management teams.

This resulted in my being able to get Steve Krumholz's support in giving Southland Canada more autonomy in its day-to-day operations. This also resulted in my title being changed to President,

7-Eleven Canada. A proud moment in my career. With this appointment, I was able to promote my key managers to new positions.

Peter Flach remained in Ontario as Vice-President Ontario Operations.

Roger Storms returned to Vancouver, as Vice-President, Gasoline Operations.

Jimmie Musselwhite was appointed Vice-President Operations for Western Canada

Chris Nicolls was appointed Vice-President, Finance

Simon Evans was appointed Vice-President, Human Resources

Jim Waldron was appointed Vice-President, Construction and Development. Jim had remained my good friend and most trusted associate for all of these years, including back in the Tamblyn and Fine Fare years, and I was so pleased to be able to appoint him to this well-deserved position.

Working with this team, we achieved the highest profitability of the twenty years that I was with 7-Eleven Canada. I was proud to be associated with such an accomplished team. I genuinely believe that we had assembled a team of individuals who were each more capable than me, in their given area of responsibility.

Vice-President, Marketing

The only position that I have not identified above, is that of marketing manager. This deserves special mention in consideration of management succession planning. Traditionally and appropriately, the marketing manager position in each division of Southland, was considered the second most senior position

I had been under some pressure from Dallas to identify and hire two or three people, who in the opinion of Dick Dole and Steve Krumholz, would be capable of running 7-Eleven Canada, should anything happen to me.

Jimmie Musselwhite had been responsible for marketing in Canada from 1978 to the LBO in 1989. I used the opportunity of promoting Jimmie to recruit a new Vice President of Marketing for Canada. I hired Vlad Romanchuk. He was a very accomplished manager, who had previously served as a vice-president of Dominion Stores, one of Canada's premier supermarket companies. Vlad was a very good manager and he did a good job, but he unfortunately crossed the line of what I could accept as a part of our values, and we had to part company.

The next executive that I hired for this position was Steve Macintyre, and he was excellent. Unfortunately for us, his heart was still with his previous employer (White Spot) and when they offered him the job as president of that company, a job that he had always wanted, he accepted it. Our loss and White Spot's gain. Steve subsequently moved on to A&W Canada, where he wrapped up his career as a part of the team that took A&W private, in what became a very successful development for that company. Steve Macintyre was a hardworking, fun guy to be around and I was sorry to lose him. However, every cloud has a silver lining.

Steve had met David Huey on a management course in Dallas and was very impressed with him. David was working in the Washington State Division. I checked with Dick Dole to obtain authorization to contact David, and I made arrangements to interview him in Vancouver

The interview went very well, and I offered David the position of vice-president, marketing for 7-Eleven Canada. He accepted and the rest is history. David proved to be an exceptional manager and a good friend. Management succession in place!

The LBO of the Southland Corporation was not going well. Although the company was always profitable, it continued to have difficulty making the payments on its massive loans. (So much for Michael Milken's advice.) It is to the credit of the Thompson family that all through this crisis, the company continued to pay its suppliers, in full and on time. At no time, were we instructed to change our policy of paying our bills on time. The problem was all with the banks.

7-Eleven Canada continued to make good progress, with record profits over the next couple of years.

A very significant event took place during one of my visits to Dallas.

Dick Dole had arranged for a dinner with all the vice-presidents of Southland. As president of 7-Eleven Canada, I was included.

All of these vice-presidents were at the dinner before Dick arrived and all of them strenuously questioned Steve Krumholz as to why he did not fire Jim Keyes. Jim reported to Steve and he was responsible for gasoline operations. He was not a vice-president, but he had gained the nick name of "The vice president of nothing, who interferes in everything."

Steve explained that he had, in fact, discussed this very issue with Jere Thompson during the week. He had told Jere that if Jim Keyes was to continue to report to him, he wanted the unquestioned right to fire him, if he continued in his disruptive ways. Jere had decided to place Jim under Dick Dole, to see if that changed anything. As soon as Dick Dole arrived, the entire group of twelve to fourteen 7-Eleven vice-presidents rounded on him, to request that he fire Jim Keyes. Dick advised the group that he had had a long conversation with Jim. He had also attended Jim's wedding a week earlier and thought that he might now change his ways and settle down. Dave Finley, Southland's vice-president of human resources gave Dick his opinion of why Jim acted like he did and why, in his opinion, he would not change.

Dick was wrong and Dave was right. Jim Keyes played a strong part in undermining Dick Dole, he absolutely undermined Steve Krumholz, and within twelve to eighteen months of him having Dick Dole's job, not one of those vice-presidents, was still working for Southland. Jim Keyes was Machiavellian to the nth degree.

Against this background, we were still shocked and disappointed when we were advised that The Southland Corporation was filing for Chapter 11 Bankruptcy Protection in the US (but with a difference). The company filed for a "pre-packaged Chapter 11" for sixty days. This gave the company sixty days to complete a refinancing. What a surprise!

Southland emerged from Chapter 11 with new owners. The company's major international licensee, Ito Yokado, of Japan, assumed responsibility for all of Southland's debt and in doing so, became the new owner of The Southland Corporation.

Ito Yokado is named after its founder, Mr. Masatoshi Ito. Ito Yokado was not the largest retailer in Japan, but it was by far the most profitable. It operated supermarkets/department stores under the name of Ito Yokado. It owned restaurants and other businesses, but its 7-Eleven stores were its most profitable asset. With over 5,000 7-Eleven stores in Japan, it dominated the Japanese convenience-store industry. The day-to-day operations of these companies were managed by Mr. Ito's deputy. Mr. Suzuki.

7-Eleven Japan

I remained with 7-Eleven until 1998 and during that time, I had a great deal of exposure to the Japanese culture, the 7-Eleven Japan culture, and the Japanese management mentality. I have to say that it was a mixture of good and bad, as the Japanese struggled to come to grips with managing a huge business in North America.

I can't summarize this in chronologic order, as everything overlaps but here are some memories to indicate how the next seven years evolved.

First meeting in Dallas—Culture Shock!

I was present for the first management meeting between the 7-Eleven team and the Japanese team in Dallas. Culture shock does not really do justice to what happened. The Japanese sent over their advance team to organize the meeting, which took place in the Joe C. Thompson meeting room in Cityplace. It was quite a shock to see that each seat on the other side of the table came with an ash tray, cigarettes, and matches. Almost all of the Japanese team smoked, and this was in a room and a building that had been smoke-free from the day that it was built. Jere Thompson was devoted to the healthy lifestyle , and he had made the bonuses for some of his key staff contingent on their commitment to give up smoking. I believe that the Japanese knew this, but wanted to make it clear that this was now their company and it would be run on their terms. I cannot imagine how offended Jere was during this meeting!

Mr. Suzuki had decided to start out the way that he intended to carry on. The meeting was a disaster, as Mr. Suzuki was abrupt to the point of rudeness, to the individual US managers, who had been selected to make presentations. He saved most of his critical remarks for Dick Dole, as he had determined to establish dominance over this key Southland Manager. I did not get to make my presentation, as Dick called for the meeting to end and rescheduled a day later.

From now on, the Thompson family involvement in the affairs of the company was limited and it eventually ceased.

It quickly became apparent that the Japanese, as an area licensee, had, over time, lost respect for the US management team. They believed that they were superior managers, and quickly and relentlessly began to demonstrate why they believed this to be true. There were many other examples of this attitude of superiority.

In some cases, it became obvious that they genuinely were superior managers, in other instances, they were not, and displayed an alarming lack of understanding of the North American marketplace.

Some examples:

Freshness

They quickly demonstrated their commitment to freshness. This is a Japanese obsession, and they try very hard to live up to their own incredibly high standards. We had a lot to learn and it was a painful process. On future visits to Japan, they repeatedly demonstrated how strong this commitment was.

Tampin Kanri *(Roughly translated as "item by item, day by day management")*

They have embraced this philosophy and continue to work at perfecting it, even though it is a never-ending process. Again, this is a primary example of their superior attention to detail. Before this time, we managed the business on a category by category, month by month basis. They were more correct than we were.

Combined Distribution Centres (CDCs)

Mr. Ito and Mr. Sam Walton were friends and as Walmart developed the "Cross-Docking" system in the US, Ito Yokado had developed a similar system in Japan, "Combined Distribution Centre" (CDC).

At the same time as the US operation was establishing its first CDC in the US, Steve Krumholz, Steve LeRoy, Jim Waldron, Frank Carey, and I, made a visit to the UK and to Copenhagen. Following this visit, we worked with Frank Carey of Wallace & Carey, Inc, to develop our own version of a CDC in Calgary.

These initiatives and others were successful. However, the new management made some missteps along the way, as the Japanese insisted on managing aspects of the business in North America along lines that had worked for them in Japan. One example was beer sales. Southland was probably the biggest seller of beer in the US; we frequently had cold displays, ambient temperature displays, and often large displays for events such as the Super Bowl

The Japanese found these levels of inventory to be ridiculous and the promoted margins too low. This caused Mr. Suzuki to make one of his "trademark" pronouncements: *"Discounting is the sign of a lazy marketing department."* While there is much truth to this, it was said in a very unsettling way and was one of the reasons that John Antioco, Southland's vice president of marketing, decided to leave (more on John Antioco later). They decided to stop the sale and promotion of beer in this manner, and Southland's beer sales collapsed, much to the pleasure of our competitors. It took two years and a reversal of policy to begin to get that business back. We did learn some lessons in the process.

The other area where they made mistakes was in the area of new store development. This was particularly true in Canada. In Japan, the business is distribution-driven and there are many good reasons for this. Therefore, they do not open stores in locations that are more than fifty miles from the nearest combined distribution centre. They instructed the Dallas management to adopt similar measure by limiting development to areas within identified "red lines." This may have worked in Japan, with its limited geography, but it was potentially disastrous for Canada with its enormous geography. In addition, we were on a roll with our rural developments.

Some of the most profitable stores that we ever opened, were opened in small towns during this period.

Fortunately, we found a way round this and with limited access to capital, we were able to open some very profitable stores. One of our innovations, spearheaded by Jim Waldron, was the development of the management contract store. This arrangement enabled us to build stores without the use of 7-Eleven's capital, at a time when this was restricted.

7-Eleven Canada Inc

Something that helped us, was our decision to move 7-Eleven Canada into the Southland International Group, managed by Steve LeRoy. This provided us with more day-to-day autonomy in the operations of the Canadian company. With Steve Krumholz's support, we created a separate management committee for Canada. The members of this committee were myself, as President of 7-Eleven Canada; Steve Krumholz; Steve LeRoy; Ezra Sashoua (lawyer); and Dave Urbel (finance).

We were given written authorization to conduct Southland's business in Canada, independently of the line management in the US, within certain limits (acquiring debt, selling assets, etc.) This worked well, as by now Steve Krumholz was the executive vice president of Southland, second only to Clark Mathews, who had been appointed president of Southland, following the departure of the Thompsons.

Steve and I got along well and I always felt uplifted following his visits to Vancouver. We both shared an inclusive style of management, which enabled us to develop a high level of mutual support. Following our meetings in Vancouver, Steve and I would usually find a local bar and enjoy a game of bar trivia. We both had a good general knowledge and Steve had an encyclopaedic knowledge of US sports and TV. We frequently won these bar games.

Visits to Japan

I had the opportunity to make two visits to 7-Eleven Japan. Both were very enlightening.

On the first meeting, about ten of Southland's senior managers were invited to visit Japan and meet with our opposite numbers within the Japanese organization. This was a very interesting visit, as we toured stores, visited the sandwich kitchen and CDC, and learned a lot more about how they ran their company. One thing that stood out was that management information had limited distribution (not unlike Canada and the UK in the '60s supermarket environment). Information was only shared on a need-to-know basis, unlike the trend that had developed in the US of sharing most information. The Japanese stores are all franchised, and the role of the store supervisor was very limited, but also very efficient.

7-Eleven Management Team in Kyoto, Japan

Golf in Japan is a very expensive and exclusive business. Some of our management team had the opportunity to play at Mr. Ito's private club. Steve Leroy was clearly the best player of the day, but I did not think that our hosts appreciated this.

On a second visit, we were invited, along with our wives, to a series of meetings in Tokyo and to a more leisurely visit to some of Japan's amazing sights in Tokyo, Kyoto, and Nara. We travelled on the famed "bullet train" and passed by Mount Fuji. I still have the commemorative desk set that we were all given at the end of this unusual visit.

During this second trip, we witnessed a most unusual sight. We had stayed at one of Tokyo's most prestigious hotels, and in the morning as we left, there was a line of what appeared to be the hotel's management seeing us off. We thought that this was a little unusual and then we discovered that this was not the hotel management, but the management of the entire hotel group, gathered to thank Mr.

Ito for his patronage (remember that Mr. ITO was currently ranked as the twelfth wealthiest man in the world).

On the final evening, we attended a gala dinner that also had some unusual features. Each table held ten people: two couples from Southland, two couples from Ito Yokado, an interpreter, and one geisha. The one thing that highlighted the difference in culture, was that the Japanese wives were so pleased to be there. Many of their husbands held very senior positions and had worked for the company for many years. However, this was the first company function that they had been invited to. This compared to the fact that our wives were frequently invited to company functions. The Japanese ladies had been invited due to the fact that the North Americans had asked that our wives be included in this trip. We saw many other examples of cultural differences on this trip.

Frank and Ann at 7-Eleven company dinner in Tokyo, Japan

On the final morning, our wives were going off on a tour and the 7-Eleven managers were going off for our last business meeting. We were leaving in separate coaches. The Japanese staff had difficulty understanding why we had one female on our coach. This was Kathleen Callahan Guion, the highly regarded manager of over 600 7-Eleven stores in the Washington DC Area. Kathleen was not amused.

During one of the dinners, I told one of the senior Japanese managers that I would welcome him and his team to visit my team in Vancouver, if the opportunity occurred. Apparently, he mentioned this at the board meeting the following day and Mr. Ito agreed that it would be a good idea to hold the next board meeting in Vancouver.

Board Meeting in Vancouver

The board meeting in Vancouver was unusual in many ways. Here is how it went:

I had learned that two previous board meetings (Dallas and Los Angeles) had gone badly, with a lot of criticism directed at the division managers. I was determined and confident that I would avoid this, at the coming board meeting in Vancouver. I was successful in this regard.

One of the things that I always do before making a presentation is to check out the room. I make sure that the mikes are working, that I know where the podium is, and that I have my notes and a glass of water available at the podium. Our meeting was at the Pan Pacific Hotel in Vancouver and a little before my appointed time, I went to check out the room. The meeting that preceded mine was still in full swing, and I could hear one of my US colleagues being subjected to some tough comments from Mr. Suzuki. I opened the meeting room door a little, to get a better understanding of what was being said.

I felt a light touch on my shoulder and turned to see a young Japanese lady. Pointing to a little old man off to one side, she said, "He is Ito, who are you?" Mr. Ito had not recognized me from previous meetings. I introduced myself and he apologized for not recognizing me.

These meetings had a ritual all of their own.

When our meeting began, Mr. Ito placed his watch on the table and then nodded for the meeting to start. He bent his head forward and closed his eyes as he listened to the interpreter speak. At the end of my presentation, he silently clapped his hands. This was a sign of approval and his entire team followed his lead. During my presentation, I had made a strong pitch for more development capital for Canada. Mr. Suzuki said that following their visits to US stores, they were concerned about Southland, but they would consider allowing 7-Eleven Canada access to its own cash-flow. I considered this a major accomplishment. Following the meeting, Clark Mathews approached me and said, "You have helped redeem our credibility. We owe you one." Unfortunately, Clark Mathews never delivered on that promise.

Following the board meeting, the entire board joined us for a store tour followed by a final dinner at the Pan Pacific.

At that dinner, I was seated with Mr. Ito, Mr. Suzuki, the interpreter, and Mr. Chai, the only Korean on the Ito Yokado board. Here are a couple of things that I remember from that dinner.

- Mr. Ito expressed the opinion that the Canadian stores that they had seen, were much better than the US stores that they had seen. If the US stores had been as attractive as the Canadian Stores, they would be less concerned than they were.

- Mr. Chai joked about the fact that in Japan, Mr. Ito and Mr. Suzuki live in fairly modest homes. (It is a Japanese custom not to flaunt wealth.) However, in Hawaii, both of them own very expensive homes and often try to outdo each other in their displays of wealth.

- Mr. Suzuki asked his interpreter to explain to me that "Although he acts like a very 'tough' man, he is not really all that tough. He just believes that you have to act that way to get things done."

- Mr. Suzuki, supported by Mr. Ito, expressed the view that the Americans were too confident that their way was the right way and the Japanese did not always agree. They felt that I should resist the US management where I thought that they were wrong as far as Canada was concerned. So much for that advice!

For the next few years, business in Canada carried on as usual. The operation of the Southland Canada management committee kept me insulated from the drama that was playing out in Dallas.

The Thompsons were no longer actively involved.

Clark Mathews was senior legal counsel to the Southland Corporation and the Japanese appointed him to the position of president. This was primarily due to the fact that until the bank loans were paid off, the company was still operating under "bank covenants" and Clark was the only person who was suited for managing this relationship with the banks. 7-Eleven Japan always had huge cash reserves and dealt with banks as little as possible. But on a personal basis, the Japanese were not happy with Clark and made it known that they would appoint a successor as soon as the bank debt was removed.

Mr. Suzuki of Ito Yukado (7-Eleven's new parent company) and Frank visiting stores in Vancouver

The potential sale of 7-Eleven Canada

It was never made public at the time, but during this period, Southland twice gave consideration to the possible sale of 7-Eleven Canada. Here is how this happened.

7-Eleven Canada continued to do well during these years with continued growth in sales and profits, although we were very restricted in the availability of capital for growth. Steve Krumholz, with the support of the Canadian management committee, obtained approval from Dick Dole and Clark Mathews to explore the possibilities of a sale of 7-Eleven Canada. Steve flew to Vancouver for a one-on-one meeting with me, away from the office.

They had agreed that I should lead the effort to find a buyer for 7-Eleven Canada, and they were okay with the suggestion that I should be encouraged to put together a buy-out offer.

Because the Canadian Imperial Bank of Commerce (CIBC) had been one of the lead financiers of the Southland LBO, and because any transaction would require their approval, they were the first people that I contacted. They made it clear that they would give serious consideration to this proposal.

For the next two months, I was very busy going between Vancouver, Toronto, and Dallas. Following several long sessions with the investment committee of CIBC, a proposal was finalized along the following lines.

- CIBC placed a value on 7-Eleven Canada of $100–120 million and they agreed to provide most of this money.

- I had to produce a business plan that would generate a twenty-percent return on capital employed for each of the following five years

- I would continue to be the president of 7-Eleven Canada and I would contribute fifty percent of my net worth to the enterprise. I could nominate any of my team to also participate and they had to contribute ten percent of their net worth. In return for this investment, I and my team, would have the right to a twenty percent interest in the company on an "earned in" basis, tied to the achievement of the business plan.

- At the end of five years, The Southland Corporation would have a "right of first refusal" to buy the company back at fair market value (FMV)

- CIBC would appoint two independent investment advisors to the board of 7-Eleven Canada.

This proposal met the initial requirements that Steve, Dick, and Clark had provided to me, and together with the senior representative of CIBC, we arranged to meet with Clark in Dallas.

The meeting was strange to say the least:

We were about one hour into the presentation when Clark asked to excuse himself for an emergency. After lunch, Clark did not return. Dick Turchi the vice-president and treasurer of Southland, chaired the afternoon meeting and following some introductory comments, he announced that Southland had decided not to go ahead with the sale of 7-Eleven Canada and apologized for taking up the bank's time.

We were left with the distinct impression that Mr. Turchi and others in the finance department had never been in favour of such a proposal, and it was not clear how much of this had been shared with them by Clark.

The Canadian Group left and returned to Canada.

Steve Krumholz and Dick Dole still believed that it made sense to allow 7-Eleven Canada to grow under new ownership, with Southland being able to buy the company back in five years.

Amazingly, they persuaded Clark to reconsider his position and six months after the original proposal, they approached me to see if I could resurrect the offer. With some embarrassment, I approached CIBC again. This was followed by further meetings with CIBC in Toronto to re-evaluate the original proposals. Fortunately, our results had improved.

On one of our visits to Toronto, Jim and I were the subject of a funny practical joke. After a long day, we returned to our hotel and settled down at our favourite bar for a well-deserved drink. As the barman greeted us with a friendly, "Good evening, sir, what would you like to drink?" we were so surprised to look up and see that it was Paul Bolus, behind the bar, wearing the barman's jacket.

Paul, who was living in England, had decided to visit us in Canada and on learning where we were, he had stopped in Toronto on his way to Vancouver, and persuaded the hotel management to allow him to impersonate their barman and pull this stunt on us. Very original and typical of Paul's sense of humour.

The investment committee of CIBC agreed to go ahead, except that they wanted a letter from Clark, confirming that Southland was negotiating in good faith. Clark provided this letter of assurance.

Reassured by this letter, we arranged to meet in Dallas and make the same proposal as we had made earlier.

This meeting was more disappointing and embarrassing than the first one. The meeting was set up to be with Clark, only this time Clark did not turn up. It was left to Dick Turchi to advise the CIBC group that the board had met to discuss this situation during the previous evening and had decided unanimously that they were not going to sell 7-Eleven Canada.

The representatives of CIBC were very annoyed and made their frustration with Clark and Dick Turchi very clear. The proposal to sell 7-Eleven Canada was never raised again, but Dick Turchi did tell me that the whole LBO process had left them with an abiding dislike of banks, to the point where they just did not want to actively partner with banks, if it could be avoided.

There were two other interactions that I had with Clark that were also disappointing.

We were making such good progress in our growth in the smaller towns in Western Canada, that I could foresee a time when these growth opportunities would become limited. What steps could we take to prepare for continued growth? I developed a discussion paper, setting out what I considered to be a big opportunity. The paper was entitled "The Urban Non-Gas Store." I put a lot of work into this paper and Steve Krumholz arranged for Clark to visit Vancouver for this discussion.

The key element of this proposal was to significantly accelerate our development of hot "food to go" alternatives and create a business model more suited to a city centre environment. It had to be one that could generate forty percent gross margins, in order to be able to justify the high rents that the city centre locations would require. Clark expressed his thanks for the proposal and promised to get back to me, "Within weeks, not months."

I was disappointed not to hear back from him and to learn that Steve Krumholz was also unable to obtain a response.

We carried on with business as usual and one year later, Steve advised me that following their routine visit to Tokyo, Clark would join him again in a visit to Vancouver. We agreed to renew the proposal for an acceleration of the " Urban Non-Gas Store" development. I made the presentation again and Clark assured me that he was very pleased with this concept. He wanted to discuss this with other stakeholders in Dallas and he would get back to me without delay.

I did not hear back from Clark on this topic.

On a subsequent visit to Dallas, Steve Krumholz and I agreed to try to meet with Clark and obtain some form of agreement. Before trying to set up the meeting, we met with one of Southland's other senior executives to ask his advice. His advice was: "You have to understand that Clark is a brilliant, psychologically confused alcoholic. He is so brilliant that he analyses things to the nth degree, and this causes him to be indecisive. You cannot change him, learn to work with him." That is a description that explains a lot of what I had seen in Clark, following the departure of the Thompsons.

Clark declined to meet with Steve and me, but he left me a message. "Your very good proposal is on my desk and it will not leave there until I have dealt with it, hopefully within days." I never heard back from Clark and I never saw him again.

It was not clear to me at the time, but the battle for a successor to Clark was in full swing. I learned that Clark had embarrassed himself in front of the Japanese on several occasions and Mr. Suzuki was signalling that a change was coming.

One day, on his swing through Vancouver, following the Tokyo board meeting, Steve shared with me that Mr. Suzuki had told him the decision was going to be made soon and that there was a good chance that he would be offered the job.

It was not to be.

Jim Keyes: Background

Up until this time, I had only had a limited, but unencouraging, exposure to Jim Keyes.

When he joined Southland as a part of the Cities Service acquisition, he was a middle-level manager. However, he had more experience than his opposite number in Southland and he was appointed to the position of gasoline manager. At his first presentation, he advocated for a stronger centralized management of gasoline purchasing and pricing. I thought that he made sense and told him so after the presentation.

Following the LBO and the ouster of Dick Turchi as treasurer, Jim was appointed to this position. Following his first visit to Japan, he made the bombshell announcement that he had concluded that "Slurpee" was unprofitable and that we should re-evaluate our support for this product. The Japanese had been unsuccessful in their efforts to promote "Slurpee" in Japan and had discontinued it. I confronted Jim on this, as it related to Canada. He claimed that although he had not studied the Canadian situation, he was sure that he was correct from a corporate perspective. I don't think that anybody in Dallas agreed with him and the idea of dropping "Slurpee" disappeared. This was an example of Jim playing to the Japanese audience, as we now had Japanese managers in Dallas.

It was not unusual in the US to see gas stations on opposite corners with a ten-cent per gallon price differential. In Canada, the competitive situation is such that gas stations do not allow competitors to have a price advantage and gas stations on opposite corners, generally sell at the same price. At one time, Jim suggested to me that we should price ourselves at ten cents (per gallon) higher than our competition and that we could increase our profits by doing so. This was clearly not the case in Canada, where we had complicated supply agreements with our major suppliers and would have placed our very valuable volume discounts at risk with such a position. Jim did not appreciate the fact that we disagreed with him, but as he had no responsibility for Canada, we were not obliged to act as he suggested.

On another occasion, I was in Dallas working with Steve Krumholz on the following year's budgets. Jim came into Steve's office and immediately suggested that I reduce my budgeted expenses by $2 million. I asked him for his justification and his reply was, "Your overhead is higher than a comparable US Division and should be reduced." This completely overlooked the requirements of 7-Eleven Canada as separate company, operating in a different country, with operations that were stretched out over 4,500 kilometres. At that time, I reported to Steve Krumholz, and Steve reported to Dick Dole. Jim had no knowledge of the Canadian market and had never visited Canada in connection with the business.

On the most ill-fated encounter, Steve Krumholz invited Jim to one of our Southland Canada management meetings, on their way back from Tokyo. This was not a good meeting!

We had just completed the most profitable three months in 7-Eleven Canada's history, and we were feeling very good. Within ten minutes of the start of the meeting, Jim had destroyed any good feelings that were present. He started by attacking Chris Nichols. This was particularly difficult, since Chris reported to Jim, following Jim's appointment as treasurer and VP of finance. I defended Chris, who at that time was one of the highest ranked financial controllers in the entire Southland Corporation. Jim's response was that none of this mattered, as he was not particularly impressed with any of 7-Eleven Canada's management and thought that we could all be doing a much better job. At this point, Steve Krumholz called for a thirty-minute adjournment.

Following the adjournment, Steve addressed the group. He stated that although Jim was entitled to his opinion, he had been invited as a guest and that following their discussion, Jim would act as an observer and not disrupt the meeting. Unfortunately, this did not stop Jim. He had come to Canada determined to act in a predetermined way and he persisted in disagreeing with every decision that we made.

At the end of the day I ended the meeting with the following comment:

"Mr. Keyes. I joined this company almost twenty years ago and together with my colleagues on the board, we represent almost 100 years of dedicated experience in providing good management to this company and its employees. When I joined this company, I was advised by the chairman and son of our founder, that respect for our employees was a cornerstone of the trust that was granted to us. You have never been to Canada on business, you have never seen our stores, and you have never met many of the employees that you are maligning. If John Thompson were here today to see your behaviour, I believe that he would fire you." I forwarded a copy of this statement to Clark Mathews

It was customary for us to try to get in a round of golf following our board meetings and we had made a reservation to play at the Coquitlam course. Steve Krumholz, ever the conciliator, suggested that we continue with our round and try to use the occasion to mend fences. Chris Nichols, David Huey, and I declined to play with a group that included Jim Keyes. Within two months of this meeting Jim arranged for Chris Nichols to be fired.

Several months later, Steve phoned me from Dallas. They had arrived back from Tokyo on the previous day and he had met with Clark in the office on the Saturday morning. He was totally blind-sided when Clark told him that he was making some changes and that Steve would not have a place in those changes. He was effectively fired.

In his conversation, Steve expressed his concern for me, in as much as Clark intended to disband the management committee of Southland Canada and there would be no one left to speak up for the various initiatives that we were implementing in Canada. (Steve LeRoy had also been side-lined. See following notes.)

Within thirty days, it was announced that Jim Keyes was taking over Steve's position as executive vice-president and it was obvious that he would be succeeding Clark as soon as the bank arrangements were cleared up.

Within a month of Steve Krumholz's departure, I received the anticipated phone call to come to Dallas for a meeting with Jim Keyes. Our meeting lasted about one hour, and Steve LeRoy joined us for a part of it. Based on our prior history, the outcome was not a surprise.

Our dialogue went along the following lines.

I explained to Jim that I understood that he now had Steve Krumholz's job. I now reported to him and asked if he had any immediate plans for Southland Canada.

He explained that with Clark Mathews' approval, he was disbanding the Canadian management committee and that he wanted changes in my management team.

I explained to him that I had been in charge of Southland Canada for twenty years, with generally good results and that I believed that I had earned the right to be consulted on matters affecting the company, though understanding that he would have the final say.

He explained that in his new position he had lots to do and did not have time for discussion. If he wanted something to happen, it should happen, with no need for discussion.

I asked him what the changes were that he wanted for Canada, bearing in mind that the Canadian operation was enjoying record results. He advised me that he wanted me to return to Canada and fire Roger Storms, Jimmie Musselwhite, Simon Evans, Mike Sugden, and our new financial controller, Arthur Mountain.

I asked him if there was any point in discussing this directive. His response was "No! I have just explained that I do not have time for these types of discussions."

I had carefully considered my options before going down to Dallas and I had decided that if things turned out as expected, I would exercise my option to take early retirement, rather than find myself in a position of having to jump when Jim Keyes said "Jump." I advised him that, subject to the appropriate severance agreement, I would prefer to take early retirement and let him have somebody else run the company the way that he wanted it to be run.

Clark Mathews remained closeted in his office twenty feet away, but chose not to participate.

That meeting was officially, the end of my association with 7-Eleven. I did stay on for another month and at the end of that time, we had two enjoyable events.

We had a going away party at the Creekside Café with all our head office staff. This was also a going away party for Paula. She had been my executive assistant for the two prior years (she did a great job), but it clearly would not work for her to remain in this position with whoever was going to take my place, and I was concerned that she might not be treated fairly.

Frank and Paula's farewell party at the 7-Eleven Head Office—March 1998

7-Eleven Recognition Plaque

FRANK FARR

We had a retirement dinner for me at the Morgan Creek Golf Club with the management team from across Canada. A couple of things have remained in my memory from this dinner. Mike Sugden rose to the occasion by giving a long, praise-filled speech, lifted from Greek mythology

Art Mountain, Roger Storms, Jim Waldron, Frank, David Huey, Jimmie Musselwhite, and Simon Evans outside the 7-Eleven Head Office

It seemed astounding that the Japanese would give such free rein to Jim Keyes, but one explanation was that Mr. Suzuki was something of a tyrant with an outsized ego. He truly believed that he had single-handedly guided Ito Yokado to its high level of success. Jim Keyes envisioned himself as the "Mr. Suzuki of North America," and the real Mr. Suzuki was willing to let him try.

Steve LeRoy lived up to his reputation for saying little by simply stating, "Frank, you did good."

Being a lawyer, Clark Mathews had developed an interesting strategy for dealing with his subordinates. He gave most of them two year's notice, while telling each of them that he would quite understand if they found other employment during this time. They would still be paid for the two years.

Dave Finley left and Steve LeRoy, Bob Baily, Adrian Evans, Terry Blocher, and many others were included in this odd procedure.

Following my departure, Terry Blocher was asked to leave Dallas and assume interim management of 7-Eleven Canada. During his period as interim manager, all the people that Jim wanted to leave Southland Canada, were let go.

Jim Keyes then set about replacing almost all of the remaining senior managers in the Southland Corporation.

Mr. Suzuki also expressed disdain for most North American retailers, and he was quite happy to see the Japanese methods put in place in the US.

Within a year David Huey was appointed as vice president and division manager for 7-Eleven Canada. In this position, David's authority was limited to operational management and all the individual departments were adjusted to report directly to the senior function in Dallas. It has essentially remained that way up until today's date, March 2020. I always had the highest regard for David, and I was genuinely pleased to see that he was the one selected to run the Canadian Operation for the next several years.

Although Jim Keyes was happy to see me go, I left with a lot of pride. During my last year, 7-Eleven Canada had the most profitable year in its history (see Appendix 3). People that I respected such as Dick Dole, Steve Krumholz, Steve LeRoy, Dave Finley, Dick Turchi, and others had expressed their appreciation for the professional manner in which I ran the Canadian operation and clearly John, Jere, and Jodie Thompson were pleased

Tim Donegan, David Huey, Terry Blocher, and Frank
(Thirty + years of 7-Eleven Canada Management)

Subsequent events

In 1998, Grace McCarthy nominated me as a candidate for The BC Businessman of the Year. However, my departure from 7-Eleven determined that I should decline this welcome gesture.

It is odd how the paths of many of the individuals who were involved in the last phase of The Southland Corporation/7-Eleven as an independent company have crossed, sometimes more than once.

Jim Keyes

The Japanese eventually fired Jim Keyes, but not before he had done much damage to the company. One of the good things that Jim Keyes did do, was to hire Joe de Pinto from Exxon to be the chief operating officer. That relationship did not work out for too long and Joe De Pinto left. However, Joe de Pinto must have made a strong impression on the Japanese management, because, as soon as they had fired Jim Keyes, they rehired Joe de Pinto as president of 7-Eleven, a position that he still holds as of September 2020.

Blockbuster

John Antioco left 7-Eleven after the Japanese acquisition in 1991. Following a short stint with Pearl Vision, he became the CEO of Circle K. Following the sale of Circle K, John became the CEO of Blockbuster.

Carl Icahn was a major investor in Blockbuster and following a very public dispute, John Antioco left Blockbuster with a significant settlement agreement. In the meantime, both Steve Krumholz and Steve LeRoy began doing some work for John at Blockbuster. At one time, Steve considered asking me if I would be interested in managing Blockbuster in Canada. Following John Antioco's departure from Blockbuster, Carl Icahn hired Jim Keyes to run the company, and both Steves found themselves working for Jim Keyes. That relationship did not last long.

Kathleen Callahan Guion left 7-Eleven and joined Dollar General in a senior position. Steve Krumholz spent some time working for Kathleen at Dollar General before retiring to his ranch in East Texas.

Steve Leroy joined Super Siete (7-Eleven Mexico) in a consulting capacity. I understand that Steve retired from Super Siete in 2019.

John Thompson died at the age of 77 in 2003.

Jodie Thompson left the company to set up his own business. I believe that he subsequently sold this business and is living a life of retirement in Texas.

Jere Thompson became involved in a company founded by his son. I believe that this company, which specialized in the reselling, or other distribution, of hydro power, was recently sold and Jere is living a life of retirement in Dallas.

Dick Dole died at the age of fifty-eight. This was after his departure from 7-Eleven and happened while he was playing in a fastball street tournament.

Adrian Evans died in 2015.

Mr. Ito is now in his nineties and living in distinguished retirement (as the advisor to the board).

Mr. Suzuki was forced to resign from Ito Yokado a couple of years ago, as a result of trying to manipulate the management succession within the company.

At the time of the Japanese acquisition of The Southland Corporation in 1991, there were approx. 14,000 stores world-wide, including, 5,000 in North America, 5,000 in Japan, and a number of area licenses in other countries, primarily in Asia.

As of September 2020, there are over 70,000 7-Eleven stores world-wide. WOW!

Alain Bouchard the founder of Couche Tarde, contacted me in 1995, regarding the possibility of 7-Eleven joining him in the purchase of Mac's. Mr. Suzuki declined. Following my retirement from 7-Eleven, we had discussions regarding the possibility of me joining the Couche Tarde board. This did not materialize, due primarily to language issues. Mr. Bouchard has gone on to build his company, Couche Tarde, into the second largest convenience store chain in the world with close to 20,000 locations. 7-Eleven remains the industry leader with over 70,000 locations

On a related note: Blockbuster went bust and yet, with more forward-looking management, it could have been the Netflix of today. Netflix is a phenomenally successful and valuable company.

A LIFE IN STAGES

Woolworth's world-wide went bust (except in Australia) and yet, with more forward-looking management, it could have been the Dollar Store of today. Dollar General and other dollar stores are phenomenally successful.

❖

"Honesty is always an option. Usually the best one." Steve Krumholz

"The sins of omission are greater than the sins of commission." Steve Krumholz

"Discounting is the sign of a lazy marketing department." Toshifumi Suzuki

"When your values are clear, decision making is easy." Roy E. Disney

CHAPTER FIFTEEN

Bosses

My departure from 7-Eleven brought an end to the time in my career when I was a part of a management structure, reporting to a boss. This is a good time for some final thoughts on the bosses that I have reported to.

I have found that people working in tandem can achieve so much more than people working individually. This is particularly true if that person is your boss. As you will have seen from my story so far, I have almost always enjoyed a good working relationship with my boss, and this has been the key to much that I have accomplished.

The key element was always trust, on both a personal and business level. They trusted me to get the job done, and I trusted them to give me the support and encouragement that I required.

As I look back, there have only been four exceptions to this trusting relationship and in three of these cases, this resulted in my leaving the company and changing my future direction.

Fortunately, these were the exceptions and for the most part, I have been very lucky, in that I have worked for, or have been influenced by many very interesting people. I have had the opportunity to learn something from each of them. Why was each one successful on their own terms, and what was I able to learn from observing their success?

Lessons Learned

Dorothy and Montague Simmons

Not really my bosses as such, but the biggest and most positive influences on my life. Although I was a "bright delinquent," they had faith in my ability to make a positive change in the events and people that would be a part of my future.—Question the status quo.—Be successful on your own terms, but do the least possible harm to others.

FRANK FARR

Norton Delaney

How do I define success? Where do you start? The first clear example for me was Norton Delaney. Nort was the manager of the Loblaw Supermarket at the Old Jockey Club location in Hamilton, Ontario when I started with Loblaws in 1957. There were many managers in the Ontario region but Nort stood out. He was a good manager, and he combined this with a decency with customers and staff that earned him instant respect. A great role model.

I mentioned Laurie Edwards, Don Neville, Werner de Smidt, Wallace Monaghan, and James Gulliver in my chapters on Fine Fare. Here are my final thoughts on these gentlemen who did play such a large part in my personal development.

Laurie Edwards—Civility

Laurie Edwards was a stand-out in the sometimes rough and tumble of the supermarket industry. He was a shining example of the fact that if you know your stuff, you don't have to go through life shouting and throwing your weight around. You can be successful and remain a gentleman at the same time.

I received a note from him together with his Fine Fare gold cuff links. They have the reversed F.F. Fine Fare logo and he remembered that these were my initials. In his note, he also sent a belated apology for delaying my promotion, so many years ago in Leamington Spa. He passed away in 2008 in his mid-nineties, a gentleman to the end.

Don Neville—Trust—Delegation.

Don Neville was a very supportive boss for several years. He had great trust in me, and he was very supportive of the merchandising teams. He taught me to delegate and he also taught me that there are always several ways to solve any problem. He helped me to adjust from the sometimes brash world of field operations to the more sophisticated approach needed to succeed in a head office environment. I stayed in touch with Don through his very happy retirement on his marina on the Great Ouse River to his subsequent passing in his late sixties.

Werner de Smidt—Intellectually Curious—Analytical.

Werner was the most intellectual of the Fine Fare directors and we had an on-again, off-again relationship during my entire time with Fine Fare. He was my boss during my final years as a director of business development. He taught me a lot, but the thing that has stayed with me the most, is the importance of being a thinking manager. I remained in close touch with Werner through to his death in 2019 at the age of ninety-four. When I visited him and his wife Joyce at their home in Huntingdon, there was always a large pork pie and a pot of tea, as we reminisced over the Fine Fare years. In his late eighties he learned to use a flight simulator on his computer. "Hello Frank, I know that you have just landed in Yerevan. I just landed at the same time. I am with you in spirit."

Wallace Monaghan—General Management

Wallace Monaghan was Fine Fare's final chairman and a strong general manager. He trusted me with continued increasing responsibility, and he encouraged me to always see the bigger picture. He also took the time to talk to me about the business and the challenges that he faced in his efforts to make Fine Fare more successful.

James Gulliver—Technocrat—Ambitious

James Gulliver was an outstanding chairman for Fine Fare and a brilliant manager in the modern technocratic style. He was a Harvard graduate. I never reported to him personally, but he identified some potential in me and was responsible for my promotion to a director of Fine Fare. He provided much guidance in understanding the techniques and responsibilities of more senior management. When I decided to leave Fine Fare, he immediately offered me the position of managing director of Oriol Foods, the new company that he was assembling with Alistair Grant. He continued to have a very distinguished career following his departure from Fine Fare.

Galen Weston—New Thinking—Big Thinking

I have mentioned Galen Weston elsewhere in these stories. For a very wealthy man, he was always polite and considerate to me. He gave me my opportunity in Canada and always enquired after my well-being. We toured stores together in England. *"Frank Farr, what's new, different, and innovative?"* He was a good man. Sadly, Galan passed away on April 13, 2021.

Dave Nichol—Originality—Marketing

I never worked directly for Dave, although I did meet him on several occasions and spent some time with him in Toronto in 1974–75. His development of own-label products in North America was a landmark achievement. (I believe that Marks & Spencer was the inspiration of his thinking in this regard.) This crystalized in the concept of developing unique products, only available in your stores and delivering higher than average margins. The "No Name" and "President's Choice" brands, developed by Dave, have become iconic throughout North America.

FRANK FARR

Serge Darkazanli—Little Stick of Dynamite—Talent—Hard Work—Brains

Unfortunately, flawed in some personal characteristics. A difficult man to work with. I did learn some things from Serge, mainly technical processes that he had learned during his time at McKinsey. They are processes that have helped me to run things or to advise others on how to run their businesses.

John Thompson—Decency—Trust

It was John who said to me on the first day that we met, *"Frank, we trust you to run our operations in Canada. Business never goes in straight lines; you will have ups and downs and when you have a bad month, you will not get any complaints from me. But if you ever betray my trust and treat our employees badly, I will fire you."* Good advice that I lived up to for my entire career with 7-Eleven.

Jere Thompson—Focus

"If it's important to me, it had better be important to you." "Don't let a big idea become a small idea." Jere was the ultimate one-minute manager. All you had to do was ask and you would have Jere's undivided attention—for a minute or two. He would pay attention and he would follow up. Jere was the strong one of the Thompson brothers. He was focused and tough minded.

Dick Dole—Dynamic Leadership—Positive, Supportive Energy

What a character—the leader at 7-Eleven in every way. I have so many good memories of Dick. He hired me and was so supportive of me and my work for 7-Eleven in Canada. Following his retirement, we were in regular and friendly contact until the day that he died, playing softball on his street. The best of the best!

Adrian Evans—Listen to Others

One of the good guys. Adrian was the best listener that I ever met. He was my predecessor at 7-Eleven Canada and a good friend for the rest of my career with the company. We had many, many good times together.

A LIFE IN STAGES

Steve Krumholz—Strong Work Ethic—Smart Thinking—Take the High Ground.

Steve was my boss and a good friend. Working together we were a dangerous combination. If we had been able to get the support from Clark Mathews when we needed it, or if Steve had succeeded Clark as president of Southland, both 7-Eleven Canada and I would be in a different position today. It is a pity that he did not get this well-deserved position. We continue to stay in touch and Steve and Scotti are enjoying a happy and fulfilling retirement on their farm property in rural East Texas.

Steve Leroy—Say Little, Do a Lot

Stick to your core values. Another one of the good guys. We gave him the title of "The man that said the least and did the most." The best golfer in Southland! In his retirement, Steve remained as an advisor to the 7-Eleven Mexico Area licensee, working out of Monterey, MX.

Mr. Ito—Appreciation of Others.

Not a lot to say here. Although I met Mr. Ito on several occasions, I cannot claim to know him. He seemed like a gentleman and he did express his appreciation of me and the work that I was doing in Canada. His first words to me (through his interpreter) were, *"I am Ito, who are you?"*

Mr. Suzuki—Power—Confidence

Mr. Suzuki was Mr. Ito's deputy and the man who ran Ito Yokado on a day-to-day basis. A very tough manager! He totally dominated the affairs of Ito Yokado and subsequently 7-Eleven. His Japanese employees called him "The Tornado." I sat next to him at dinner in Vancouver and he told his interpreter to tell me, "Mr. Suzuki would like you to know that he is not really a tyrant in person, he just believes that in a big organization, you have to be tough to get things done." I think that James Gulliver would have agreed with that sentiment.

"If it's important to me, it needs to be important to you." Jere Thompson

"The man that knows how, will always have a job. The man that knows why, will always be his boss." Werner de Smidt—Frank Farr

In business, "That which gets measured, gets done" James Gulliver

CHAPTER SIXTEEN

West Van to Morgan Creek— Building our Retirement Home

During 1995, Ann and I started to think of our next move. Paula had left home and was living in Burnaby. West Vancouver was changing quickly, as many empty nesters decided to downsize and friends and neighbours were moving on. Many of our English group of friends lived in Delta/South Surrey, and we thought it would be a good move to be closer to that area.

View from 2398 Westhill Drive, West Vancouver

Paula at 2398 Westhill Drive, West Vancouver

Paula's 1988 Camaro

Pauline Elsby (Ann's sister), Paula, Ann, Alex Elsby and Terry Elsby—Christmas at 2398 Westhill Drive

197

FRANK FARR

We spent a lot of time looking at homes throughout the Lower Mainland, but had difficulty finding anywhere that could compare with West Vancouver. During this time, our good friends, Bernie and Gerry Finan, decided to build a home in the Morgan Creek development in South Surrey, surrounding the new Morgan Creek Golf Course. The idea of building a new home in the middle of a golf course development attracted us and we soon settled on buying a lot at 16028 Delsey Place. This was a third of an acre, south-facing lot, backing on to the seventeenth fairway and within a few hundred yards of the new clubhouse.

We decided on the design of our "retirement home" and engaged a local architect to turn our design into reality. We quickly learned the golden rule of house building: "Everything takes longer than you expect, and everything costs more than you expect." . We moved into our new home in August of 1997 and in March of 1998 I retired from 7-Eleven and began to settle into our new community

❖

Delsey Place, under construction in 1997

The house was 5,400 square feet and took almost two years to build. It was quite exciting to visit our new home on a very frequent basis and to see how a new building of this type comes together. One of the surprising things for us was to see how much wood is required in a house like this. The roof structure alone was quite amazing. In finalizing the details of the house, we were fortunate to have the services of Judy Christopherson. Judy acted as the project manager and was able to help us think carefully as we chose the finishing details.

16028 Delsey Place, Morgan Creek Golf Course, South Surrey

One of the other features was the large amount of "carved" glass for the huge double-height living room windows and other feature windows around the house. The living room window carving featured a beautiful, twenty-foot-high tree carved into the glass and continued on the adjacent wall. We included a gorgeous eagle in the window of the main bathroom.

However, the "piece de resistance" was the unique bar that we designed for the rec room. This bar immediately became the focal point of the house. It was a ten-foot-long curved bar. The bar top was a solid sheet of copper and over the bar, we had an acrylic glass rack. This really was a spectacular bar and the scene of so many good times with our friends. In one corner of the bar, we placed a small metal plaque: "Snarler's Corner." This was in honour of Ann's dad, as his usual place in his local pub also had this same nickname.

Frank's Pub at Delsey Place

A LIFE IN STAGES

Judy's husband, Chris, was a master electrical engineer and he did us proud. The lighting system was quite amazing. The home was divided into zones and each zone had its own controls, offering a never-ending variety of lighting options. The result was like having two homes, one through the day and an entirely different look at night-time.

The lighting to the exterior of the house was also very attractive. Chris explained the concept of "architectural delineation" and showed us how to highlight the exterior architectural features of the home. The result was quite extraordinary.

We designed the exterior to resemble a mini spa. The garden had over 5,000 square feet of pressed concrete terracing, surrounding a 36' x 20' pool, and included an eight-person hot tub, a sauna and changing room, and a commercial-sized, built-in BBQ.

All considered, building this house was an enjoyable, once-in-a-lifetime experience. For the most part, the contractors were good and the workmanship was exceptional. The only disappointments were the endless delays and two or three disappointing contractors.

By August of 1997, we had to move in, although the house was still not finished. George and Esther moved in with us and it was a pleasure to share our first few weeks with them. In March of 1998, I retired from 7-Eleven after twenty amazing years and we settled down, ready to see what "retirement" would bring.

George and Esther Pope

Our home became the focal point of our lives and we were able to host so many parties and get-togethers—too many to mention. We managed to get into a routine of at least one summer BBQ/pool party and one Valentine's party, where Ann decorated the home in a blaze of red. These were large parties. We also had a steady stream of get-togethers with our smaller group of close friends.

Although George passed way in June of 1998, we had the pleasure of Esther's company at Christmas for most years, until the travel became a little too much and Ann started to visit her mum back in England. Those final times with Esther in Delsey Place were very special for all of us. During one memorable visit, we had the opportunity to have an eightieth birthday party for her, which included a video presentation of her life.

BBQ with friends at Delsey Place

Esther's Sentimental Journey video

Esther and Ann – New Year's Eve 2000

Paula - Horses

Paula at Leeds Riding School

During our years at Delsey Place, Paula avidly got back into horse riding. Back in England in about 1970 she'd had her first experience with horse riding with her cousin Jacqueline at Leeds Riding School. She continued with riding lessons at Sandridgebury Riding School throughout our time living in Welwyn Garden City. (Paula visited these stables again in 2016 with her best friend Jo Eden.) During our time in West Vancouver she kept up her riding at Lynn Valley Stables.

When Paula stopped working at 7-Eleven head office in 1998, she started volunteering at Pacific Riding for the Disabled in Maple Ridge, which eventually became North Fraser Therapeutic, where she became the program co-ordinator. Paula also worked at Valley Therapeutic Equestrian as their office manager and got certified to teach therapeutic riding through CanTRA (Canadian Therapeutic Riding Association). She taught at Valley Therapeutic and Pacific Riding for Development Abilities in Langley.

However, her final joy in riding and horses came together when she purchased her own horse "Galeano," an eight-year-old, registered Canadian warmblood. Paula had the love and enjoyment of this wonderful horse until the day he laid down and peacefully passed over the rainbow bridge on June 10, 2019.

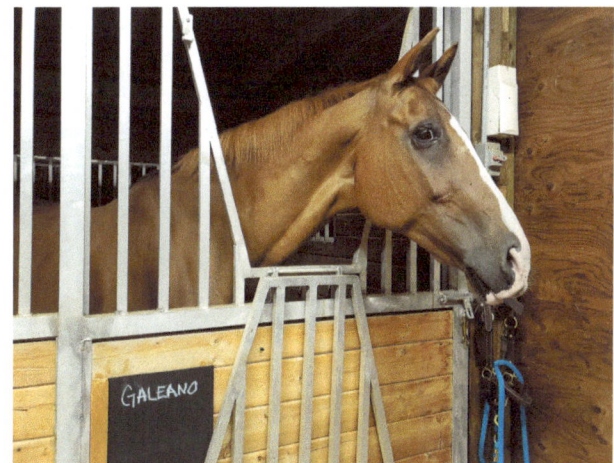

Paula and Galeano at a horse show at Rosewyn Stables

Paula and her "heart horse," Galeano

During our time at Delsey Place, we also had three lovely cats: Callie, Kia, and Suzi. Paula also bought home an old rescue dog, a golden retriever named Harley.

Callie 1997–2014   **Kia 2000–2015**   **Suzi 2006–2021**

Harley 1997–2010

Christmas card from Paula's friend, Dolores Scott, December 2020 with Suzi, Galeano, and Harley and his swan

When we planned our move to Delsey Place, we anticipated staying there for maybe ten years. As it turned out, we lived in this wonderful home for almost twenty years, finally selling the house and moving out in March 2017

"Building your own home will always take longer and cost more." Frank Farr

CHAPTER SEVENTEEN

Retirement (NOT)
1998–2010

My Sixties

In March of 1998, I retired from 7-Eleven, after an amazing, twenty-year career. I had just turned sixty and realized that my healthiest and most productive days were behind me. However, I still felt very confident and that there was more to come. I believed that my experience could be put to some good use.

What to do now?

I had always assumed that I would work part-time in some advisory capacity, possibly as a government advisor to small business. Many years ago, I'd had a last conversation with Mr. Perkins, Fine Fare's Director of Produce Operations, and he told me that he was going to work for the UK government's small-business advisory service. It had always stuck in my mind that I might do something similar when my time came.

I should note at this point that for the first time in my life, health issues began to have an impact on my life. I had been incredibly fortunate in not having any serious health issues in the prior forty years. I never even caught a cold that I can recall, and I never had one hour off for any illness-related reason. Then, over the course of the next few years, I had three serious issues to deal with.

- In 1999, it was determined that I had "Barret's Oesophagus." This is a potentially dangerous condition that can result from frequent and repeated acid reflux. Fortunately, I qualified for a test program at St Paul's Hospital. The treatment was successful, the "Barret's" disappeared and has not reappeared in the twenty years since the procedure.

- During my annual medical exam in October 2001, my doctor recommended that I have an ultra-fast CT scan on my heart. These scans were not readily available in BC at that time, so off I went to San Francisco. We received the results within one week. The usual "plaque count" in the coronary arteries is 200 or less. At 400 or more, there is a need for remedial treatment. I had a count of over 800 and needed an angiogram ASAP. This was arranged within a month and the result was clear. I needed heart bypass surgery. This was January 2002.

- The surgery was scheduled for March. Unfortunately, due to the high waiting list for these surgeries, I was 'bumped' until June. Then again in June, I was bumped until August. My cardiologist was quite concerned and asked me if I would be willing to pay, if he could schedule an operation earlier in the US. Without any real thought, I said YES! "Good," he replied. "I thought that you would agree. I have booked you into the Virginia Mason Hospital in Seattle for next week." WOW! Following a special effort by my cardiologist, BC Medical agreed to cover the cost of this operation.

- I underwent the operation on the third of July 2002. It was successful and I do believe that my BC cardiologist saved my life. Ann and Paula came to Seattle with me and stayed in an apartment close to the hospital. I had the operation on a Tuesday, and I was home the following Monday.

- In April of 2006, I had a bad accident involving my pool equipment. I was on my own at the time. Ann was in England visiting her mother, and Paula was in Coquitlam visiting her boyfriend. The pool heating equipment "exploded" and I suffered severe scalding steam burns to my stomach and right leg. This required hospitalization and skin grafts to repair the damage.

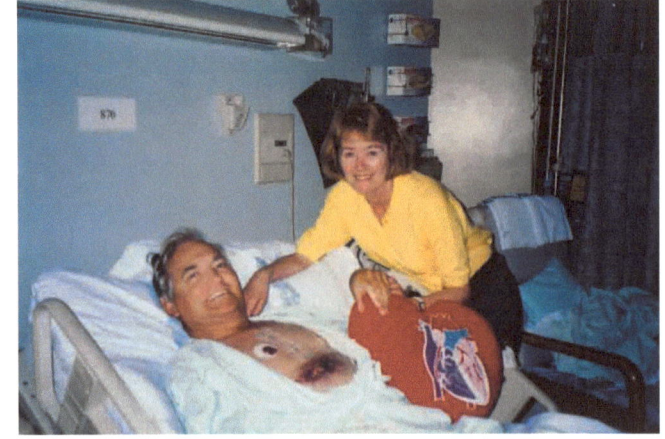

Frank in recovery following his quadruple bypass heart surgery at the Virginia Mason Hospital in Seattle

- In 2018, again in a routine examination, I discovered that I was suffering from atrial fibrillation (periods of irregular heartbeat). During the tests for this, I had another angiogram examination of my heart. The surgeon who performed this latest angiogram declared that he could see the work from my by-pass operation of sixteen years before and that physically, my heart was in good shape. They did good work back at Virginia Mason Hospital in 2002.

- Apart from any lingering effects from these incidents, I am in generally good health.

A LIFE IN STAGES

Morgan Creek Men's Club

I joined the Morgan Creek Men's Golf Club and was appointed secretary/treasurer. I enjoyed that position for three years and it was a good opportunity to wind down from my business life and get to know the 100-140 members of this newly formed club. I particularly enjoyed working with Mike Ellam, who was the club captain for two of my three years in this position.

The Osborne Consulting Group

I am not sure how I was introduced to the Osborne Consulting Group, but I was offered an opportunity to become a principal of this group. We used to meet monthly in the downtown offices, as a group of sixteen or so ex-senior executives and we worked individually or as small teams, to provide assistance/advice, usually to start-up groups.

I also did some consulting work on my own. One interesting and successful project was to advise the owner of property located at the SW corner of 152nd St and 32nd Avenue in Surrey. Following a lead from my good friend Bernie Finan, this is now the location of a very successful Keg Restaurant and I take some pleasure from knowing that this restaurant would not be there, without my efforts on behalf of the developer.

British Columbia Assessment Authority: (BCAA) (2002–2003)

Shortly after joining the Osborne Group, I was asked to join the British Columbia Assessment Authority as Chairman of the Board of Directors. This was a part-time job, as the day-to-day management of the authority is managed by a president and his staff. I agreed and this became a very interesting occupation for the next year of my life.

BCAA is the government agency charged with determining the value (for taxation purposes) of all "real property" in British Columbia. This is a mammoth task, which must be completed each year within tight and predetermined deadlines. It was a pleasure to be associated with this very dedicated group of professionals. We often referred to "the long skinny things" as being the most difficult to value. Long skinny things was their term for such things as waterfront, railways, rivers, canals, hydro lines, oil pipelines, etc.

I will say that Gordon Campbell, the premier of BC at the time, did an excellent job and in my opinion, has seldom received fair credit for the work that he did while in office.

By the end of my first year at BCAA, I had decided to dedicate all of my time to my new venture, Immediate Images Inc. and I resigned from BCAA.

Canada
Province of British Columbia

PURSUANT to the *Assessment Authority Act*, and
Order in Council 208, approved and ordered March 6, 2003,

FRANK FARR

was appointed a member and chair of the
BC Assessment Authority Board
for a period of one year.

Minister of Sustainable Resource Management

Premier and President of the Executive Council

A LIFE IN STAGES

Immediate Images Inc: (2003–Present)

During my time with BCAA, as member of the consulting company, I continued to deal with some clients. One of those clients was DMS Controls, a Victoria-based company that had developed a proprietary system for the management of content on remote/multiple digital displays.

DMS had been founded by Rod Cummings, a recent arrival from South Africa. He was a good man with an interesting business background and a thorough knowledge of computer technology and computerized education. My initial role with DMS was to assist them in their search for funding, and at the same time, assist them in negotiating an area license for Washington State in the US.

The outcome of this work was that I decided to go into the business myself, having negotiated an exclusive agreement for DMS technology for the whole of Canada. I formed this company in 2003 and it is still in operation eighteen years later in 2021.

A lot has happened with Immediate Images during its eighteen-year life.

Here are the main milestones

- My original thought was that I would spend two or three years to establish the company and then retire from active involvement. I needed somebody younger than me, with sales experience, and I offered an equal partnership in the company to Peter Hucul. Together, we came up with the title of Immediate Images Inc.

- We hired a small group of people to help develop sales. I also persuaded Paula to join us as administrator and co-owner. I wanted somebody competent that I could trust to control the company's cash.

- Peter hired a man named Cal Sucher to assist him on the technical side of the business. This turned out to be a disaster. We also hired Lee Taal to work with Peter on the sales side and subsequently, we hired Casey Jones to succeed Lee as our director of sales.

- These were busy times as we crisscrossed the country in search of new business.

- However, within a couple of years, we ran into trouble. Peter and Cal were racking up expenses that exceeded our sales, and it was clear that they would not respond positively to my requests for improvement. I decided to make changes.

- I arranged to buy Peter out and I fired Cal Sucher. Cal subsequently sued me for wrongful dismissal and lost. The judge's ruling from that trial makes fascinating reading (Madam Justice Fisher).

- Following the departure of Peter and Cal, Lee and his team, including Casey, led us to higher sales. We achieved close to $1 million in sales in 2010. At that time we owned or managed almost 400 digital displays located across Canada from Victoria on Vancouver Island to Ottawa, Ontario. During this time, we became involved with a company known as SIMS (Student Information Systems) and we formed a successor company, ChatterHigh Communications Inc. Lee subsequently resigned from Immediate to chase his dream of making ChatterHigh a success. He is still working at this and the company continues to grow. I wish Lee every success.

- Following Lee's departure, we were very fortunate to be able to rely on Casey to continue the development of Immediate. Casey's hard work and dedicated support of Immediate, has opened new doors for Immediate, as he has continued to use his sales experience and co-operative personality to grow sales and expand the company's professional profile. Kim Yawney has also been instrumental in providing us with accounting support over the years.

Casey Jones, Frank, Peet, and Paula at Victoria International Airport

Immediate Images is owned by P.A.F. Investments, which in turn is owned by Frank, Ann, and Paula. I have gradually pulled back from the company and it is now effectively managed by Paula and Casey.

A LIFE IN STAGES

Casey Jones, Partner with Immediate Images Inc.

Immediate Images outdoor LED screen at Hwy #91 (Alex Fraser Bridge)

Immediate Images outdoor LED screen at Hwy #99 (Massey Tunnel)

Frank and Ann with Peter and Jo Flach

In 2009, Peter Flach, my friend from the 7-Eleven days, suggested that I should consider becoming involved in a venture that he was involved in. He thought that it would suit me. This was the European Bank for Reconstruction and Development (EBRD). I was very busy at the time and did not take the suggestion seriously. I was wrong and I am thankful to Peter for bringing this opportunity to my attention.

So much for retirement!

❖

"Anticipation is the art of management.
See over the horizon. Avoid the bad news that lies out there
and embrace the good news and all that it brings." Frank Farr

CHAPTER EIGHTEEN

Glow of Ownership—English Language

At this point, you might expect me to comment on my hobbies: gardening, carpentry, etc. Unfortunately, I never had the aptitude for these types of activities and I was always so busy working that I never developed any hobbies, unless you count travel and reading as hobbies.

However…

Here are a couple of issues that have frequently interested me over the years.

The Glow of Ownership (a hobby)

The closest that I have come to a hobby, is that I have spent a lifetime studying retail companies and trying to understand why some succeed and what sets them apart. What do the following leading companies (and many more) have in common? Walmart—Tesco—7-Eleven—Sainsbury's—Marks & Spencer—Shoppers Drug Mart—Disney—Ito Yokado—Four Seasons Hotels.

Answer

They were controlled by a single individual, or family, during their formative years. This allowed them to grow, flourish, and prosper under a set of rules, guidelines, and values that were instilled into the culture of the organization from the day that it was founded. This is what I mean by "The Glow of Ownership." It is a little hard to describe in detail, but it is unmistakable in practice.

Walmart was founded by Sam Walton. What began as a small-town discount department-store chain, is now the largest retailer in the world. Sam had the foresight to see the opportunity of developing mid-sized, low-cost department stores in the smaller towns of middle America, at a time when the giant retailers were focused on the major cities. By the time that the rest of the industry began to notice them, Walmart already had a monopoly on these hundreds of small towns. As the era of the large city-centre department stores came to an end, Walmart, with its huge, low-cost base, was able to go to the cities and repeat the success that they had had in the small towns. Sam Walton and his team were able to perfect the cross-docking system that improved their efficiency, and all the time they were guided by Sam's retail philosophies, which included "managing by wandering around" and the "ten-foot rule." Basically, this meant get out of the office, get to know your customers, and provide personal service.

Tesco was founded by Jack Cohen. What began as a small number of market stalls in St. Albans, England in 1919 is now the second-largest food retailer in the world (after Carrefour). Following Jack Cohen's retirement in 1970, the company was controlled by his son-in-law Leslie Porter.

Jack had two mottos that he used to get his values entrenched in the company's culture.

He used to distribute ties with these bold initials, "YCDBSOYA" (you can't do business by sitting on your arse), and he would also say, "Pile it High and Sell it Cheap," (we are discounters).

Sainsbury's was founded in 1869 by John Sainsbury and the family controlled the company for over 100 years until 1998. They still control fifteen percent of the company. The company, which became dominant in the south of England, was famous for its high standards and fresh foods. The owning family made sure that these values were maintained and today, Sainsbury's is the second largest food retailer in the UK, following Tesco.

Fine Fare. During the early 1960s Tesco, Fine Fare, and Sainsbury's were the three leading food retailers in the UK. Tesco and Sainsbury's were family-run businesses and they are still the two biggest food retailers in the UK. Tesco stayed close to the founder's discount principles and Sainsbury's stayed close to its founding family's principles of freshness and quality. They continue to prosper.

Although Fine Fare was owned by the Weston family, it was never managed closely by the family, and it always remained a distant third in sales and never managed to create that "bond" with consumers. The company was sold in 1986 by its parent company, Associated British Foods, and by 1988, the brand had disappeared.

Although Mr. Garfield Weston bought and controlled large supermarket groups on a global basis, he was never actively involved in the management of these companies. He relied on a frequently changing group of senior managers who usually failed to achieve market dominance. James Gulliver at Fine Fare was an exception, although he was a technocrat rather than a grocer, but he was not there long enough to achieve his ambition to make Fine Fare the leader that he wanted it to be.

In this context, it is interesting to note that following Garfield Weston's passing, his two sons, Gary and Galen, assumed personal responsibility for the operation of the UK and Canadian companies, where they have established market dominance. "The Glow of Ownership" is a huge contributing factor to their continued success.

Marks & Spencer was founded in 1884 by Michael Marks (originally as a "Penny Bazaar," a forerunner of Woolworth's Nickel and Dime Stores and today's Dollar Stores) and was controlled by the Marks family (and subsequently by the Sieff family) until the mid-sixties.

Marks & Spencer achieved a unique dominance and acceptance by the British public that was unequalled by any other retailer of its day. It was universally acknowledged as one of the leading retail companies in the word and probably more than any other example that I could provide, it was guided to this success by its values and by "The Glow of Ownership." Lord Sieff described the guiding principles as "Providing high quality production at reasonable prices, simplicity in administration, welfare for the employees, and a belief in modern science and technology."

Shoppers Drug Mart was founded by Murray Koffler in 1962 and over the next twenty-four years grew into Canada's dominant drug store chain. Following Koffler's retirement in 1986 the company was acquired by IMASCO (British American Tobacco) and eventually the company was purchased by Loblaw's in 2013. The key to SDM's early success was the unique franchising formula that Murray Koffler developed. This was continued by Murray's successor, David Bloom, who also launched the Optimum Loyalty Program that quickly became the most successful loyalty program in Canadian retailing history.

Murray Koffler and David Bloom provided that "Glow of Ownership" for the several decades that they controlled this very successful company.

7-Eleven was founded in 1927 by Joe C. Thompson in Dallas, Texas. Following Joe's death in 1961, the company was controlled and managed by his three sons. Chairman John Thompson, President Jere Thompson, and Executive Vice- President Jodie Thompson.

The family owned or controlled this company for over seventy years, until the control was acquired by Ito Yokado of Japan in 1991. Ito Yokado was 7-Eleven's largest international area licensee.

7-Eleven is probably one of the best examples of the "Glow of Ownership" in the retail world. The Thompson family established clear values, standards, and objectives for their company and the company achieved multi-year success and dominance of the industry. 7-Eleven is firmly established as America's Neighbourhood Store. The 7-Eleven name and logo is one of the most recognized trade names in the world, and its signature products, "Slurpee" and "Big Gulp" are a part of the American vernacular.

Even as the company grew in size to over 6,000 stores in the US and Canada, the Thompsons managed to retain a "family" approach to running the company. As a senior manager, I, along with my colleagues, was on a first-name basis with John, Jere, and Jodie and at the same time they ensured that the family's values were well communicated and sustained. This was a big key to their success.

7-Eleven's success in North America and internationally was so good that Ito Yokado, its Japanese Area licensee, outgrew the originator (The Southland Corporation) and in 1991 managed to gain control of Southland. At that time, there were approx. 14,000 7-Eleven stores worldwide.

Ito Yokado was founded in 1947 as a tiny haberdashery store by Masatoshi Ito and his family. By the time that the Ito Yokado Group acquired the control of The Southland Corporation in 1991, Ito Yokado was not the largest retailer in Japan, but it was by far the most profitable. Mr. Ito was ably supported by his deputy, Toshifumi Suzuki. They had built up a huge retail conglomerate that included department stores, supermarkets, restaurants, and 7-Eleven convenience stores. The convenience stores were the most profitable segment of this retail empire. Since acquiring 7-Eleven in 1991, Ito Yokado has gone on to oversee the growth of this company and as of 2020, 7-Eleven is the world's largest chain of convenience stores. It has been the largest for many years and with a current total of 70,000 stores in seventeen countries, it is likely to retain this position

The Disney Company was founded by Walt and Roy Disney in 1923 and it would be hard to find another company that has been as defined by the vision and values of its founders.

Walt, the creative genius, and Roy, the businessman, managed and directed this unique company until the death of Walt in 1966 and Roy in 1971. "The Glow of Ownership" at Disney resonates through everything that they accomplished during those fifty years, from their insistence that employees at Disneyland understood that they were always "performers," once they donned their uniforms and emerged from backstage, to the clear business methods taught at The Disney Learning Centre and the evolvement of their value system of decision making. *"When your values are clear, decision making is easy."*

Four Seasons Hotels—founded by Issy Sharp in 1960. The first location was the Four Seasons Motor Hotel, which opened on Jarvis St. in Toronto in 1961. By the time of my return visits to Toronto in 1968 and 1972, this location was already established as the place to stay in Toronto. It was not a "posh" hotel, but a hotel already renowned for a high level of service.

Issy Sharp recognized the high risk and the high capital cost of building and owning hotels, and he changed the business model to one of managing hotel properties under contract. As of 2020 the company manages 117 properties in forty-seven countries

Issy Sharp maintained control of the company through to 2007, building the company into one of the world's leading hotel brands. As of 2020, The Four Seasons Hotel & Resort chain is owned jointly by Bill Gates and a member of the Saudi royal family. It is still operated under the principles established by its founder. "The Glow of Ownership" as established by Issy Sharp is frequently quoted as one of the best examples in the business world. The idea of excellent service, to be exemplified from the minute a guest has a first contact with an employee, to the minute that the guest departs the premises, has become a standard by which many organizations measure their success. The key to it all, as set out by the founder is defining standards and maintaining those standards through training, training, and more training.

So how do you sum up "The Glow of Ownership"? I usually have no difficulty recognizing the unseen beneficial presence of an "owner." It's that certain X-factor, from the original Joe Troll in his fish restaurant in Horseshoe Bay, West Vancouver, to Ruth Fertel at her Ruth's Chris Steak House in New Orleans, to John and Jere Thompson at 7-Eleven, to Issy Sharp at Four Seasons, to Walt and Roy Disney at Disneyland. It's a belief in clear values and consistently communicated standards, and it's supported by a strong commitment to training.

❖

"When faced with the challenge to reduce expenses, training is an easy target. Big mistake." Frank Farr

A LIFE IN STAGES

The English Language (a Fascination)

The second issue that I think about frequently is the English language and the use of words.

Ever since my early childhood, I have enjoyed reading, and over time I have come to have a fine appreciation of words. Unfortunately, I have never learned a second language and therefore I am limited to my understanding of English, but what an astounding language it is. In English there are so many words of a similar meaning, and yet each one can provide such penetrating clarity and insight. The power of words is simply amazing. The more that I read, the more I appreciate English in its simplest form.

I recently reread Winston Churchill's *A History of the English-Speaking Peoples* and his *The Second World War*. They are complex stories, told in the simplest of language. You have to search hard to find examples of the multi-syllable jargon that has become so common in much of today's writing. The other best example that I can think of, is to read the first and last chapter of Charles Dickens' *A Tale of Two Cities*.

So many times over the past years, I have read articles that should interest and inform me, only to have to go back and reread them, in order to try to understand the point. Too many multi-syllable words, the more the better, and even better if they are couched in popular jargon. And yet, I am always impressed on those occasions when I hear people, often with no formal education or qualifications, speak or write with great clarity.

I also think that the simple language of song and poetry, adds so much to our culture without confusing the message.

I understand and actually enjoy, the complexity of legalese in contracts and other legal documents. In this context, it is usually necessary and helps to clarify, but in so many other instances, it is gratuitous and unclear. There is real value in plain speaking.

I wish that the people who write in this manner would go back to basic English. They could do no better than to consider the strength, power, and clarity of Lincoln's Gettysburg Address or Martin Luther King's epic "I have a dream" speech, or to reread almost any of President Barak Obama's speeches, or to listen again to Nelson Mandela speaking.

"The beauty of the English language has enriched my life and I am so grateful for the encouragement to read, that was the ever-lasting gift from my mother, Olive Farr."

CHAPTER NINETEEN

The European Bank for Reconciliation and Development 2010–2021

My Seventies

In 2010 I was seventy-two years of age and looking forward to what the next decade would bring. Clearly, I would no longer want to put in the hours, nor could I, but my brain was still active and the thought of assisting formative retailers through the European Bank for Reconstruction and Development (EBRD) programme, seemed like it might be the perfect next challenge. Not too arduous, but mentally stimulating and rewarding. A perfect solution.

Frank "the traveling man," leaving on one of his many trips with EBRD

FRANK FARR

European Bank
for Reconstruction and Development

TurnAround Management and Business Advisory Services Programmes (TAM/BAS)

London, 18 January, 2011

To Whom it May Concern,

TurnAround Management (TAM) Programme

Mr Frank Farr

UNITED KINGDOM Passport: 704268280

This is to certify that **Mr Frank Farr** (hereinafter referred to as the "Expert") is travelling to **GEORGIA** as a **TAM Team Advisor** under contract with the Bank's TAM Programme and that the Expert will be regularly visiting **GEORGIA** during the next 12 months, on behalf of the Bank's TAM Programme.

The Executive Directors of the Bank's TAM Programme request that the Expert be given every facility necessary to enable the Expert to carry out the assignment on behalf of the European Bank for Reconstruction and Development in **GEORGIA**.

Charlotte Ruhe
Director
TAM Programme

Article 4 (Schedule C)

The Expert's Contract with the Bank states in Article 4 Schedule C that:

"In addition to any privileges, exemptions or immunities which the Bank may have arranged with the Government of **GEORGIA** to be extended to the **TAM Team Advisor** in connection with the Services, the Bank shall make all reasonable endeavours to ensure that the **TAM Team Advisor** receives in member countries of the Bank the privileges, immunities and exemptions accorded to an expert performing a mission for the Bank under Articles 51 and 52 of the Agreement Establishing the Bank."

European Bank for Reconstruction and Development Certification

A LIFE IN STAGES

This next chapter covers my ten years of experience working for EBRD.

I have had difficulty in trying to paint a full picture of this experience. I could have just listed the places where I worked and the work that I have done. However, once I include the historical and political background to these adventures, a much fuller picture emerges. I hope that I have done justice to the people that I have met on this remarkable journey and to their backgrounds, and I hope that you will find this both informative and interesting.

Background

The European Bank for Reconstruction and Development (EBRD) is based in London. The EBRD was founded to support countries of the former Eastern Bloc in the process of establishing their private sectors. To that end, it offers "project financing" and "advisory support" for banks, industries, and businesses, for new ventures or existing companies.

Utilizing funds from a variety of sources, EBRD provides funding and consultancy services to the previous Soviet Bloc countries and beyond. e.g.: Egypt, Mongolia, and others. However, the bulk of its activity still takes place in support of previously communist economies that are working to grow and develop under a more contemporary and free society.

I have now completed an amazing ten years, working with the people of these ex-communist countries, assisting in the development of their businesses and gaining some limited, but enlightening insight into their history and their current challenges and aspirations. It's been a real privilege.

In each case, the political background and current political situation play such a strong role that I must acknowledge them, in order for the work that I do to fit into an understandable context. It also helps that I have always been interested in history.

These countries are what we describe as "emerging economies," and this is an apt description. Following the collapse of the Soviet Union, or their declarations of independence, these countries were essentially left to fend for themselves with depleted infrastructure and little in the way of democratic or functioning government.

This has been a history lesson for me.

During the first decade following the collapse of the Soviet Union in 1991, there was a significant rise in lawlessness, as ruthless people enriched themselves, often with the use of violence and gangsterism—the rise of the oligarchs.

During the second decade, the institutions of government gradually took over. However, in many cases, corruption had become so entrenched that it has taken an enormous effort on the part of the Common Market and other institutions, to help these governments to reduce corruption at the highest levels. This fight continues.

One other thought prevails. For those of us who never lived in a communist state, here is one of the ways that It has been described to me:

> *"Under the communists, we were not paid very much, but we were not expected to do very much. Timekeeping and absenteeism were not regulated and the general idea of efficiency, at the level of the average citizen, was non-existent."*

This makes me think back to the efficient, hard-working, "can do" environment that I had encountered in Canada and the US back in 1957. There should be no surprise at the outcome of the Cold War and the collapse of the Soviet Union.

One of the more pleasant aspects of doing this work for EBRD is that it has provided many personal opportunities that I might not otherwise have had.

It gave me the opportunity to spend a very enjoyable week working with Peter Flach in Moldova.

It has given me the opportunity to strengthen my friendship with Tony Murray and at the same time, to assist Tony in adding another chapter in his career. I was able to get Tony registered with EBRD and then he worked with me on two assignments. One was in the Republic of Georgia and one was in Kosovo. The one in Tbilisi, Georgia was a lot of fun, as this was during the time that I discovered the Hanger Bar (Rebecca's Bar). I don't know how many hours that we spent at this bar, but it really was a fun time. Working with Tony was a genuine pleasure and his expertise in inventory management, merchandising techniques, and category management proved to be invaluable.

Tony continued to work for EBRD for some time, with several assignments on his own. I remember that he worked in Serbia, Montenegro, and Mongolia, of all places. I remember telling him to "be careful of eating the boiled sheep-eyes and rancid yak's milk."

EBRD also gave me the opportunity to renew my friendship with Jim Humphrey. Jim, who had worked with me during the 7-Eleven days, was able to join me on two projects in Georgia and Kosovo. Jim even moved to Kosovo, where he and Andrea lived for a year. They made the most of their year there by taking the opportunity to tour Europe between work assignments. They were able to visit Albania, Montenegro, Malta, Greece, Croatia, Italy, and the Czech Republic. Jim also spent some time in Germany and Austria.

In addition, Jim completed a project on his own in Ukraine. On one trip with me, he enjoyed his first visit to London, which was quite an eye opener for him. Jim's energetic leadership and innovative marketing ideas added an extra dimension to the success of these projects.

EBRD has given me the opportunity to work with Mark Cousineau, also from 7-Eleven, both in Kosovo and in Ukraine. Mark is excellent and thorough in his knowledge of food service issues in convenience stores. He has also proved to be very helpful and capable of providing advice and training to the staff of Meridian Express and Clever Stores. His support has been invaluable and was very much appreciated by our clients. Mark also enjoyed his first visit to London with me, during one of these trips.

One name from the past is Brian Hielbron. Brian was one of the early members of the merchandising teams at Fine Fare and he went on to have a successful career in retail, primarily in the fashion side of the business. Tony passed on Brian's contact information and although I could not get him involved in any of my projects, I did help to get him registered with EBRD and he completed one project in Mongolia.

Although the work that I do on behalf of EBRD can best be described as "consulting," I am frequently asked, "What exactly do you do?" Over the past ten years, I have developed several key elements to my work: Basically, I am a retail corporate planner working with the company stakeholders to develop and execute a business plan.

1. I assess the potential of client companies and assist the owners in producing a series of business plans (see the attached planning chart).

2. I work with the owners of the client company to assist them in structuring their enterprise, in a manner best suited to achieving the objectives of the plan.

3. I review the results and assist them in adjusting and preparing for the next plan review.

4. I act as a confidant and advisor to the owners of the client enterprises.

Business Plans - Organisational Flow Chart and Ownership of Plans

3-5 Year Business Plan
(The Board)
Sets out the Revenue, Expenses and Profit /Loss Expectations for The Plan period including growth in number of stores, any possible acquisitions and the development and protection of the company's Brand

The Marketing Plan
(The CEO & Marketing Director)
Explains source of the revenue anticipated in The Plan Period
By year, by category, by number and type of stores

Management of Vendor relations & Corporate Distribution Centre
All products intended to be sold in stores will be included in Category Manager's Plans, with allowance r for Products and categories not yet developed

Finance Plan - (CFO)
How we will fund the the planned activities
Source an Use of Funds
Return on Capital Employed ROCE
Return on Capital Investment ROI
Cash Flow, Ebitda

Individual Category Plans
To be produced by the Category Managers working with the Director of Marketing and approved by the CEO

Human Resources Plan
(CEO and HR Director)
How we will identify, hire, train & retain The Human Resources required to Execute the Plan

Advertising & Sales Prom. Plan. (Marketing Manager)
How we will create and maintain our Loyalty Programs
Explains strategic & tactical communication plan.
Establishes Advertising budget and sets out framework for planned advertising expenditures in support of marketing objectives and development of the company's Brands

Retail Operations Plan
(CEO & Director of Operations)
How we will manage product ordering and maximinse Return on Inventory Investment (ROII) (Turns X Margin) by staying in stock of best sellers, while reducing stock of slow sellers.
How we will merchandise our stores to obtain optimum levels of sales and profits in support of our marketing objectives
How we will optimise store standards while controlling labour costs
How we will maintain the security of our physical assets, including inventory
How we will provide superior customer service, exceeding our customer's expectations and providing them with an experience that will retain the customers we have and attract new customers from our competition

Merchandising Plan
(Cat. Mgrs & Mktg. Mgr.)
Store Layouts, Plan-o-Grams
Promotional Displays
Re-Merchandising.
New Store Preparation
in cooperation with Operations

Business Planning Process Chart

A LIFE IN STAGES

It was Pater Flach who introduced me to EBRD. During a visit to Vancouver in 2009, he described the work that he was doing for this organization and said that he thought that it was something that I should consider. I was very busy with Immediate Images at the time and didn't really give serious thought to this suggestion.

I understood that Peter had completed consulting assignments as a senior industrial advisor on behalf of EBRD, primarily in the Balkan countries and I know that he subsequently did work, as far away as Mongolia.

In 2010, Peter told me that he had accepted a project with a supermarket company in Moldova and wondered if I would consider joining him as a technical specialist to assist in their retail marketing operations. I was still unconvinced about this work, but faced with the opportunity to travel and to spend some time with Peter, I agreed and off we went to Moldova.

Peter was correct. This project was a revelation for me. I found the work very interesting and I decided that I would submit my resume to EBRD for future consideration.

As of January 2020, over a ten-year period, I have completed fifty trips to Europe on behalf of EBRD and its clients. I did have eight additional trips planned for 2020 but the pandemic made them impossible. I wish that I could have started this work earlier and I am very thankful to Peter for making this connection between myself and EBRD.

Each of these countries has a very complicated past and a precarious future. Here are the projects that I have completed so far and my impressions from these countries.

I have come to be very fond of the people that I have met and worked with and I can only hope that they will be allowed to grow in freedom, to develop their societies in the ways that are best suited for the wishes of their peoples. As I write this, Ukraine is in a "hot war" with invading forces from Russia. Moldova and Georgia live with a constant threat to their independence, and their future freedom from Russian interference is not guaranteed. Kosovo is negatively impacted by the actions of Serbia, and there is a continuing potential for violence between Armenia and Azerbaijan.

The fact that these countries were all recently a part of the Soviet Union or in the case of Kosovo, a part of communist Yugoslavia, results in there being a strong political undercurrent to all that goes on in these emerging democracies. In most cases, the past and present actions of the central government have a large impact on the day to day lives of the citizens and their business activities.

FRANK FARR

Moldova: 2010 Population, 3.55 Million

I joined Peter for one visit to this interesting but fragile country. We were assisting Mr. Adrian Casenco of IMC Supermarkets in the development of a supermarket chain.

Moldova is a small country situated between Romania to the south and Ukraine to the north. Its access to the Black Sea was cut off when the previous USSR gave the land with access to the sea to Ukraine. There is a small sliver of land known as Transnistria, between Moldova and Ukraine. I wanted to visit this, but was advised that this is a lawless place, primarily ruled by smugglers, moving products to and from Ukraine into Romania and The European Common Market.

We did go out for a fantastic drive into the countryside, away from the capital of Chisinau. This trip included a visit to the state winery where there's an unbelievable arrangement of tunnels dug into a limestone cliff (several kilometres long and big enough to take a bus). Alcoholism has long been a problem in the USSR and at one time President Gorbachev decided to reduce this by destroying stocks of alcohol. The Moldovans were advised that the Red Army, was coming to destroy the stocks in this winery and they contrived to seal off secret tunnels to preserve their best stocks. They succeeded, and today you can enjoy these treasures in a huge underground banquet room. Quite a story.

We also visited another winery, this one owned by a Russian oligarch. He only visits this place once or twice each year, but in the meantime, the entire estate is maintained in an unbelievably immaculate condition. There are villas and a very nice restaurant on site and we were the only guests.

During this trip, we were run off the road by a large oncoming truck with no lights. A close call.

To place Moldova's vulnerability in perspective, under the USSR, Moldova was designated as a wine-producing region, and wine production is its only industry. As a punishment for not following Russian policies, it was suddenly declared that their wine was "substandard" and could no longer be imported into Russia. The country is left as a producer of good-quality wines, hoping to sell into the common market, but in truth, dependent on Russia, who expects compliance with Russian policies.

The most positive future for Moldova is to become an autonomous region of Romania and have access to the Common Market. It does not look as if this will happen.

A LIFE IN STAGES

Armenia: 2011. Population Three Million

This was my second assignment and again this is a country full of opportunities and yet with a number of seriously unresolved issues.

Here are some of them:

Political – Historical background

Armenia once covered a much larger territory. A great deal of this was in what is now Turkey and includes the famous Mount Ararat. There were two instances of mass deportations and atrocities committed by Turkey against the Armenians, once around 1890 and again around 1920. Millions of Armenians were slaughtered and displaced. If anybody doubts that this occurred, they should visit the Armenian Holocaust Museum on the outskirts of Yerevan.

This has led to a large Armenian diaspora, as they fled at first to Egypt and then around the world. Armenians are very talented businesspeople, and they have achieved a high degree of success in most of the countries where they have settled.

In more recent times, the related Armenian population of Iran was also persecuted and many moved north to Azerbaijan, where again they were persecuted by the Muslim Azeris. In 1994, Armenia went to war with Azerbaijan, to protect the Armenian population. The Armenian Army prevailed, and today there is an enclave (Nagorno-Karabakh) of Armenians living in Azerbaijan under Armenian protection. This is a fragile situation. Although the Armenian Army was successful, the situation is fluid. In addition, as a result of Armenia's war with Azerbaijan, Turkey closed its borders with Armenia, and this is a constant source of problems. Azerbaijan is rich with oil and therefore in a position to rearm its forces with the most modern and expensive equipment. Armenia is not as wealthy.

Note: in 2020, there was new armed conflict between these two countries. This has resulted in some of the territory controlled by Armenia since 1994 being returned to Azerbaijan.

I was asked by EBRD to join in a project already in progress. The client was Alpha Pharmaceuticals, a retail chain with approximately thirty-five retail stores, which was basically having problems achieving acceptable gross margins. I was able to assist CEO Artur Gregorian to achieve his sales and margin objectives, and we have remained in touch over these past nine years.

Here are some recollections:

Armenia's capital city of Yerevan was a fascinating mixture of old and new. It has one million people with a fabulous old opera house and gardens in the centre of the city. Thousands of people enjoy the open air in the centre of the city well into the night and the early hours of the morning

My initial impression of the pharmaceutical business in Armenia was a shocker. I remember e-mailing Ann to say that I felt as if I had returned to England of the '40s and '50s. Artur was a US-educated professional, operating in the middle of an almost gangster-like environment. His chairman complained that he should be "More like Stalin."

One highlight of this trip was my opportunity to be introduced to Vahan Kerobian, a friend of Peter's. It was a real pleasure to meet Vahan, a very smart, hard-working executive. He was the CEO of a supermarket chain that was an EBRD client.

Peter had told Vahan that he should speak to me as I was the one that had taught him much of what he knew about retailing.

I met Vahan in the lobby of my hotel. He leapt forward to hug me with the greeting, "Hello Grandfather." Puzzling, but eventually it was explained by the comment, "Peter is my retail father; he tells me that you taught him everything, therefore, you must be my retail grandfather."

Vahan took me to a very impressive jazz bar in central Yerevan, where we enjoyed a famous jazz orchestra.

Vahan has gone on to bigger and better things in business. He recently served in the Armenian Army during the short war with Azerbaijan and he has subsequently ventured into national politics. His leadership qualities have been quickly recognized and he has been appointed Minister of Economic Development for the national government of Armenia. He still refers to me as "Grandfather."

I wish him and his family all the very best.

Republic of Georgia. EBRD and Private 2011–2014. Population 3.71 Million

Georgia sits between Russia on the north, with Armenia and Turkey on the south. The Black Sea is to the west and Azerbaijan is to the east. Russia essentially occupies two enclaves in the northern border with Russia, Abkhazia, and South Ossetia. These enclaves were seized by Russia, following a short but bloody seven-day war in 2008.

Political

Georgia was always a central part of Russian history. Stalin's mother was born there and Stalin himself may have been born there. It is a country with a rich and long history, and it shares its patron saint with England (St. George).

This can be a confusing place in dealing with individuals. The men all seem to be called George, David, or Zurab and this devolves into nick-names: David/Davit, George/Giorgi or Goga, etc. The women are often called Tamara or Tamuna or Nino. These names are taken from ex-kings or queens of ancient Georgia.

Adding to this potential for confusion, was the fact that many of the people concerned were relatives, with the same surname.

I completed three projects with the Georgia Pharmaceutical Company (GPC). Two were with EBRD and one was under a private contract.

The capital city of Georgia is Tbilisi and I had a couple of very odd experiences there.

The Zoo and the National Day Parade

The Zoo

I arrived one Sunday morning to find a chaotic situation. Heavy rains on the previous day had caused floods and a mini landslide in one of the many ravines. One of them contained the city zoo and the zoo had flooded. Many animals had drowned but many more had escaped and there was a frantic search and capture effort underway.

Imagine everything from tigers, crocodiles, a rhinoceros, wolves, and other dangerous animals being loose in a large city, with people trying to live their lives, getting children to school, etc.

There was one tragic follow-up to this.

On the Wednesday, I had organized a board meeting and I was particularly concerned that the entire board should attend. As I got the meeting underway, I realized that one of our members, George (Goga) Gordaze, was missing. Shortly after we started, Goga's brother, David Gordaze, who was at the meeting, answered his cell phone with a cry: "He's been eaten by a tiger!" and ran out of the room. Based on the little that I understood, I believed that "Goga" had indeed been eaten by a tiger.

A little later, as things became clearer, the following story surfaced. Goga had gone to check on one of the outbuildings (only 400 yards from where we were meeting) to check on some pharmaceutical stock that had been damaged in the flood. He had taken two assistants to help him. As they entered the shed, the first helper was attacked by a tiger that had taken refuge there. The tiger had not eaten in several days and instantly killed the poor man. I believe that Goga fainted.

Rounding up the animals following the Zoo disaster in Tbilisi, Georgia

The zoo had been established there by the Russians and nobody had thought to clear out the debris from the ravine above it. The landslide broke through with this devastating result.

There is a plan in place to reopen the zoo in a safe location where such a tragedy cannot happen again.

The National Day Parade

Georgia's "Freedom Day" is a national holiday and I had an opportunity to witness, close-up, some of the peculiarities of modern-day Georgia. I had asked Tamuna, the secretary to David Kiladze, the chairman of GPC, to arrange for me to see the national parade that was due to take place that day. This exposed me to a peculiarity of Georgian politics. In most democracies, following an election, one party is declared the winner and the other parties retire to lick their wounds, and prepare for the next election in a few years' time.

Not in Georgia. Immediately following an election, a winner may be declared, but then the opposition takes to the streets to demonstrate against the results (maybe with justification) and to declare resistance to the new regime. (**Writing this seems odd, considering recent developments in US politics.**)

This process was in place when I decided to view the parade. I had been in the Hanger Bar (Rebecca's Bar) the night before, when all the expats in the bar declared that they were going home early, to avoid potential violence in the streets. I went to the Presidente Hotel, next to the bar, completely unaware that violence was indeed about to take over in the streets.

Frank and Tony downtown Tbilisi

Frank at the Hanger Bar (Rebecca's), Tbilisi

I met Tamuna at 10:00 am and she explained that during the night's violence, several thousand people had been demonstrating. Many had been injured by the police, four civilians had been killed, and one policeman had also been killed before the streets were cleared by the army. The protestors were advised to move, as tanks would be coming down the main street in a matter of hours.

As we approached the main street, we were initially turned back by army personnel. I remember Tamuna being adamant. "This gentleman has come all the way from Canada to see our parade. You must let him through."

This was greeted by a gruff demand for "Documents." I had no documents with me, my passport was back at the hotel. The only thing that I had was my Canadian driving license. The young conscript did not read English, so he took my driver's license to his superior. I don't think that he understood English either, but after some consideration, he waved us through. This same process happened at two more checkpoints, until I found myself standing not more than twenty yards away from the country's president. If I had been someone who meant to harm him, I am sure that I could have done it. All based on a driving license.

The National Parade

The parade was due to start at 10:00 but in true Georgian fashion, it was delayed until 11:30. The president spoke at length (almost ninety minutes, through a loudspeaker system set up on the streets). His deep, booming voice seemed to go on forever—pure Russian style. The parade included the usual array of soldiers and other servicemen and military hardware. There were a couple of peculiarities.

I noticed the soldiers lining up on the main street and then marching off in formation. Except that they merely marched around the block and then came back again several times. What looked like thousands of armed forces personnel, was several hundred, repeatedly passing by the president's dais.

I also noticed the crowd, and Tamuna advised me that the better dressed ones were really government office workers who had been given the day off and told to attend. The more poorly dressed ones were groups of villagers, who had been bussed in for the occasion and given flags. Typical Soviet-style pageantry.

Also, while I was working in Georgia, there was an election that overturned the previous government. This time, Georgia's wealthiest man, Bidzina Ivanishvili, an oligarch with ties to Russia, used his immense wealth and influence to take over the government. This really was bizarre. He was not necessarily a bad guy, but he ran the country in a totalitarian manner, immediately issuing decrees against what he saw as past injustices. When he was done, he stepped back, and passed on the leadership of the government to a hand-picked successor.

While he was president, he declined to live in the huge president's palace, recently constructed in the centre of Tbilisi. Instead he ran the country from his fortified, mountaintop mansion (a futuristic circular building reminiscent of something out of a James Bond movie).

As far as the work was involved, the EBRD client was the Georgia Pharmaceutical Company. The chairman was David Kiladze, and we became good friends. There was one major problem. The Georgians are notoriously poor at timekeeping and meetings often started up to an hour late, and in this company decision-making was difficult. The twelve shareholders were the original founders and out of a sense of fairness, they liked to make decisions by mutual agreement. However, it was next to impossible to get a quorum for a board meeting, even though I arranged for them to receive a 1,000-Euro bonus to attend meetings, and gave them one month's notice.

The chairman's brother, George Kiladze was the director of retail operations. His office was next door to mine but in my four years with the company, I never met him. He never attended one meeting and he used to arrange to be away on most of my visits. The excuse given was, "That's my brother, he does not like meetings."

Before my visits, they had never had a formal or documented board meeting, or a business plan. I was appointed to their board and organized quarterly board meetings. We completed a business plan, a marketing plan, and a human resource plan. The staff was hard-working and quite competent. However, as a result of the delays in decision making, I offered to quit on several occasions. The reply was always the same: "Please don't leave. Although decision making is a problem, you are changing our thinking and we need your help."

I think that it is fair to say that they were trapped in the old Soviet style that they had grown up with, and they were having a lot of difficulty in adjusting to a more modern way of conducting business. As they were a big part of the health community, they were also subject to continual and sometimes unreasonable requests from the Health Ministry.

The end-result of all this is that shortly after I completed my final assignment, GPC was acquired by a more aggressive, forward-looking competitor, and all of the shareholders were bought out.

Republic of Kosovo, Pop. approx. Two Million: EBRD and Private 2014–Present.

Political

Kosovo has a two-thousand-year-old history, but it has seldom been independent. It has continually been overrun and ruled by its much larger neighbours and yet somehow, it has managed to maintain a distinct identity and its close relationship to its ethnic cousins in Albania.

Its most recent experience of upheaval was in the turmoil that followed the collapse of Yugoslavia after the death of Marshall Tito, as the area, known as the Balkans, violently split into its different ethnic identities: Slovenia, Croatia, Bosnia, Serbia, Montenegro, and Macedonia. The situation with Kosovo became more desperate. As a semi-autonomous province of Serbia, the ethnic majority of Albanian/Kosovars were increasingly discriminated against by the minority Serbian authorities in the general areas of education, jobs, and governance. The Kosovars are also eighty percent Muslim, following their previous occupation by Turkey. The Serbs are mainly Orthodox Christians.

A LIFE IN STAGES

This situation accelerated from 1991 onwards, as the Kosovars asserted their independence from Serbia. The bloody reprisals by Serbia were only ended by the actions of a US-led, NATO military action in the war of 1998, which forced the Serbs to retreat to Serbia.

Kosovo's independence from Serbia has won recognition from most western countries, but Serbia and several other countries in the region have never recognized Kosovo's independence. This is a situation with many complications.

With a population a little under two million, Kosovo continues to struggle economically and has only a small industrial and manufacturing base. I have found the Kosovar population to be a very good natured, friendly, people and I really do wish them the best, as they continue to develop the society that they desire.

Although my work with EBRD is primarily focused on business matters, it has been a great pleasure for me to get to know and work with the Gashi Family in Pristina. The parent company, Meridian Corporation was founded by Hakif Gashi in 1992 and the company has grown to become Kosovo's leading distributor of beverages and other related products. Meridian is proving to be one of Kosovo's outstanding corporate entities, operating a successful enterprise, founded on sound, consistent family values and playing a positive role in Kosovo's emerging economy.

My continued involvement has been with Hakif's brother, Agon Gashi, the CEO of Meridian Express and this involvement has continued from 2013 through to 2021. Our personal friendship extends beyond business.

Meridian Express C-Store with food service in Pristina, Kosovo

I have had a number of particularly enjoyable experiences working in Kosovo.

The capital city of Pristina has developed a long pedestrian street in the centre of the city, Mother Theresa Boulevard (Mother Theresa was an Albanian). It is a great pleasure, particularly in summer, to stroll down this boulevard during the evening to see thousands of Kosovars and their families out and about, enjoying a well-deserved peaceful life.

On a personal basis, I have enjoyed the pleasure of Agon's company (and his two crazy friends, Fisi and Fatos) during the six years that I have worked with Meridian. Agon is blessed with an intelligent mind combined with a broad range of interests. It is going to be interesting to see where this leads him as his future unfolds.

In 2019, I attended Agon's wedding to Fjolla. WOW— 550 guests in an enormous hotel ballroom, dancing the night away. The ladies were dressed in their best and I have to admit, they looked marvellous. The festivities lasted for three days.

What a wonderful couple they are. Fjolla is a beautiful, intelligent, young woman and Agon must have been Kosovo's most eligible bachelor. (He's only thirty-two.) I can only wish them all the happiness and good fortune that life has to offer.

Oma Gashi: a beautiful baby girl with an amazing future ahead of her.

I have had the good fortune to travel with Agon and his team during my time working with Meridian. We have held budget retreats to Durres in Albania and also in the snowy mountains in south Kosovo, close to Prizren.

I also had the opportunity to visit Tirana, the capital of Albania, an attractive modern city and a place that I never expected to visit.

One trip stands out and that was to Montenegro. This is an amazingly old small country, to the north-west of Kosovo on the coast of the Adriatic Sea. The coastline is simply beautiful and the old town of Budva is exceptional.

Meridian Express Budget Meeting in Prizren, Kosovo

Porto Montenegro

A wealthy Canadian businessman, Peter Munk, purchased a no longer used ex-Soviet submarine base and entered into an agreement with the government of Montenegro to develop it into the Mediterranean's most prestigious marina.

He has succeeded! This place is amazingly impressive. The word "expensive" does not really explain what has been accomplished here. One example would be that the Saudi royal family moor their yachts here. There were three of them there at the time of my visit. They are simply more luxurious than I can describe. Peter Munk, who is retiring, has agreed to sell Porto Montenegro to the sovereign fund of Dubai, and they have agreed to invest the several hundred million euros, that will be required to bring this amazing development to its final form.

Another unforgettable memory is the weekend that I spent with Agon, Arben, Kemajl, and Valon in Budapest. What a wonderful old city. The architecture of the major buildings is as good as anything that I have seen and in what is now typical of the great European cities, many of the city centre streets have been pedestrianized. The result is wonderful, and very enjoyable. The two old cities of Buda and Pest are on either side of

Arben, Frank, Agon, Kemajl, and Valon in Budapest on the Danube River

the great Danube river. The river cruise boats are very impressive. I think that it would be a great trip to go on one of these cruises in the future.

We also visited the famous old market in the centre of Budapest. It reminded me of the Kirkgate Market in Leeds, and I enjoyed telling my friend Steve Lovas, about this visit. He grew up in Budapest and has fond memories of this market.

Work

I have developed a strong, friendly working relationship with the owners, the Gashi family. Hakif Gashi is the chairman of The Meridian Corporation and Agon Gashi is the CEO of Meridian Express (a retail food store chain with approximately forty locations). Hidajete (Hida) Gashi is their sister, and she is the CFO. for the organization. Another brother, Raif Gashi, runs the family bakery business (Kosovo Foods).

During the seven years that I have been working with Meridian Express, Agon has visited Vancouver twice. Initially, he came on his own and subsequently he came with Hakif and Hida. I was able to show them many of the interesting food stores in the Vancouver region and to introduce them to Mark Cousineau at the 7-Eleven Food Centre. We also took the opportunity to include some sight-seeing: Whistler, Grouse Mountain, etc. Paula was our driver and guide for much of this second visit.

Hakif, Agon, Paula, Hida, Frank, and a local resident at Whistler, BC

A LIFE IN STAGES

BBQ at Delsey Place with Karen Shellenberg Empey, Liz Murray, Casey Jones, Frank, Brian Empey, Hakif Gashi, Agon Gashi, Hida Gashi, Tony Murray and Mark Cousineau

Agon, Jim Humphrey, and Frank on a visit to the 7-Eleven Food Centre in Richmond, BC

Agon and Frank at the Boathouse in New Westminster, BC

I have completed two projects sponsored by EBRD with Meridian Express as their client. I have also completed a project sponsored by a Swiss non-profit organization and I have completed one additional project, working directly with Meridian Express. I am currently involved with a more extensive "Blue Ribbon" Program with EBRD and The Meridian Corporation. This project is due to finish at the end of 2021

During my time working with Meridian, we have been able to create a new type of combination convenience food store and food service cafeteria. These stores are remarkably popular. They are the most attractive stores of their type in Kosovo and are comparable with many of the Retail Food/Food Service developments that are growing on a global basis.

We have developed successive business plans, marketing plans and human resource plans and at the same time, we have developed plans for a proprietary food centre.

Kosovo is a relatively small country with a population of a little under two million and this crates some unique problems:

- Most requirements have to be imported. Supply chains are costly and frequently unreliable.

- Kosovo's strained relationship with Serbia is the source of ongoing problems. Political strains, supply, customs duty difficulties, and a lack of recognition of Kosovo by other European countries, all contribute to challenging circumstances.

The good news is that the new stores are very attractive. This has provided EBRD with the confidence to designate The Meridian Corporation as a candidate for its "Blue Ribbon Program." This is intended to assist Meridian in arranging long-term financing, as it works to emerge from its current position. As an additional part of this program, EBRD is also committed to providing additional consulting services. We have already contracted for two additional consultants and this phase may be completed after the travel restrictions from the pandemic are lifted.

In February 2020, I returned from a visit to Meridian, followed by a visit to Euroshop in Dusseldorf. This gave me a good opportunity to discuss the next steps that we plan to take with Meridian and I am more hopeful that 2021 will prove to be a more progressive year. During our visit to Euroshop, I was able to introduce Agon to the team from my client in Ukraine, as they were also attending this huge tradeshow.

Having attended Euroshop 2020 in February, it was a little odd to realize that I had previously attended this trade show as a part of my responsibilities with Fine Fare back in 1972 and 1974—almost fifty years ago.

Since March of 2020, the Covid 19 pandemic has affected Kosovo in the same way that it has affected all European countries and my visits to Pristina have been postponed. I will have to work with Agon and his family to re-evaluate the company's short to medium-term priorities once the situation returns to normal.

We have recently opened four new stores. They will add further credibility to the Meridian Express brand in Kosovo.

In completing a final review of this section, I am pleased to note that Agon has succeeded in acquiring the SPAR license for Kosovo. SPAR is one of Europe's leading retail organizations. This is a significant development and a tribute to Agon's growing entrepreneurial skills. Agon and the Gashi family will be faced with some major decisions during the next two to three years. It is too early to say where this will lead, but it will change the future direction of Meridian and presents some exciting opportunities.

Also, as I celebrated my eighty-second birthday, I was very pleased to receive the following accolades from my colleagues in Meridian Express.

Agon sent me the following message.

Hi Frank

First of all, thank you for all of your support. You have been a role model to me, and I have learned so much over the last seven years that we have known each other. You have always helped me with your support and advice during my difficult times. You pushed me to become a better person and your stories always inspired me. You are a true inspiration for any young leader and your hard work, patience, positive energy, knowledge and support are one of a kind. For me and everyone else at Meridian, you are the retailer with the longest and best experience worldwide. I wish and hope to have you with us for many years to come. I wish you health, happiness and fun times in the years to come. Your professional help towards others, your commitment to work, your support towards family and friends, your successful life, and your ability to give hope and ability to help others succeed and develop professionally, is what makes you one of a kind and the best food retailer in the world.

Thank you!

Agon

Lirim, the head of Management Information Services (MIS) and internal control sent me the following message as he was preparing to leave Meridian to join a company in the Netherlands.

Hello Frank,

Leaving Meridian is one of the most difficult decisions that I have had to make in my life. I owe the Gashi family a lot for giving me the opportunity to meet people like you, who have had a profound impact on my personal and professional development.

Thank you very much for everything that you have done for me and Meridian. Your wise words will continue to motivate and inspire me throughout my career and your legacy will be remembered for future generations in every place you have been.

Sincerely

Lirim

Arben Idrizi, ME's Director of Retail Operations with his collection of Frank's sayings" October 2021.

Ukraine Pop. Approx. 42 Million: EBRD and Private 2016–Present

The Blue and Yellow flag of Ukraine celebrates the open skies and the neverending fields of yellow and gold wheat. It really is a joyful sight to see these miles and miles of golden fields at the end of summer, just before the harvest!!!

At the outset, I have to say that I did not want to be involved in this project. I honestly thought that I would get it started and then pass it on to Tony or another EBRD consultant. Instead, I have become deeply involved in the future direction of this enterprise. This is mainly due to the hard working, decisive, and dedicated Ukrainians that I have come to know and respect.

Through my visits to Kyiv, Lviv, and Lutsk, combined with my reading of Ukrainian history during the tumultuous twentieth century. I have become aware of the incredible struggles that Ukraine has endured and continues to endure. I am full of admiration for the Ukrainian people and their ability to overcome adversity.

A LIFE IN STAGES

Politics

Ukraine is the most complex of all the countries that I have been involved in. It is a massive country in central Europe, that until 2000 had a population of almost fifty million. Although it is historically at the heart of what was the USSR, it has suffered grievously over the decades, as a country subservient to the dominance of Russia.

Its background is too complicated to go into here, but it must always be remembered that three to four million Ukrainians were deliberately killed or starved to death during 1933-34 as a direct result of decisions made in Moscow by Stalin. (the Holodomor). During the Second World War between five and seven million Ukrainians perished. During the period from the turn of the century until the years following the Second World War, huge numbers of Ukrainians fled their homeland. Canada has the largest ex-pat population of Ukrainians anywhere in the world except Russia.

Although Ukraine gained its independence from Russia following the collapse of the Soviet Union in 1991, its relationship with Russia has remained difficult. On the one hand, Russia deeply resents the loss of its largest previously subject-state and many Ukrainians, particularly in Eastern Ukraine are of Russian origin. On the other hand, Ukraine wants to follow its instincts and align itself with the European Common Market and other Western Institutions. Ukraine has the right to control its own destiny.

Matters were brought to a head when Russia annexed the Ukrainian province of Crimea in 2014 and then proceeded to foment a war in the Donbas region of Eastern Ukraine, which has cost 15,000 lives and continues to this day.

As a result of this loss of territory and other ongoing demographic changes, the population under the control of the Ukrainian government has declined from 50 million in 2000 to approximately 43 million as of 2020.

During one of my visits to Ukraine, I travelled via its capital, Kyiv. Wow! This is an amazing, major European city with a long history. Very attractive, and despite the war and other distractions, a surprisingly prosperous-looking city.

I had the opportunity to visit the "Maidan" or Independence Square, that was the centre of the Revolution of Dignity that overthrew the recent pro-Russian president. Tragically, many people were killed or wounded during this popular uprising. On the side of the main square, there is a very moving tribute (photos, flowers etc.) to the hundred martyrs who were killed there, while protesting for their freedom. Also close-by is a street dedicated to remembering the soldiers and others who are currently dying on a weekly basis in the Donbas Region. Mostly young men and women. A very moving experience.

My lasting hope is that the long- suffering and heroic people of Ukraine can enjoy the freedom that they deserve and build the society that that their people want and deserve.

Glory to Ukraine!

Note

I had a memorable dinner with Oleg, Serhiy and Inna, during which I was able to outline Britain's historic involvement in the Crimea, including the battle of Balaclava and "The Charge of the Light Brigade."

Note: Russia – US Intrigue

In a very unfortunate development, the previous administration of the US government under the direction of President Trump "the worst president in the history of the Unites States" was involved in ongoing intrigue with both Russia and Ukraine.

This is too complicated to describe here. It is the subject of endless debate on TV and the truth of the matter will not be fully known, until long after President Trump has left office.

The key issue is that the Ukrainians did not want to be involved in any of this and this is taking place against a background of Ukraine's new government, which is trying hard to reduce corruption and retain the support of the United States in its ongoing struggles with Russia.

The Work

The company is registered as Clever Stores LLC, trading as Sim/23 (7/23) which is as close to 7- Eleven as you can get.

Frank presenting Oleg with "Oh Thank Heaven" – The Story of 7-Eleven/Southland Corporation

On my first visit, I almost despaired. The stores that I saw were very small, mostly in the basements of high-rise apartment blocks and very reminiscent of the Becker Stores in Ontario (circa 1960).

I tried to explain that these were stores built for the past, and that they would not be able to compete with any new, more contemporary, competitors. They had virtually no food service, and the entire operational side of the business had fatal flaws in the way in which it was being managed.

I tried to outline what I thought the future convenience stores should look like, and I highlighted the problems that they had on the operating side. I left with no confidence whatsoever. All my communication was done through an interpreter and I did not know for sure if they fully understood what I was saying.

A LIFE IN STAGES

I did not come up with an alternative consultant for me before the next visit was due, and I headed back, not knowing what to do. I got a big and welcome surprise.

Oleg Merchenko was the founder and majority owner. Up until my first visit, he had only played a limited role in how the company was being developed. There was a big difference that was apparent on my second visit. Oleg had gone back into the business and was aggressively working to change things around.

Serhiy Kykinov, one of the other founders and the executive responsible for marketing, was working on a plan for a new concept store. I reviewed the plan and I was impressed. It quickly became clear to me that Serhiy is one of those individuals that I am always looking to meet in these client companies. He has a good "marketing brain" with the ability to juggle all of the components of category management, pricing, promotional policy, and new product development, while maintaining a clear view of the impact of all of these actions on sales and gross profit. This ability is not common, but it is an essential component of good marketing practice.

The new concept store was an improved take-off on a new 7-Eleven Store, and they were confident that they could pull it off. Oleg assumed responsibility for the operational side of the business and immediately began to make improvements.

I was very impressed and realized that these two men were true professionals, who could quickly relate to and react to the guidance that I was offering. This was made workable by the incredible job that Ms. Inna Zholob, the interpreter, did. She quickly caught on to my way of talking and was able to translate in paragraphs, while retaining the emphasis that I was placing on various aspects of the business.

Frank and Serhiy Kykinov wearing their Vyshyvankas (Ukrainian national costume)

I was encouraged to stay with the project and see what we could accomplish.

For the remainder of the initial EBRD project, things went very well and at times they were moving much faster than I expected. The new concept store was an instant success, and other new stores got off to a good start. One of the big wins was the change in demographics. The original stores were demographically targeting housewives and the elderly, shopping for their daily grocery requirements. The new stores quickly, and obviously, became a hit with younger customers, particularly students. Our future!

I was hooked, and we arranged for Oleg, Serhiy, and Inna to visit Vancouver, see a range of stores and meet with Mark Cousineau at the 7-Eleven Food Centre. They were impressed with what they saw, and this gave them a greater appreciation of the opportunities that would lie ahead.

The first phase of this EBRD project was completed early in 2017. At the end of the first EBRD project, Mr. Merchenko's report to EBRD, was as follows:

> "We were proud and honoured to be advised by Mr. Frank Farr. His advice and recommendations were useful and invaluable for both our professional and personal growth. Best practices that were shared with us were of particular interest and benefit to us. We appreciate Mr. Farr's time and effort during this project, and we'll be looking forward to the opportunity to continue our fruitful cooperation during phase two."

Oleg made a request to EBRD to go ahead with a second phase. Based on the progress that we had achieved, EBRD approved. In December 2019, we completed the second phase of the EBRD project, and it has been a resounding success.

Unfortunately, there was one incredibly sad event in November 2019. On Wednesday, November the sixth, Inna emailed me with the terrible news that there had been a tragic car crash on the previous day. Our regular driver, Volodia, had been returning from L'viv to Lutsk with two passengers, Stanislav, a company director, and Sasha, the real estate manager. It was dark and raining and the car was involved in a head-on collision. All three were killed.

I knew Stanislav and I had met him and his wife (Helen) on numerous occasions. They were both in their thirties with two young children. I knew Sasha, too. I had spent several days with him, working on real estate issues. He was also in his thirties, married with one child and one on the way!!! We had just been to Rivne together during my last visit.

The driver, Volodia, did not speak English, but he had driven me along that same road. on twenty or so occasions. I can see their faces and I can hear their voices. Volodia was a very fast driver; we all knew it, and at some point, we even laughed about it. We are not laughing now. So sad!

It is clear that this tragedy could just as easily involved me and Inna on our way to and from L'viv Airport to Lutsk. Scary. As Ann is always reminding me, speed kills—slow down.

At the end of the second EBRD project, Mr. Merchenko's comments, in his report to EBRD were as follows:

> "Working with both the SIA, Frank Farr, and the Field Specialist, Mark Cousineau, has been exceptionally productive and enjoyable. Mr. Farr is tremendously professional in company Strategic Development and Corporate Planning. Mr. Cousineau is particularly experienced in developing and managing the Food Service Category, which is strategically important for the Seven. 23 new store concept. The amount of business knowledge, professional experience and successful solutions that they shared with us cannot be acquired in any of the world's best- known universities. Every associate of our company who has had a great opportunity to work with them will remember such a unique experience for the rest of their lives. It's been a genuine honour and an utmost delight to have known Mr. Farr and Mr. Cousineau and to have worked with them during these two EBRD projects. This kind of professional and interpersonal relationships is one of the most valuable and the most remarkable things one can experience in their lives. Every member of our team

and myself are immensely thankful to Mr. Farr and Mr. Cousineau for teaching and guiding us throughout both of the EBRD projects. I am sure that our further professional cooperation and friendly relationships will continue lasting, regardless of the end of the EBRD Advisory Projects.

Oleg Merchenko, *Chairman Clever Stores LLC. Lutsk, Ukraine December 11th, 2019.*

Frank in the first "new concept" store in Lutsk, Ukraine

Serhiy Kikiniov, Inna Zholab, Frank, Brian Ballingall, and Oleg Merchenko in Lutsk, Ukraine

Apart from Mr. Merchenko's praise for us, it is worth noting that the "New Concept" 7-23 stores are achieving a high level of praise from various segments of the Ukrainian retail community.

We have new business plans in place, we have a new marketing plan and a new human resources plan. The company has opened its own proprietary food centre, and this has been expanded to include key elements of a combined distribution facility (CDC).

The new-store approval process is well understood. Mark has made a second visit and provided ongoing guidance with regard to growing the sales and profitability of the food service categories. The company is well positioned for sustainable, profitable growth.

Oleg has asked me to continue working with them on a private basis, and subject to any health concerns, I have agreed to do so.

The focus now must be on growth, probably including franchising, and this growth, in whatever form it takes, will be my major focus during this next phase. This will be tied to Oleg's success in obtaining capital funds for new stores and identifying potential partners for whatever franchising program we can develop.

I had scheduled four visits in 2020 with the first one at the end of March. Unfortunately due to the pandemic, these visits are on hold.

I celebrated my eighty-second birthday in October 2020 and it is not clear how long I will be able to continue my work for EBRD and its clients. However, I hope to complete my assignments with

Meridian Express in Kosovo and Clever Stores in Ukraine in the near future. I will continue as long as my health and ability to make a positive contribution continues.

In December 2020, Oleg confirmed that he was finalizing an initial franchising proposal that may result in up to fifteen franchised locations opening in 2021. I am meeting with Oleg, Serhiy, and Inna on regular Zoom meetings and this will probably continue until the risks from Covid 19 have passed.

Note: During June of 2021, Clever Stores has opened the company's 100th corporate store. They are to be congratulated on reaching this milestone. I have also confirmed my intention to re-start my visits to Ukraine in September.

Frank visiting school children in Lutsk, Ukraine

Inna, Frank, Oleg, and Serhiy

A LIFE IN STAGES

Liberia: Population Five Million

I was asked to attend a week-long series of meetings in Liberia on Africa's west coast. The meetings were related to the National Oil Company of Liberia, (Nocal).

This was my first and only visit to Africa and I am certainly left with some lasting impressions. I only visited the capital, Monrovia, but I had a distinct impression that following successive civil wars, the country was still in a very fragile state. The president, Ellen Johnson Sirleaf, the first female leader of an African country, was a competent and honest politician, from an established and prominent family, but she was due to leave office and the future was unclear.

During my visit, the Ebola crisis erupted, and I was pleased to leave before it invaded the capital. While I was there, I did have an opportunity to tour the city. The major market in the centre of the city was a hive of activity. I also got to see (from a safe distance) the "West Point enclave." I had not appreciated that this was one of the largest urban slums in the whole of Africa and I shuddered to think what Ebola could do if it got loose in such a place. Fortunately, the Ebola outbreak was contained before it could take a hold in "West Point."

View of West Point in Monrovia, Liberia— thousands of people live in this area, in a self-regulated, semi-lawless environment

The resort hotel where I stayed on the outskirts of the city, had been developed by an African American entrepreneur (the founder of Black Entertainment Television (BET) in the US). I had the opportunity to enjoy not one, but two, wonderful lobster dinners at this unusual hotl/resort.

I am pleased that I had the opportunity to see another part of the world, but I am happy to have been there and to have returned home safely. Not to be repeated.

FRANK FARR

One of the other advantages of my involvement with EBRD was that during the months leading up to my brother Michael's death from cancer, I was able to visit him and his wife Elaine on a frequent basis. It was a great pleasure to see the genuine love that Michael and Elaine enjoyed during their many years together. I really do think that they were made for each other. These visits also gave me the opportunity to renew my friendship with my nieces, Pauline, Jacqueline and Suzanne and their families, and I enjoyed their company.

Harry Kinghorn, Suzanne Dickinson, Peter Kinghorn, Frank, Jacqueline Dickinson, and Pauline Dickinson-Kinghorn at the funeral of Frank's brother (Michael Farr)

Jacqueline, Pauline, Suzanne and David Dickinson (nieces and nephew) on one of Frank's visits to Leeds

"Develop the plan—obtain buy-in from all stakeholders—execute the plan—review the plan—start again." Frank Farr

"The best ideas are easy to describe, but incredibly difficult to execute." Frank Farr

CHAPTER TWENTY

Mexico and the Caribbean

During the decade that I worked with EBRD, Ann and I rediscovered the beauty and fun of Mexico and the Caribbean. I also bought my second and third (last) Rolls Royce cars. The last one is a beautiful, deep-burgundy 2000 Silver Seraph. This is probably the last personal car that I will own. Paula immediately christened it "Ruby."

In 1998, we rediscovered Mexico. We had visited Mexico twice at the 7-Eleven properties in Cuernavaca and Acapulco and on two other occasions in Puerto Vallarta. Once was with Jim and Angela and their daughter Louise and later, we went for the wedding of Charlotte Murray and Jorge.

Bernie and Gerry Finan, Angela and Jim Waldron, Ron and June Pellegrin, and Ann in Puerto Vallarta, Mexico

However, following my retirement from 7-Eleven and my sixtieth birthday, Ann and I decided to go to Cabo San Lucas. We stayed at the Rui Palace, a five-star all-inclusive hotel and we were hooked. We thought that the hotel was fabulous, we loved the food, and the nightly entertainment was very enjoyable.

Since that vacation in 1998, we have been on numerous similar vacations to Mexico, both to Cabo San Lucas and many other destinations. I am not sure of the order, but I know that we have been to Puerto Vallarta; Huatulco; Ixtapa; Mazatlán, on the Pacific Coast; and Cancun and Playa Del Carmen on the Atlantic Coast on several occasions.

Ann and Paula Ixtapa 2015

Frank and Ann at the Riu Palace in Cabo San Lucas 2019

Frank and Ann in Cancun, Mexico 2014

Mexico has an incredibly warm, colourful, and historic culture and the people are exceptionally friendly.

Each one of these destinations has its own charm and we have enjoyed each one in its turn, including seeing the Mayan pyramids at Chichen Itza, close to Cancun.

A LIFE IN STAGES

Dominican Republic and Cuba

Mixed in with our trips to Mexico, Ann and I have also taken vacations in the Dominican Republic and in Cuba.

There is not much to be said about the Dominican Republic, but Cuba is a different story.

Cuba was still ruled by the Castros. Fidel was still alive when we visited, and it is a very fascinating, but difficult, country to understand. The communist government has clearly provided a good education system and a good health service. They are justifiably proud of this. However, the standard of living is poor and there is still a high level of political oppression. The most important part of this trip was Havana.

Havana

This must have been a wonderful city (maybe in the 1930s and '40s). It has street after street of magnificent Spanish-style mansions and broad boulevards. Incredibly it is all crumbling into ruins. Some of them may be restored, but there are too many and most of them will eventually fall down. It is a strange, sad, but amazing sight to see all of these buildings in this state. It seems that following the Communist revolution, these buildings were confiscated from their original owners and given to multiple poor families to live in. However, poor people cannot afford to keep up these fine properties and they have gradually become ruins over the past fifty years. This is quite an amazing sight to see. Sad, but strangely attractive.

The other famous oddity of Havana is the cars. Following the revolution, there has been no trade with America and yet somehow the Cubans have managed to keep hundreds of old American cars running and in almost perfect condition. They are everywhere in the centre of Havana and they are now a tourist attraction. (For a suitable fee, you can ride in one.) I was delighted to see a couple of my original 1959 Ford Fairlanes still in that unique shade of light blue, the same as my first car back in Canada in 1959. It is a remarkable sight to see dozens of these cars lined up along the main street in the city centre.

The main boulevard along the ocean is known as The Malecon and it is still very attractive. (I ran for ten yards!) just to say that I had ran the Malecon.)

There are several other memories:

The huge murals of Fidel and Che Guevara are everywhere, particularly Che.

Books seem to be in short supply and at the two bookstores that I checked, they had very little except revolutionary tales.

We spoke to one waitress in one of the hotel bars and she explained that almost all people enjoyed the same salary of $200 per month. She did, as a barmaid, and her husband had the same pay as an entertainer in one of the hotel shows. This type of communist equality is still very much the rule. It is difficult to get by on these salaries, but most basic food items are heavily subsidized by the government and these prices have been the same for years.

Cuba is famous for its cigars and they are prized outside of Cuba. I managed to buy a box at what seemed like a good price and brought them back to give to Tony. I think that he enjoyed them for many months.

It did seem to us, that the few Cubans that we spoke to, were genuinely proud of their country, while acknowledging that living standards were relatively poor. Yet another clear example of the overall failure of the Communist ideology.

I think that Ann and I would both go back to Cuba if there was an opportunity to do so.

Cabo San Lucas

One day in 2017, I was talking to Paula about her plans for the future. Her response was that she would like to "buy a house in Cabo San Lucas." My first thought was that this would not make sense. Owning property in a foreign country did not seem like a good idea.

One year later, I asked her the same question. She gave me the same answer. Paula had been to Cabo San Lucas on several occasions and had met Canadians there who owned their own homes. She liked their lifestyle and if it was her decision, she said that was what she would do.

The three of us continued these discussions and eventually decided that this might make sense, as all three of us liked the idea of being able to get away to somewhere on the Pacific Coast, within a few hours flying time. We also liked the opportunity for us to have somewhere to stay either as a family, or for Paula to be able to stay and enjoy the company of her friends.

Following several exploratory visits to Cabo, Paula and Ann bought a very attractive condo. This condo is located in the La Vista Development, on the hills overlooking Cabo, with a fabulous view of the harbour, cruise ships arriving and departing, and the famous Arches and Land's End.

A LIFE IN STAGES

View from the pool/palapa at La Vista, Cabo San Lucas

Casa Farr Away at La Vista

View from the patio at Casa Farr Away

Casa Farr Away Patio, overlooking the Sea of Cortez

It's a three-bedroom condo of 1,800 square feet with a large deck and a communal pool only yards away. So far this is working out well. Paula has named her home "Casa Farr Away," and has had many of her friends visit her there over the last three years: Casey, Alana, and Liam; Dave and Vania; Karen; etc. and also some of her high school friends: Chris, Leona, Jill, Pam, Michele, and Kim. Apart from the condo, we have spent many, many nights enjoying the live music and bars in Cabo.

Frank and Ann at the Jungle Bar in Cabo San Lucas

Casey Jones, Paula, Ann, and Frank at Cabo Wabo Bar

Dave Hidbur, Rody, Sylvia, Sildia, Sharon, Maelet, Leon, Jamie, Vania Hidbur, and Leo (the Rivas-Heredia Family), Los Leones/The Lions Band

Sunset dinner boat cruise on the Sea of Cortez, in Cabo San Lucas

A LIFE IN STAGES

The main thing is that Paula is very happy during the times that she is able to be there. Unfortunately, the coronavirus pandemic is sweeping the globe and to be on the safe side, Paula returned home in March 2020. I am sure that as soon as this terrible pandemic is behind us, Paula will be off to Cabo again.

Paula's Friendships

On reflection, it is interesting to see that Paula has a similar trait to me, in that she is very loyal to her friends and has remained on friendly terms with almost all of her friends, male and female over the years. Many of them have already visited her at Casa Farr Away.

Starting over fifty years ago, with her best friend, Jo Eden, in Welwyn Garden City and including most of her friends from Westcot School and Sentinel High School in West Vancouver, Ann and I have always enjoyed the company of Paula's friends at our homes, over the years.

Paula has an outgoing personality that allows her to make new friends wherever she goes. She is continuing to display this quality as she widens her circle of friends in her new "home away from home" in Cabo San Lucas. She and her friends have always been there for each other and I am sure that she will retain this trait and enjoy the pleasure of so many of these amazing friends for the rest of her life.

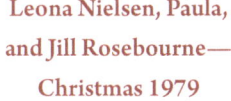

Leona Nielsen, Paula, and Jill Rosebourne— Christmas 1979

Paula, Leona and Jill— Princeton, BC 2018

Tracey Phillips, Jacquie Ray, Pam Barton, Andrea Solnes, Karen Ergas, Kim Little, Corinne Carpenter, Paula, Penny Mullan, Cherrie Dechenes, Michele Moore—"Bad Ass Traveling Mamas" Playa Del Carmen/Mexico celebrating their fiftieth birthdays

Paula and Kevin Shaughnessy 1985

CHAPTER TWENTY ONE

Close Friends, Good Company and Many, Many Parties

Although work has been the dominant factor in my life, I cannot bring this story to a close, without writing about close friends, good company and the many, many parties that have also been such a part of this life.

The biggest problem in writing this, is that there is no way that I can do justice to all of the people that I am going to mention. so just as I remember it, here goes.

Leaving aside family, I think that it would be best to start this chapter at the time that we arrived back in Canada in January of 1975.

Jim and Angela, together with Steve and Mary, joined us in May 1975, and Steve's brothers, Tony, (Liz) Martin (Sandra) and Andrew, subsequently emigrated to Canada and also became good friends. Apart from friends that I made at work, the next close friends that we made were Bernie and Gerry Finan and over time this group has grown to include Mike and Debbie McKay-Dunn, Ron and June Pellegrin, Harry and Pat White, Bobbie and Helen Park, and David and Terri Mayer.

There are many others, too many to mention. However, it is time to talk about the fun part:

The Parties

The first thing that I have to acknowledge here is Jim Waldron's determination to always find that right balance between work life and home life. This is a balance that eludes many, but Jim and Angela always got this right, and their home has been at the centre of the innumerable parties and get-togethers that we and our group have enjoyed over the years. There were also parties at our homes and parties at Steve and Mary's, Bernie and Gerry's, Ron and June's, and Pat and Harry's.

257

FRANK FARR

As most of us were from the UK, we missed our opportunity to go to the local pub, but we made up for it by setting up our own bars in our homes. Martin Murray proved to be very good at this and apart from his own bar, he was instrumental in helping Jim and Steve to build theirs. These bars have remained the focal point of our many parties.

We gradually developed a round of parties that started on New Year's Eve at Jim and Angela's, continued at our house on Valentine's Day, Steve and Mary's for St. Patrick's Day, Pat and Harry's for St. George's Day, Bernie and Gerry's for summer BBQs and a round of parties at many of our houses for the Christmas season, before starting again at Jim and Angela's to celebrate Jim's January 1st birthday at Midnight on New Year's Eve. beginning the circle one more time.

Many people joined us for these parties, too many to mention, and the group grew and changed over the years. The main thing that I remember is the good nature of all of these get-togethers, good food, lots to drink, and great company at all times.

Many of the parties at Jim and Angela's were theme parties, and again this provided an opportunity for much improvisation. We had "Vicars and Tarts," "Roaring Twenties," "Swinging Sixties," and many more, including at least two "Treasure Hunts" around the Surrey-Delta Area. Jim and Angela did a remarkable job of decorating their home in keeping with these themes. A lot of work, but always much appreciated.

A LIFE IN STAGES

Steve Murray, Frank, Jim Waldron – New Year's Eve Party

Ann and Frank on New Year's Eve 2019

It is an unfortunate reality that as our group has grown older, we have had to experience the loss of some of our closest friends. Our entire group was incredibly saddened by the passing of Angela in 2012. Our hearts went out to Jim, Nick, and Louise. Following several years of grieving, Jim has become close to his new partner, Rebecca Fry. We wish Jim and Rebecca all that they wish for themselves and the happiness that they richly deserve.

We were fortunate to enjoy several celebratory parties at our homes, and here are some of the ones that I remember:

We had some great parties at our Westhill home in West Vancouver.

- Celebrating my tenth anniversary with 7-Eleven. Ann and Paula organized this one and I was completely unaware until I arrived home to find such a large group of friends on our pool deck outside the front of the house.

- George and Esther's fiftieth wedding anniversary party, before we left for a fabulous vacation in the Orient.

- Paula's pre-Grad party with so many of her friends that have remained close over all these years.

- A very enjoyable party to celebrate the "burning of our final mortgage." Paid for by the proceeds from 7-Eleven's LBO.

A LIFE IN STAGES

Our home on Delsey Place in South Surrey was designed with entertaining in mind and during our nineteen years there, we made the most of it. We had many get-togethers, but we usually had two main parties each year.

- Our Valentines parties were always lots of fun and Ann did an unbelievable job of decorating the entire house in a blaze of RED!!!!! The food was always outstanding and the result of a lot of work on Ann's part.

- The summer weather in Vancouver can be a little unpredictable, but we usually managed to have an outdoors BBQ and pool party in the summer. Again these were lots of fun and always, with lots of work and preparation, mainly by Ann.

The Covid 19 Pandemic of 2020 has put a temporary hold on parties, but I hope that once this is over, we can take up where we left off.

Good Friends—Good Company—Great Parties. How fortunate we have been to have had a bounty of good times!

❖

"There are Friends, there is Family and then there are Friends that become Family."

CHAPTER TWENTY TWO

Golf

It was during my time with EBRD, that I played my last round of golf.

It is a fact of my life that I have never had any particular affinity to activities that involve hand/eye coordination. This may be related to being left-handed, or as they used to say in England "cack-handed." The one exception is golf (NOT!!!) and yet, I have spent a lot of time on golf courses and enjoyed playing on many of the leading courses in North America.

To begin at the beginning, when I grew up in Leeds, it was unheard of for a working-class boy to play golf. Golf was for wealthy people.

My lack of hand/eye coordination has also manifested itself in the fact that I never learned to ride a bike and I am probably the only person that I have ever met that has this claim to distinction.

However, I digress.

I had no exposure to golf until I joined 7-Eleven in 1978. Adrian Evans, my first boss at 7-Eleven, had started to play golf with his good friend, Bill Prokop, in Calgary and I occasionally joined them. Also, Adrian, who was based in Chicago, used to arrange for his group to play golf on a frequent basis and I was always asked to join in.

Not quite mastering the art, though, I usually found myself sitting in the clubhouse nursing a sore back. This back issue became so bad that on business trips, I would often stay in my hotel room, working on my presentations, and I'd meet the others after they had finished their round.

But I persisted, and finally figured out how to swing a club without pulling my back out. So, for the next few years, I enjoyed the occasional round with my various 7-Eleven colleagues. I played frequently (but badly) with Adrian Evans, Steve Krumholz, and of course Steve LeRoy.

Playing with Steve LeRoy was always a treat. He was the best golfer in Southland (a Plus 2) He had such patience with hackers like me, and at the same time was able to exemplify all that is great about golf. The best shots that I can recall from my time playing, were usually shots made by Steve, often from what looked like impossible positions.

Our annual golf trips to Phoenix became one of the most popular events on our annual calendar. This was particularly enjoyable, as we were able to take our wives and make a really good weekend out of it. Those weekends at The Point at Squaw Peak, The Pointe at South Mountain, and The Pointe at

FRANK FARR

Tapatio, will stay in my memory forever. Sitting in the hot tub, free drinks at happy hour and dining in the numerous restaurants.

Later, I also enjoyed many a long weekend, joining in Frank Carey's fabulous golf weekends out of Calgary on long trips to marvellous courses. Lots to eat and drink and good company. Later, Frank built a professional, nine-hole executive course, on the grounds of his new house in North Calgary and I enjoyed playing this course on my occasional visits to the Carey home.

During this time, we also started our annual golf trips with our group here in BC.

The founding members were Bernie, Jim, Steve, Tony, Mike, Harry, Tom, David, and me. This group grew and changed over the years, with Bobby Park being a most welcome addition. Fairview Mountain, Ink'meep, and Osoyoos are still the favourite venues. I dropped out about three years ago, due to conflicts with my EBRD visits, and my concern with A-fib and a leaky heart valve.

One of the odd outcomes from our group trips was that Steve, who never took golf that seriously, still managed to play most holes, except the par threes, with a score of six! Remarkably consistent.

Bernie, who did take his golf seriously, was always the best player in this group and in subsequent years went on to become the vice-captain and the club captain at Morgan Creek Men's Club for four years. Bernie was also our joker-in-chief, his steady stream of jokes entertained us for many years.

Tony, who started slowly, but always played honestly, would probably qualify for the most improved golfer of this group.

Mike is also a decent golfer, but his main claim to fame is as our resident musician, songwriter, story-teller, and all-round funny companion. "Bernie and The Dykes" and "Harry Forgot to Pay his Bill" are two of his creations that spring to mind.

The Okanagan Golf Group: Tony Murray, Frank, David Myer, Bernie Finan, Chuck Giese, Mike McKayDunn, and Jim Waldron—19th hole Inkameep Golf Course, Oliver, BC

Everybody in this group has a story to tell and a memory to savour, and some have the distinction of winning "The Wanker's Cup," one of the more prestigious awards in amateur golf.

I have so many fond memories of these times. The camaraderie and good-natured bantering within the BC group, led to a special type of male bonding that will last a lifetime. Some of the early trips to Sequim have become entrenched in our minds, and as the venue changed to the Okanagan, we enjoyed many "pub nights" at The Olde Welcome

A LIFE IN STAGES

Inn over the road from Gallagher's Lake Lodge. Tom Proctor (RIP) was a fine singer and often led our sing-alongs with a local pianist. These pub nights were always followed by a long, drinking and BS session around the fire on the beach. This brings some other memories to mind.

I have never been a big beer drinker and after one or two beers, I would usually switch to a more enjoyable "Monte Christo," (Grand Marnier and Khalua). As the bill was usually being shared by twelve guys, the extra cost was negligible. (On the basis of twelve to one, it may have been twenty five cents) However, on one occasion, a guest of Tom's took exception to paying his extra share of this cost. Jim soon put him right and reminded him that he was getting good value for his trip and that he always had the option not to come again. He never did.

On another occasion, the barmaid joined in our fun (the landlord was not there) and I went behind the bar to assist in dispensing our own drinks. The barmaid got a big tip on that night.

We also discovered that Bobby had amazing agility. He displayed this by falling down the steps to the beach fire, and rolling over, while at the same time keeping the pizzas that he was carrying in an upright and safe position. A feat never duplicated.

The Okanagan Golf Group – Osoyoos Golf & Country Club, BC

2008 Oliver Golf Tournament

When I retired from 7-Eleven, everybody told me, "Join a club, buy new equipment, and take lessons, your game will improve." (NOT!) However, I did act on this advice. We built a new home on Morgan Creek Golf Course and I joined the men's club.

That was a great experience. After my first year, I was elected to the men's club executive as club secretary and treasurer. In this role, it became my job to organize many of the activities, and I applied myself to the task with some notable success.

The club did not have a written constitution, so I wrote one. They are still using this version, over twenty years later.

I learned the rules of golf and wrote the club's rules, including the local "rules." Working with the club captains, we organized most of the functions, including the annual general meeting and the annual awards banquet. We also introduced a "Green Blazer" Award for the winner of the Men's Club Championship. They elected me for three years running and the members always joked about appointing me "Secretary for Life." Of course, this had nothing to do with my playing ability, although, I did win one of the club tournaments, "The Eclectic" and my name is inscribed on the cup in the trophy case. I worked with two club captains, Mike Ellam and Peter Hucul. All considered, it was a very enjoyable experience. It was a pleasure to get to know so many of the members. They were a very diverse group. Lots of fun and plenty to drink, in the clubhouse following our Saturday rounds

As a result of these experiences, I clearly understand the special attraction of golf. It is a game based on personal integrity and individual ability. The skill level required to succeed at the professional level is exceptional and at its peak, it is such a pleasure to enjoy.

Two related golf stories come to mind from my time at Morgan Creek:

At the club, we had several teaching professionals. They were always offering to teach me (for a fee) and promising that they could improve my game. One day, I decided to take them up on it, my way, "Double or nothing."

My proposal was, you teach me, and if, following your lessons, I can break 100 on three successive Saturdays, playing from the blue tees, I will pay you double. If not, I won't pay. Nobody took me up on this very fair offer. This told me all that I needed to know about my game. Notwithstanding this, I must admit that there is quite the thrill in hitting a good shot or playing what for me was a good round.

Here is my funniest golf story of all. I was beginning to ease back on my Saturday morning rounds and one Saturday morning, as I watched the players go past my window, I was busy checking the financial accounts of my EBRD client in Tbilisi, Georgia and noticed, what I thought was an obvious error. I was leaving for Georgia the following week.

When I arrived in Georgia, I was quite annoyed to learn that not only was the error quite large, but that neither of the two managers involved were aware of it. (One of them was the chief accountant!)

I was chairing a board meeting the following day and decided to let them know how I felt. "When I work here in Georgia, you pay me; however, when I work from home, I do it for free! It is appalling that, working for free, I find significant errors in your accounts and when I check with you, you are

A LIFE IN STAGES

not aware. What makes this even worse is that, in Vancouver, I live on a golf course, I am a member of the men's club and I have the highest handicap in the club for the past ten years. I am having to give up playing golf, so that I can pay attention to your business from 10,000 kilometres away, and you can't be bothered to look after your own business."

They were quite embarrassed, but the point of this is that there are no golf courses in Georgia and their understanding of the game is very limited. They had no idea that my having the highest handicap in the club, meant that I was the worst. They assumed that having the highest handicap meant that I was the best.

❖

"They call it golf because all of the other four-letter word were taken." Ray Floyd

"If you want to hide your character, do not play golf." Percy Bomer

"Don't play too much golf. Two rounds a day is plenty." Harry Vardon

"The more I play, the luckier I get." Gary Player

"Golf is the most fun you can have without taking your clothes off." Chi Chi Rodriguez

"Golf is a fascinating game. It has taken me forty years to discover that I can't play." Ted Ray.

"If you're caught on a golf course in a thunderstorm and are afraid of lightning, hold up a 1-iron. Not even God can hit a 1 iron." Lee Trevino

CHAPTER TWENTY THREE

❖

2199 179th Street, South Surrey

In October of 2016, we made the decision to sell our home on Morgan Creek Golf Course. We had lived there for twenty years and although we had designed and built this beautiful home, we felt that it was time for a move and we should probably downsize. We believed that the housing market had reached one of its "five-year peaks," and that the time was right to sell. Our timing could not have been better. We received a very acceptable offer within three days of the listing and the attractive bonus was that the buyer did not want possession for five months. This gave us lots of time to consider our alternatives. We considered buying two town houses and other options but nothing that we saw appealed to us.

Then we got lucky!

I was away from home, on an assignment in Kosovo, when Ann contacted me to say that she had found a house that might meet all of our requirements. Within a week of my return, we had made the decision to move to 2199 179th Street in South Surrey, very close to the US border. We moved into this house in March 2017.

2199 179th Street is a larger home than we planned, with a huge, beautifully landscaped garden and a pool with a built-in grotto and jacuzzi. Lots of wildlife, some more welcome than others. Deer, owls, coyotes, rabbits, and a varied range of birds. Paula has developed a particular passion for the garden and spends a lot of her time outside growing her own flowers and vegetables.

269

"Olive" the owl   The "famous five" coyote pups

Paula organized a "Twenty Year" 7-Eleven reunion party and it was a great pleasure to host so many of our old colleagues from 7-Eleven. A party to remember.

7-Eleven Twenty-Year Reunion Party 2018

Paula has put so much work into improving the garden and she has hosted many parties (too many to count!) It has been such fun to see so many of her friends, many from her school days, come over for pool days and parties.

A LIFE IN STAGES

The "grotto" pool

Pool day with the Murrays
Mary Murray, Frank and Ann, Liz and Tony Murray, Jim Waldron and Rebecca Fry

Steve Murray and Frank

Charlotte Murray-Marrujo, Steve Murray, Pauline Moore, Paula, Jo Murray-Devine, Sinead Murray-Ryan, Mary Murray, Ann 2019

FRANK FARR

Mary Murray with Jo,
Charlotte and Sinead

Gerry Finan, Ann, Steve Murray,
Harry White, Mary Murray

Paula and her high school friends—Jacqueline Ray,
Andrea Solnes, Corinne Carpenter, Penny Mullan, Paula,
Michele Moore, Tracey Phillips, Cherrie Deschenes,
Pam Barton – "Bad Ass Traveling Mamas"

Ann and Frank

Frank and Ann's fifty-sixth wedding anniversary
at Charlie's Don't Surf Restaurant in White Rock
with Jim Waldron, Steve and Mary Murray, Bernie
and Gerry Finan, and Tony and Liz Murray

CHAPTER TWENTY FOUR

On Eighty

On Thursday, October 16th, 2018, I celebrated my eightieth birthday. I am happy to be alive and this seems like a good time for reflection. This is also a little long, but then I have been able to pack a lot into my eighty years since being born in Lewisham, London, England in 1938.

On Dying

I see that so many men die in their late seventies and early eighties that I am reminded that we cannot live forever. I am thankful for having made it to eighty and I plan to go on and stay active, for as long as I am able.

I do not want to die, but I am somewhat philosophical about the prospect. I just hope that when my time comes, I still have my faculties and am able to go as peacefully as possible and with the least distress to Ann and Paula.

I have never tried recreational drugs, but I have wondered what it would be like to follow Aldous Huxley's example and finish with a gentle dose of LSD and move into an incredible space of light and beauty.

On Religion

Religion has not played a role in my life. I was born into a Catholic family, christened as a Catholic (Francis) received a confirmation name (Vincent), attended a Catholic church (St. Anne's) in Leeds, and went to a Catholic junior school.

However, my mother had a falling out with the church at the time of my father's death and this falling out was never repaired.

I understand the concept of God and Godliness, or Good and Goodness and I have the greatest respect for the saintly acts of such people as Mother Theresa in India and Albert Schweitzer in Africa, but I have never reconciled the evil that has been perpetrated throughout history (and to this day) in the name of religion.

During these past few years, I have had the opportunity to enjoy the company of many people of the Muslim faith and I have realized that there is so much that is similar in the foundation of both the Muslim and Christian faiths.

While I can accept the good that is done by many faiths, I have to say that ultimately, I am an agnostic atheist. A religious sceptic, having difficulty accepting the idea of a deity.

On The Good Life—Well lived

I truly believe that I am fortunate to have lived the life that I have. On the whole, it has been a good life, far more eventful than I ever anticipated growing up in a single parent, poor working-class family in Leeds, during and after the Second World War. For the most part, our futures are unpredictable, and I have been so lucky to have enjoyed good health and endless support from friends, family, and many people from all walks of life, whose paths have crossed mine throughout this amazing journey.

On Happiness

I am and always have been, a happy and positive person.

There is a saying that "Happiness is a state of mind, not a result of circumstances." There is much truth in this. Although I have been fortunate to live most of my adult life in good circumstances, I believe that my basic happiness stems from having a positive and enthusiastic approach towards most things that a long life has thrown at me.

I do believe in planning for the future, but also in living in the moment, and reacting positively to the opportunities that present themselves. To quote. "Life is not a rehearsal. *Carpe Diem!*

On Maintaining a Positive Attitude

There are times when it is near impossible to remain happy and positive, particularly in the face of a cruel illness or other calamity. While this is quite understandable, we can, for the most part, defeat negativism, by remembering that ultimately, we are in control of our own minds and our emotions.

I believe strongly that each of us is in charge of and responsible for ourselves. So often, I hear people say, "Such and such a person has made me angry, or such an event has made me frustrated." In the words of Marcus Aurelius, *"Problems are created in the mind."* We can remain happy and maintain a good disposition, if we remember not to allow others to determine our attitude and our frame of mind. Stay positive!

I have to say that I do not remember being as happy and relaxed as I am now. I am in reasonably good health, and I am not under any stress. We are currently living in a wonderful house. The house and garden seem magical and Paula is even growing her own vegetables! Paula and Ann have the home in Cabo San Lucas, and it seems to be giving Paula the pleasure that she deserves.

We all have differing degrees of ability, but so much comes back to attitude. It is your attitude that allows you to get up each day and to go out and overcome whatever challenges come your way.

On Good Luck

There is a saying that "Good luck is where preparation meets opportunity," and that sentiment has played a big part in my life.

However, there is also pure good luck and I have had more than my share.

I am very lucky that the following events occurred:

- That somebody decided to administer that IQ test back in 1953.

- That I went to Kneesworth Hall and enjoyed the patronage of Montague and Dorothy Simmons.

- That Doreen Abbot's family decided to emigrate to Canada.

- That Mr. Garfield Weston decided to send some young Canadians to Fine Fare in England.

Dorothy Simmons and Frank in Victoria, BC 1993
(forty years after our first meeting in 1953)

- That Fine Fare asked me to manage the supermarket in Maghull and I met Ann.

- That Ann and I are the parents of Paula; they are the most important people in my life.

- That Fine Fare asked me to manage the store at Crossgates in Leeds. This opened the door for my friendship with Jim and Steve and all of the good times that have resulted from this friendship.

- That Mr. Jones and Mr. Shelley made their surprise visit to Crossgates Fine Fare.

- That Mr. Galen Weston made that phone call to Wallace Monaghan at the time when I was leaving Fine Fare.
- That Dez Hubble introduced me to 7-Eleven.
- That Peter Flach introduced me to EBRD.

I played no part in bringing these individual events together and yet cumulatively, these have been the "lucky breaks" that we all need, as we make our way forward.

On Food

I am probably the pickiest eater that I know, although Paula was always a close second. Ann, on the other hand, has always been willing to try any food and usually enjoy it. The three main things that I will not eat are onions, garlic, and mustard. Unfortunately, I have never been willing to eat most vegetables, cabbage, sprouts, cauliflower and most pickles are among the foods that I avoid, but there are lots more.

This results in my not being adventurous in trying new foods and this is a pity since I have had lots of opportunity to try new tastes on my extensive travels. I actually like spicy food, depending on the type of spice used.

Fortunately, there is a lot that I do like and I have managed to enjoy good food in most of the places that I have visited. Some of the stand-outs have been Ruth's Chris mouth-watering steaks, lots of seafood in the Orient, and recently, a delicious, slow-roasted duck in Lutsk, Ukraine.

I am also fortunate that Ann has cared enough over all these years to constantly prepare wonderful food that I thoroughly enjoy and look forward to each and every day.

Paula has dramatically increased the range of food that she enjoys, particularly now that she spends so much time in Mexico.

On Music

Music is so individual, but I must say how much I have enjoyed listening to Frank Sinatra, Tony Bennett, Ella Fitzgerald, Sarah Vaughan, and Billie Holiday. They seem like voices from another time now and yet they have never been equalled. The genius of Ray Charles, Louis Armstrong, and Duke Ellington and the pure American talent of Willie Nelson will remain in my mind forever. The remarkable baritone voices of Billy Eckstine, Ed Townsend, Lou Rawls, Nat King Cole and of course the incomparable Sammy Davis Jr. continue to provide such pleasure. I must also admit that I enjoy a great orchestral symphony (Tchaikovsky) and many of the arias from the great operas. (Pavarotti)

A LIFE IN STAGES

On Films

I have lived through the great era of filmmaking. I grew up with many cinemas close to where I lived. They usually showed one movie on Monday, Tuesday, Wednesday and then another on Thursday, Friday, Saturday with yet another one on Sunday. Somehow, we managed to see most of them. I have always had a passion for the musicals of the '50s and '60s and for huge historical dramas. *Dr. Zhivago*, *Lawrence of Arabia* and *Ghandi,* are three that come to mind. Although I recently watched the original *Godfather* movie again and I think this is one of the best movies ever made.

On Books

Where to start? I have read everything that I could lay my eyes on since I was a young child. Too many to mention, but still a big passion. Everything from historical biographies (Nelson, Wellington, Aldous Huxley, Bertrand Russell, Mountbatten, Krishnamurti) to spy novels and more lately, histories of Armenia, Georgia, Kosovo and Ukraine, plus all the latest books on the recent US political upheavals. It's a question of too little time—too many books.

On Humour

Humour is such an odd thing. What one person sees as funny, the next one does not.

I have enjoyed many funny American comedies, from *Cheers*, to *Seinfeld* and others, but being English, I always have to go back to my roots.

- The original lunacy of *The Goon Show*
- The clever madness of *Monty Python*
- The originality of the *Peter Cook & Dudley Moore Show*
- The amazing word play of the *Two Ronnies*
- And more recently the incredibly funny Katherine Tate

All of these can still have me in stitches to this day.

Here is my version of a true funny story.

One day, I received an official looking e-mail from a department of the US government. "Do your duty and join the US Naval Reserve." I thought that this was silly. I was over seventy and a Canadian citizen, so I paid no notice.

A few months later, I received that same e-mail again. "Do your duty and join the US Naval Reserve."

This time, I could not resist replying.

Dear Sir,

I have now received your second request to join the US Naval Reserve. I have decided to accept your kind offer. This assumes that you can resolve the initial problems that result from the fact, that I am over 70 years of age and a Canadian Citizen.

However, due to my unique qualifications listed below, I would expect to receive the initial rank of vice-admiral.

- *I have sailed the Atlantic, both ways on three occasions. (Without becoming sea-sick).*
- *I have sailed to many of the islands in the Caribbean.*
- *I have circumnavigated the Island of Catalina.*
- *I have spent time on cruise ships at the Olympics in Los Angeles and the Olympics in Barcelona.*
- *I have studied the biography of Admiral Lord Nelson and I know the battle order of his famous triumphs at The Battle of the Nile, The Battle of Copenhagen, and of course, The Battle of Trafalgar.*
- *And as an added accomplishment, I once had a very intense personal relationship with a female naval officer.*

I look forward to hearing from you at your earliest convenience.

Sincerely

Frank Farr

I was disappointed not to hear back. And then approx. a year later, I received the following e-mail. Somebody at the other end had seen the funny side to this.

Dear Mr. Farr,

We have finally reviewed your request for a position in the US Naval Reserve. Following a lengthy search, we think that we may have something suited to your unique experience.

The role would be purely ceremonial, and would involve you wearing period dress uniform, and acting the part of your naval hero Admiral Lord Nelson. To play this part authentically, you would need to have your left eye removed and also, the right arm below the elbow.

If this proposal is acceptable to you, please advise and we will set up your first appointment

Sincerely

US Naval Reserve Academy.

A LIFE IN STAGES

All I could do was return the e-mail marked, "Touché." This seemed funny to me at the time. Still does.

On Health, Energy, Work

I do believe that subject to good luck and good health, life is what you make of it.

Despite some age-related concerns, I feel relatively healthy. I don't think that I could work sixty hours-plus weeks on a regular basis, as I did when I was working full time. However, I work at my own pace in preparation for my consulting trips to Europe and when I am there, I put in a solid week's work and often surprise my clients with my ability to keep up and stay ahead in hours worked and issues under consideration. I find this very satisfying and I am sure that it contributes to my general well-being.

I am sure that health is a combination of genetic and environmental factors. My mother lived to the ripe old age of ninety-two, and although the last few years were a challenge, I do not recall her being ill at any time as we were growing up.

Olive Farr at ninety

I have been extremely fortunate in that I did not have one hour off work due to illness during forty-five years of full-time work. Never had an injury and never even caught the flu. Ann has also been very fortunate in this regard.

I have been asked if I consider myself a workaholic. The answer is no. There are many negative attributes to workaholism and fortunately, I don't have any of them. The truth is that I have always enjoyed my work and the challenges that come with it

It's true that I have worked long and hard for most of my working life, but this was due to the amount of work and responsibility that came with the job. As the years have gone by, I have gradually cut back on the time that I have spent working, usually five days per week and seldom on a weekend, unless I was travelling and had nothing else to do.

We will have to see what the next few years bring, but I have always been both optimistic and enthusiastic. In so many ways, I have been fortunate to have a positive approach to my work and I genuinely looked forward to going to work each day. I always have and I hope that I always will, through to the very end.

On Influences

Ann and Paula

First and foremost, is the influence of my wife of fifty-eight years, Ann, who has given me a well-deserved taste of humility, combined with a constant dose of common sense (from her father George). Ann has had the patience to stand by me all these years, often at times when I have not deserved her support, but I do believe that she understands that I have done my best. Most important of all, we had Paula; she has blessed our lives with a genuine kindness, combined with an example of strength, intelligence, and loyalty of spirit that is a joy to see. They say that she resembles me in some of her ways. I don't know if that is true, but I continue to be proud of her for so many reasons. Paula has also developed a good use of words and some of her comments are very insightful.

Frank and Ann New Year's Eve 2020

Paula and Frank, Christmas 2020

Christmas 2020 –
our board games tradition

Jim Waldron and Steve Murray

Jim and Steven have been at my side for most of my adult life through thick and thin, through (mostly) highs and the occasional lows: almost fourteen years with Fine Fare, four years with Tamblyn and then twenty years with 7-Eleven. They have taught me the value of friendships that endure. Jim epitomized the importance of finding that elusive balance in life, between work and home. Unfortunately, I never did get this right. Steve has always defined true friendship, reliability of character, and family values. I have been, and I remain, privileged to have enjoyed their friendship for over fifty years.

New Friends

I am fortunate that my work at EBRD has helped me to make new friends. Also, due to the fact that these new friends are from more distant countries, I get to see many things from a new perspective. I am greatly influenced by the opportunity to see life from this different perspective. I have come to appreciate the culture and struggles of others, and not to take for granted the rights and privileges that are a part of living in Canada. What good luck!

Ann and Paula organized a tremendous eightieth birthday party for me, and once again the good food and the company created an evening to treasure.

❖

"Approach life with an open and curious mind. Be prepared to react to all of the wonderful opportunities that lie ahead." Frank Farr

"Believe in young people; they are the future and given the opportunity, they will usually exceed your expectations." Frank Farr

CHAPTER TWENTY FIVE

❖

Epilogue: No End in Sight—Just Yet!!!!!!

On October 16th, 2020, I celebrated my eighty-second birthday.

What lies ahead? I am happily looking forward to more adventures, with an open mind and continued enthusiasm for the opportunities to give of my experience and to learn from my exposure to all that a long life can bring.

In February of 2020, I completed my fiftieth consulting visit to Eastern Europe and if the Covid 19 pandemic had not changed things, I would have completed seven more trips in 2020. Now that we are emerging from the dark cloud of the pandemic, I am hoping to fit in one trip to Kosovo and one trip to Ukraine before the end of 2021.

Many of my friends and acquaintances suggest that I should more fully retire, but I enjoy what I do so much, and I am stimulated by the challenging process. However, age, health, or the pandemic may limit my options.

How and why do I still want to do this?

I am not too sure, but I think that it somehow relates to what I call the "X" Factor.

For me, the "X" Factor is that extra dimension to things.

Frank at 82

- That extra thought that makes me want to get up in the morning and deal with whatever the day will bring.

- That extra effort that allows me to understand difficult things, more clearly.

- That extra step that seems to make each project better.

- That extra feature that makes initiatives more likely to succeed.

Just when you are about to conclude a discussion paper, or a project proposal, that quiet thought: *What have we missed? What have we overlooked that would make this better?* I have lost count of how many times this extra effort has made the difference on so many initiatives that I have been involved with.

There have been so many times that others have advised me not to go to that extra length, and against all advice to the contrary, I have pushed further, and in doing so, I have found a better solution. For me this is the only way.

This helps me to understand myself and my underlying drive to succeed, in dealing with the responsibilities that have fallen my way. As long as I am searching for a better understanding of things and finding the "X" factor that will be a part of my unique contribution to life, then I will have no difficulty finding that extra effort to keep going on!

I am eighty-two and I can remember a time when that seemed like a very old age. And yet, I do not find that my mental abilities are too diminished, and I still look forward to each day. It may be unreasonable, but I go to bed each night, expecting to wake up in the morning and to carry on with my life as usual. I hope that this expectation can continue for as long as possible.

There are four things that will determine the next steps.

1) **My Attitude**: I am so fortunate to have reached this point in life and to be so happy. This allows me to continue to maintain my positive approach in all that I do, and if I am lucky, I will be able to retain this positive approach for some years to come.

2) **My Health**: Although I think that I am in relatively good health considering my age, I am acutely aware that this will not continue. I am hopeful that my heart conditions: leaky heart valve and A-Fib, do not deteriorate too quickly. I am also aware that I do not do as much as I should to keep myself fit, but so far, so good. I do manage to get in a mile a day on my treadmill (most days).

3) **Covid 19**: Now that we have been vaccinated and the risk of contracting Covid 19 is diminished, our plans are falling in place. Paula, Ann, and I have already confirmed our plans to get back to Cabo San Lucas, in October – November 2021 and I have set provisional dates to visit Kosovo in July and Ukraine in September.

4) **Clever Stores (Ukraine) and Meridian Express (Kosovo)** Both Oleg and Agon want me to continue to advise/consult to them and I want to return. On an interim basis, we are holding frequent Zoom or Skype meetings, and this is allowing me to continue to help. As in most things, timing is everything and circumstances could change. The best thing for me is to stay informed and keep my mind active, so that I can still make a positive contribution if the opportunity occurs.

The Covid pandemic has been, and remains an international disaster. However, on a personal level, there have been some benefits.

A LIFE IN STAGES

I enjoy my consulting work in Europe, and during this past year, had there been no Covid, I would have made at least six more trips to Kosovo and Ukraine and spent many days away from home. As a direct result of the pandemic, Paula, Ann, and I have spent more time together during this past year. More family time has allowed us to become closer in the process.

This biography, which started out with a simple request from Paula, has turned into a more significant task than I originally imagined. A true labour of love. Completing this story has taken many hours and days, starting in April of 2020 and finishing over one year later in June 2021

Paula on her birthday—February 19, 2021

Paula "hitching" a ride to Cabo—March 2021

Recalling so many events from my eighty-two years of life. *It has been time well spent.*

Paula and Ann have acted as editors and "fact checkers" for my sometimes faulty memory.

I hope that readers of this story will enjoy this trip down Memory Lane, as much as we did in getting it down on paper. I also hope that you will also recognize the times when I have appreciated the positive contribution that so many people have added to my life's story.

I have tried to make these recollections as accurate as my memory will allow, please accept my apologies for any errors or omissions.

Early on in this story, I mentioned the young girl living in Maghull Lancashire, England. Ann Pope, who was a fan of Elvis Presley and had the five shilling piece souvenir from Queen Elizabeth's coronation in 1953.

Frank and Ann, Easter April 2021

Frank and Ann, April 2021

Ann and I have just celebrated our fifty-eighth wedding anniversary and here we are "in the autumn of our years." We have travelled the world and enjoyed the everlasting pleasure of family and good friends. We are happy and generally in good health, apart from a small number of minor age-related concerns. We are not under any particular stress, and we have been vaccinated for Covid 19.

Together, we face whatever comes next, relying on each other, as we have done successfully, for these past fifty-eight years.

We have each other, and we do complement each other so well. My daily enjoyment comes from seeing Ann take the *Globe and Mail* crossword from the paper, sit down with her morning coffee, and complete the cryptic puzzle. I'm always embarrassed that I usually cannot answer a single clue.

And it all started at the entrance to Deyes Lane, Fine Fare Supermarket in Maghull, February 1962. How could we have guessed?

I have been so lucky to have been married to Ann for all these years, and I would not change anything.

To be continued…

APPENDICES

The following appendices don't fit neatly into the main body of my story. Some of them are primarily lists; however, they are there for reference for Paula, and any other readers who might appreciate some additional details.

APPENDIX 1

Fish and Chips (Part 2)

Before I bring this story to its end, I should finish my comments re. fish and chips, which I started in an earlier chapter.

I've had the good fortune to travel widely and to have eaten gourmet food at some of the most famous places in the world: Beautifully prepared continental cuisine at Gaddi's in Hong Kong, gourmet buffet at the Oriental in Bangkok, Ruth's Chris Steak House in Dallas and elsewhere, seafood in New Orleans, but at the end of the day, for me, there's nothing quite like a really good plate of fish and chips.

I don't know which potatoes make the best chips, but I believe that it probably has to do with the amount of sugar and starch in the potatoes. As for the fish, cod is the one used most, haddock has a far superior taste and of course here in Canada we are blessed with bountiful supplies of pure, white, tender halibut.

The worst and the best

I have probably tasted every type and kind of fish and chips imaginable. The worst that I can remember was upon my arrival in Canada in 1957. In downtown Toronto, feeling somewhat homesick, my spirits were lifted by a sign, a block or so away flashing "Fish and Chips" in red neon. I can honestly say that they were, until recently, the worst fish and chips that I have ever experienced. Decency will not allow me to say what happened to them, but they were not consumed. The worst recently, unbelievably, were at Troll's in White Rock. They left me quite sick for a couple of days.

The best fish and chips ever? …I'll save that till later.

I came back to Canada in 1975, to Vancouver. There is a strong tradition of fish and chips in Vancouver and some very good fish and chip restaurants. My first good experience was at the original Troll's in Horseshoe Bay. Joe Troll, the proprietor, would come out from behind the fryer and make his way around his restaurant checking that the customers were happy, before going back to work at the fryer. Sadly, after his passing, the restaurants were franchised, and the quality deteriorated.

The finest fish and chips available in Vancouver in recent years were produced by people who came from Pudsey between Leeds and Bradford. One of them was Petticoat Lane in West Vancouver. The owner is related to the owners of Uncle Herbert's in Ladner and to my knowledge they are the only places where you could still get those old-time Yorkshire fish cakes that I used to get at the Blackman Lane Fish shop back in Leeds in the late forties. Petticoat Lane also featured a "Bradford Special," which is a large piece of cod requiring a larger plate. As an aside, as I grew up, Pudsey was known as the place where "pigs fly backwards." Never did discover the origin of that one. Unfortunately, both of these fish and chip shops are no longer in operation.

There are numerous fish and chip shops along the front in White Rock and many people say they are very good but so far, I have not found one that I would rate that high.

Going back home

I still go back to Leeds occasionally, and to Maghull in Lancashire. In Maghull, there are two fish and chip shops that I recall. The one at the top of Esther's street, Green Lane, is run by an incredibly entrepreneurial man who manages to run a busy shop with a menu comprising fifty or sixty items, most of which he can conjure up at your request. The fish and chips there are quite good, but you can't excel without focus. The fish and chip shop on Deyes Lane next to the old Fine Fare is much better.

I find that same lack of focus in the large number of fish and chip shops that now sell curry items and other delicacies. Tasty food no doubt, but they will never be remembered for their great fish and chips.

I mentioned that Michael had taken me back to a very good fish and chip shop by Kirkgate Market on a recent trip back. One of the funnier experiences that I have had recently came on just such a trip. I was staying with Michael and Elaine and enjoying a late-night Canadian Club and Coke, when Michael suggested we go out for some fish and chips to bring back for a late supper. We had to leave right away to catch them before they closed.

What a riot! I took my large, strong, rye and Coke with me, not my first of the night, and we headed off to this busy, noisy, and very funny fish and chip shop. The place was bustling, and the female staff were in good form with lots of good-natured banter back and forth with the customers. One lady asked me what I was drinking, to which I replied, "Coke." Not believing me, she asked for a taste and then proceeded to pass my drink around for all the staff to taste.

In the meantime, I had studied the menu board to order a special. The menu board featured " Regulars," "Specials" and "Firkins" I know that a firkin is a large-size barrel. When I enquired as to what a "Firkin" Fish was I was told loud and clear that it was so big "you would not firkin believe it." It was big, it was good, and I went back to that fish and chip shop for the next two nights prior to leaving. I brought them a large rye and Coke; they had my "Firkin" ready.

A good example of clean Yorkshire fun and great fish and chips.

A LIFE IN STAGES

In May 2016 I was going back to Leeds on a frequent basis. Unfortunately, my brother, Michael, had terminal cancer and he would not be with us much longer. Just before he became ill, Michael took me to Murgatroyd's. It's on a round-about close to Yeadon Airport. They have magnificent fish and chips and best of all, they have the largest haddock "Special" I have ever seen. If you are ever in the area, don't miss it.

So, there you are. I believe that I qualify as a fish and chip connoisseur. I've had the best and I've had the worst.

And the best? By far the best fish and chips in the world are available to me year in and year out.

My wife Ann actually does make the best fish and chips in the world. And that includes Harry Ramsden's!!! I'm not just saying this to earn brownie points on the home front. Prepared from fresh tender halibut in a light, crispy golden batter with perfect chips, they are without a doubt the best fish and chips in the whole world.

If I have the good fortune to choose my last meal, it will be Ann's fish and chips prepared with TLC and me in mind.

What a way to go!

I love fish and chips.

APPENDIX 2

❖

2020 - The Covid 19 Pandemic and Donald Trump

The year 2020 has proven to be a watershed year in many ways that have impacted our lives.

At the start of this year, there were rumours of a new virus that was emerging from China. At first, it was assumed that this would just be the latest in a number of viruses such as SARS and Swine Flu, that had emerged from China in the past decade.

These previous epidemics had run their course and the assumption was that this one, Covid 19 would be similar. Nothing could be further from the truth. This virus is now a true pandemic. It has swept the entire world to a degree not seen in a century. The last such pandemic was the so called "Spanish Flu" of 1917–1918. That flu caused the death of many millions of people around the globe.

The Covid 19 pandemic has affected populations around the world, starting during the first quarter of 2020, and as of March 2021, 133 million people have been affected around the world. There have been over 2.89 million deaths attributed to this virus and this number is clearly understated.

The impact has not been evenly spread, with some countries faring far better than others. This is primarily due to the different approach and relative efficiency of the actions taken by respective governments. Some countries, New Zealand, Taiwan, Singapore, and South Korea have done very well.

Europe has had mixed results, with Germany and the UK initially doing very badly. This is still a moving target as Europe is now entering its second phase and seeing huge increases. The United States, Brazil, and India seem to be doing the worst, and this is particularly surprising, as the US has the most advanced medical systems in the world and also many of the world's leading epidemiologists.

There is a general consensus that the US, under the leadership of President Trump, has failed to address this crisis. His administration has absolutely failed to provide leadership, at a time of utmost need. Either non-responses, or ever-changing misdirection and outright denial of the facts and the best scientific advice has caused America to suffer many hundreds, or perhaps thousands of unnecessary deaths in a system that has frequently been overwhelmed.

The situation in the US is a national disgrace. There have been over 30 million people affected in that country. As of this writing, the number of deaths in the US has now exceeded 600,000. This exceeds the number of deaths from World War One, World War Two, Korea and Vietnam combined, and , it is possible that the US could reach the number of 650,000 that perished in the 1918 pandemic.

Two vaccines have proven effective and more will be approved during the coming months. The US, Canada, and most of the developed countries are making rapid progress in the roll-out of these vaccines and the rate of vaccination is increasing each week. There is some uncertainty regarding the availability of large amounts of these vaccines for the developing countries, and it may be the end of 2022 before global vaccination can be at an acceptable level.

It is unclear how many people will perish before these vaccines can have their anticipated affect. The major responsibility for the situation in the US rests squarely on Mr. Trump. The details of this failure are too numerous to mention. However, there seems to be a general recognition, that although Mr. Trump did not cause the virus, his approach to dealing with it, is negligent to the point of criminality.

This played a major role in the results of the November 2020 presidential election and he has been thrown out of office.

The economic impact of this pandemic has been catastrophic

On a world-wide basis, people have had to remain home, or at least severely limit their movements. Businesses have closed down, sports events and other gatherings have been cancelled, and the resulting record levels of unemployment have been devastating.

However, I find it amazing that so many people are complaining in such strong terms about having to comply with some of the recommended restrictions such as wearing masks, social distancing, and avoiding groups. I think that some people will always find reasons to protest on the restrictions to their civil liberties. I wonder how these same people would cope if they had to deal with the type of war-time restrictions that really were difficult to deal with.

Despite government measures to ease the financial pain and stimulate the economies, there are incredible levels of distress. The financial impact of these stimulus measures and the resulting debt will impact government's policies for many years.

Specifically, in the US, the medical and financial impact has fallen disproportionally on minorities and the poor. This has amplified the growing disparity of affordable health care and wealth among Americans. One of the results of this may well be that in the next few years, we will see a social revolution in taxation and the availability of universal health care, across the entire US population.

While the pandemic and all of the restrictions that have been required as a result of it, have not impacted our family too much, one of the unfortunate aspects is that my twice weekly cardiac exercise classes were canceled. Apart from the health concerns, I have missed the friendship of the sixteen or so of the other members of this group of cardiac survivors. We have managed to stay in touch and recently (Sep21) we managed a short get together, hosted by John Oliver. It was a pleasure to see all of these friends still safe and healthy, after a two year break.

A LIFE IN STAGES

It is terribly disappointing to learn that a variant of the original Covid19 virus (Delta) has turned up and is rapidly advancing throughout the US. This is particularly distressing, as it is almost exclusively affecting unvaccinated people, at a time when vaccination is widely available in the US at no cost. This is primarily due to the fact that the Covid pandemic has become politicized to the point that many people, mainly Republicans, are refusing to get this life saving vaccination.

It will take future generations to understand this sad phenomenon, but the origin is Trumpism. Yet another tragedy that this incompetent, evil, self- serving person is responsible for.

Donald Trump

The other big event of 2020 was the US presidential election on November 3rd. The potential re-election of Donald Trump was an alarming possibility, and thankfully, this has been avoided.

There is a general consensus, both in the US and around the world, that Trump's presidency has been an unparalleled disaster. His defeat in the 2020 election has been a cause of celebration on a global basis.

And yet, through all of the unbelievably bad events of his first term, he remains popular with approximately thirty to thirty-five percent of the voting base in America. There is no simple explanation for this, but it is a fact. He exemplifies all that is bad about America.

For the past several years, I have lumped this together under the umbrella of "The Dumbing Down of America." As I see it, there is a definite correlation between the lowering of educational standards, the generally poor standard of the "entertainment" segment of TV and movies, and the overall decline of literacy, connected to the less desirable aspect of social media and its ability to disseminate lies and untruths linked to incomprehensible conspiracy theories. The FOX news channel (Owned by Rupert Murdoch) has been a truly disgraceful source of much of the disinformation that has permeated the mindset of so many of its viewers.

In addition, as political divisions have made the US less governable, there has been a failure to acknowledge and retrain large segments of the workforce to adapt to the changing needs of a global economy. This has left so many Americans feeling left behind and forgotten.

Fortunately, Trump's supporters are in the minority. Hopefully, those Republicans that have supported and enabled him will also be rejected as they come up for re-election.

January 6th 2021

President Trump and some of his sycophants incited a mob of several thousand of his most ardent supporters to storm the US Capitol, during the joint meeting of the US Congress, to ratify the vote of the Electoral College and declare Joe Biden to be the president-elect and the forty-sixth president of the United States.

This violent storming of the Capitol was the most dramatic event of its type since the British sacked it in 1814. Fortunately, control of the Capitol was restored later the same day.

Although this riot was incited by the president, in the hope that it would in some way rally his support, it has in fact resulted in a dramatic reversal of support for him.

The Electoral College vote was ratified by Congress, confirming the results of the election and that Joe Biden had won a clear victory. However, Trump repeatedly took the position that he would not hand over power smoothly and he appealed the results all of the way to the US Supreme Court. The courts have consistently and overwhelmingly rejected his appeals.

The House of Representatives has passed an unprecedented second article of impeachment against President Trump. The following trial in the Senate resulted in an acquittal, as the Democrats were unable to obtain the two-thirds majority required for a guilty verdict. It is clear that the majority do believe that he was guilty but out of political expediency they voted to acquit him. What a disgraceful verdict on the US political system.

On January 20th President Joe Biden and Vice-President Kamala Harris were sworn into office and the majority of the US population and most of the world heaved a great sigh of relief.

As of June 2021, there is a general acceptance that President Biden has got off to a stronger start than expected. However, with the Republicans committed to blocking much of what he plans to do, the political short- term future is uncertain.

APPENDIX 3

My Final Staff Communication as President of 7-Eleven Canada

I left 7-Eleven on a high note and I tried to reflect this in my final message to all of our staff in March 1998.

> As many of you know by now, I am in the process of retiring from Southland Canada. I wanted to take this last opportunity to thank all of you for your support and friendship during these past twenty years.
>
> I feel very privileged to have been able to lead this organization for so long. We have grown from just over 70 stores with total annual sales of approximately $40 Million to our present number of 470 stores with total annual sales exceeding $1 Billion. Together, we have survived two major recessions and at the same time, we have created a Canadian retail success story. There are many factors that must converge for a company to enjoy long-term success.
>
> 1) We have to secure the very best locations. We have always had a well thought out Development Strategy. This strategy has been consistently executed and I would like to thank Jim Waldron, our Vice-President of Development, who, together with Steve Murray, our Construction Manager, Fred Meester, Paul Jhooty and Mebs Jiwa, has done such a good job of making sure that we operate from the best locations possible.
>
> 2) Our professional approach to gasoline marketing has allowed us to establish credibility with our major oil company partners, providing the basis for a profitable gas retailing business and supporting our ability to obtain valuable oil company-controlled locations. I would like the thank Roger Storms, our Vice-President of Gasoline Operations, who together with Bill Runciman, Gord Groff and Skip Walsh has done such a great job over all these years.

3) We have enjoyed consistent innovative leadership in marketing. These initiatives have been the envy of our competitors and they have earned us the admiration and support of our suppliers. We have had fun with such temporary opportunities as 3D Glasses, while building sustainable leadership in such areas as Slurpee – Big Gulp - Coffee – Sandwiches - Chicken – Fast Food – Newspapers – Magazines. As well as services – Retail Postal Outlets, A.T.M's – Lottery and Phone Cards.

In addition, our Food Centres, together with our recent CDC development in Calgary have given us unbeatable competitive advantages.

For all this and much more, I would like to thank David Huey, our Senior Vice-President of Marketing and his key support staff. They have been remarkable. Thank you to Jim Humphrey, Trish Lee, Chuck Hutcheson, Glen Riley, Ron Muller, Grant Richards, Mark Cousineau, Norm Dickinson, Mike McIsaac, Tony Murray, Roger Barret, Raj Gill, Shahbu Dhanai and Susannah Kirkland. You are all winners and your individual achievements are too numerous to mention.

4) Somebody has to keep track of all that we do and make some financial sense of it all. Thank you to Chris Nicolls our Vice-President of Finance (and Chris's successor Art Mountain) together with Phil Morgan, Kirk Pinneo, Mal McPhail, Bev Skazlic, Maureen Lepard and Kathy Nicholson. They have provided the very necessary support and control without which none of us can succeed.

5) Probably the most important is our Human Resource and Operations capability. While it is essential to have leadership in Development, Marketing and Accounting, at the end of the day it all comes down to execution. This is the area where you have all excelled the most. With our Human Resources ably led by Simon Evans, our Vice-President of Human Resources, we have been able to recruit, train and retain excellent staff at all levels of our store operations. Thank you to Barb Boon, Brenda Jones, Len McGeouch, Chris Webber, Barb Smith, Pat Hopkins, Mary Benassi, Gerry Collinge, Arly Dobson and Derek Perks.

6) The Operational Leadership provided over the years by the unique Jimmie D Musselwhite, Mike Sugden and Greg Ross has been outstanding. Our market managers and their teams continue to provide strong leadership and I am particularly grateful to them for their unwavering support. Thank you, Curtis Clairmont, James Ferguson, Kate Keillor, Blair Magnusson, Dale Shaw, Wayne Pelletier, Laurie Smith, Brian Bovencamp and Lawrence Richler.

A LIFE IN STAGES

I would also like to acknowledge the support that I have enjoyed from the people to whom I have reported over the years. Adrian Evans, Steve Krumholz, Steve LeRoy and the late, great Dick Dole, have been so supportive of my efforts and of Southland Canada, that words cannot describe the debt that we owe to these gentlemen.

The Field Consultants, our Store Managers and their hard-working staff have never ceased to amaze me with their dedication and enthusiasm. You are what makes this company what it is, and you can take great pride in what you have accomplished. Running great stores, that are the best in the business, by any objective measurement, exceeding our customer's expectations, raising funds for MDA and other worthy causes while usually having such fun doing it.

I have also been very well supported by my daughter Paula. She has had the unenviable job of being my Executive Assistant for the past three years. Thank you, Paula, for a job well done.

Surrounded by such capable people, it was impossible for me to fail and it is nice to leave on such a high note.

- Twenty successive months of leading the entire Southland Corporation in sales growth.
- The highest average store sales of any Division of Southland (without the benefit of beer and wine sales)
- The fastest rate of profit growth of any Division of Southland
- Double the rate of Food Service Sales of any Southland Division
- Record profits in three of the past four years and a high probability of another record year in 1998.

These are achievements of which you can and should be so proud and they form the base for your future achievements. The future of Southland Canada is unlimited, and I wish all of you good health and good luck for the future.

Before I decide which direction to take next, I intend to take things easy for a while, spend more time with my often-neglected family, and try to improve my very poor golf game!!

Once again, thank you for your friendship and your support.

Sincerely

Frank V Farr

President

Southland Canada Inc, March 1998.

APPENDIX 4

Schools and Education: A Slow Start and a Strong Finish

St. Anne's Roman Catholic Children's School

The first school that I attended was St. Ann's Roman Catholic Children's School in Leeds. I was only three years old.

St. Anne's Primary School

Later, I moved to the building next door, St. Ann's Roman Catholic Primary School and I remained there until I was eight years old. There was a shop close by, that made fresh pikelets (flat muffins) and we used to buy them for our lunch (a half penny or one penny).

It was on the way home from this school that we found the house, frequented by US soldiers and young local women and we could knock on the door and ask, "Got any gum, chum?" This was an irresistible opportunity for a young boy, when there were no sweets or gum available in the shops.

I was also at this school when we moved to Coburg St. and Stanley Dickinson gave me the ride to our new house on the front of his delivery bike.

I got a school award for writing an essay on Gandhi and during this time I became an avid reader of anything that I could get a hold of.

Both of these schools were a mile or so from where we lived.

Blenheim Secondary School

When I was nine years old, I changed schools and started at Blenheim Secondary School. This was much closer to my home at 14 Hillary St. I don't really have very many memories of Blenheim except that they also had a children's school and as soon as he was old enough, my younger brother Michael, started to attend.

The kind teacher that I had at Blenheim was Mr. Frank Cooper and he was the first person that encouraged me to do my best at my schoolwork. It was Mr. Cooper that advised me that I had passed the 11 Plus exam and qualified for a scholarship to go to the grammar school at the start of the next school year.

In England at that time, the 11 Plus exam was the exam that determined what type of education you would receive from then on. Those that passed the 11 Plus would be offered a place in a grammar school (although this was not certain, as there were limited places available). Although I lived in the centre of Leeds and there were several grammar schools closer, I was assigned to Leeds Modern School, on the northern edge of the city.

Leeds Modern School

Leeds Modern School was a boy's-only school, with the Lawnswood Girls Grammar School next door. Both were at the northern edge of Leeds, just past the Leeds Ring Road at Adel. Each school had approximately 500 pupils.

My experience at Leeds Modern School was mixed. Being one of the poorer boys from the city centre, I did not fit in (fortunately, there were a few others). I always did very well at English Language, English Literature, Geography, and History. I was good at Geometry and Algebra but not so good at Arithmetic.

It seems so odd to be as old as I am, and to find myself describing myself as a rebellious youth during my time at Leeds Modern. I was twelve years old when I went there and fifteen years old when I left, and I have to admit, I was not an ideal pupil for any of that time. My preoccupation was getting up to mischief, chasing girls, and going to dances. Although the official drinking age was eighteen, we were able to get into certain pubs from fourteen onwards. Efforts to succeed at school took second place to these more interesting pastimes.

I hated homework and avoided it at every opportunity. I don't know how many times I would get off the tram at the school, to disappear into the bushes on the round-about and come out without my satchel, only to claim that I had left it on the tram. Then I'd collect it from the bushes at the end of school and fabricate some story about not being able to find it at the tram terminus for several days.

And then I left for Kneesworth Hall.

Kneesworth Hall

All of this changed when I went to Kneesworth Hall. I have covered this in my story, but you have to consider the contrast.

Leeds Modern School: A big school, on the outskirts of a big city. There were 500 pupils and I was a rebel that did not fit in.

Kneesworth Hall: A hundred and fifty acres in the countryside with thirty-five to fifty pupils—twelve to fifteen to a class. First class, dedicated teachers and all of the boys were generally intelligent. An environment designed to provoke intellectual curiosity and an accelerated education.

It was at Kneesworth that "I learned to learn." By that, I mean that I went from "skimming" and hoping to remember, to "focusing" on what I was studying and not moving on until I understood.

At Kneesworth, we were exposed to a first-class education, under almost perfect conditions. This was a residential school, so our education in a broader sense was 24/7. I obtained six "O" level GCE Certificates and two "A" level GCE certificates. Under ordinary circumstances, this would have been sufficient to get me started on the route to university. However, we were still a poor family and I needed to contribute by earning a living.

Leeds College of Commerce

After Kneesworth, I returned to Leeds and began working at a menswear store. I also attended Leeds College of Commerce. I did very well, as I studied two subjects that I enjoyed. One was Textiles and the other was Retail Organization.

Following this, I emigrated to Canada, but my education continued after I had returned and started working for Fine Fare

Barneswood

Fine Fare's chairman, James Gulliver arranged for Fine Fare to purchase a large private house just outside of Welwyn Garden City and to convert it into a residential training centre. As director of merchandising, it was a part of my responsibilities to provide merchandising training to a range of Fine Fare staff.

This provided me the opportunity to sit in on any of the courses that interested me. A good opportunity. I attended courses on Business Planning, Management by Objectives, Budgeting, Statistics, Marketing and Sales Promotion, Retail Accounting, Category Management, and other retail related subjects.

British Institute of Management

At the same time, I was mixing with most of the senior management of Fine Fare and I was very pleased when our chairman, James Gulliver sponsored my membership in The British Institute of Management. This provided me with an ongoing opportunity to receive books and manuals and attend courses on a whole range of management subjects. I still have many of the books in my library today.

This exposure and training came a little later in my life than for most people, but it also came at the time when I was most eager to learn and it helped me to become a more informed, professional manager, at a time when I needed it.

This also set the scene for my opportunities to assume more senior general management roles as my career in Fine Fare progressed, through senior vice-president at Tamblyn's to president of 7-Eleven Canada, and on to my career as a senior international consultant, with The European Bank for Reconstruction and Development (EBRD)

To all of this you can add forty years of practical experience in retail management up to and including serving at the board level for over ten different organizations, including one year, serving as chairman of The British Columbia Assessment Authority, a Crown Corporation, of the Government of British Columbia.

A slow start and a strong finish!

❖

"Happiness is a state of mind, not a result of circumstances." Anonymous

"Most problems are created in the head." Marcus Aurelius

APPENDIX 5

My Work History (CV)

This was produced at the time that I joined EBRD and has since been updated to include my EBRD experience.

Frank Farr is an experienced retail executive, having operated at the most senior levels in food and drug retailing in the U.K., USA, Canada and Internationally for 36 years.

1961-1974. Fine Fare Supermarkets Ltd.

Starting as an executive trainee in 1961 Frank moved through the company to become the youngest director of this $2 billion company. At the time that he left Fine Fare to relocate to Canada in 1975, Frank was Fine Fare's *Director of Merchandising* with responsibility for the effective merchandising policy for over 500 supermarkets. Frank was also a *Director of Fine Fare Business Development Ltd., Fine Fare Discount Ltd., and Fine Fare Superstores Ltd.*

During his service to Fine Fare, Frank had personal responsibility for the planning and opening/reopening, of over 350 of Fine Fare's Supermarkets, along with many other unique projects, all of which were successfully completed. Frank was one of the key people involved in developing the first Superstores in The U.K. during the early 1970s.

1974-1978 Tamblyn Drugmarts

As *Senior Vice-President* of this Weston Companies subsidiary, Frank was one of a three-member team charged with turning around this money-losing subsidiary. This 150-store chain was returned to profitability within one year and then enjoyed three successive years of increased profit improvement, prior to being successfully sold to Boots P.L.C. of Britain.

FRANK FARR

1978-1998 Southland Canada Inc.

Southland Canada Inc. trading as 7-Eleven Convenience Stores, is a wholly owned subsidiary of the Southland Corporation of Dallas, Texas. Southland is the world's largest operator and franchisor of convenience stores.

Frank joined 7-Eleven as *Canadian Division Manager*. Consistent improvement in sales and profits allowed Frank to obtain increased autonomy for Canadian Management and led to Frank's appointment first as *Vice-President/General Manager* and then as *President of Southland Canada Inc.*

When Frank joined 7-Eleven Canada in 1978 the Canadian operation had approx. 75 stores with sales of $40 million. With a mandate to grow the business and a high degree of autonomy, Frank was able to attract a team of competent retail professionals, who, with Frank's leadership were able to develop 7-Eleven into a major Canadian retail success story.

As President of Southland Canada, Frank represented 7-Eleven Canada in meetings and conferences throughout North America, The UK, Denmark, Hong Kong and Tokyo and hosted 7-Eleven delegations from Mexico, Australia, The Philippines, Taiwan and Thailand.

At the time of Frank's retirement, Southland Canada, with over 475 stores and gross sales in excess of $1billion, was the 9th largest food retailer in Canada. Southland Canada was the 185th largest company in Canada, the 76th largest private company in Canada and the 5th largest private company in B.C. Based in Vancouver. Southland operated in five provinces and employed over 6,000 Canadians.

The Canadian 7-Eleven stores had the highest average sales of any convenience stores in North America. In Canada, 7-Eleven's average store sales and profitability significantly exceeded that of any other Canadian C-store chain, and they led the Canadian C-store industry in every objective measure of performance.

2000 – 2003 The Osbourne Group.

As a Principal of the Osbourne Group based in Vancouver BC. Frank provided Executive Consulting services to numerous clients in the Vancouver Region.

2003 – 2004 British Columbia Assessment Authority

As Chair of the British Columbia Assessment Authority, Frank, together with the board, provided oversight to the management of the assessment authority, which is charged with providing the property assessments for all real property in the Province of British Columbia.

A LIFE IN STAGES

2003 – Present: Immediate Images Inc.

As President and controlling shareholder, Frank has steered this start-up digital signage company from zero revenue in 2003 to revenues in excess of $ 1 Million.

2010 – Present: European Bank for Reconstruction and Development (EBRD)

As a Senior International Advisor, Frank has successfully completed assignments on behalf of EBRD in Moldova (IMC Markets) Armenia (Alfa-Pharm JSC), Republic of Georgia (GPC Pharmaceuticals JSC – 2 Assignments) and is currently providing Consulting advice in Kosovo (Meridian Corporation - 4 Assignments) and Ukraine (Clever Stores LLC. - 3 Assignments).

Frank also served on the Board of Supervisors of GPC Pharmaceuticals JSC. and was Chairman of the Compensation Committee.

Personal Strengths

- **Strategic Thinking**

  Develop a strategic plan; obtain buy-in from Stakeholders, Shareholders, Management and Staff. Execute the Plan, guided by consistent values.

- **Hands on, Results Oriented Management.**

  Thorough, Detailed, Consistent, Accountable.

- **The ability to attract, retain and develop high calibre managers**

  Fair, open and honest approach to managing subordinates.

  Competitive Teamwork

  High, incentive-based compensation, tied to results.

  Develop a clear sense of corporate values.

- **Community Service.**

  A commitment to pro-active community involvement.

  Director of the Muscular Dystrophy Association of Canada from 1980 -1998

  Member of the Capital Steering Committee for The Arts Umbrella Group in Vancouver BC from 1994 – 1996

  Secretary/Treasurer Morgan Creek Golf Club 2002 – 2005

Work Hard, Have fun…Share fun.!!!

APPENDIX 6

Family Tree

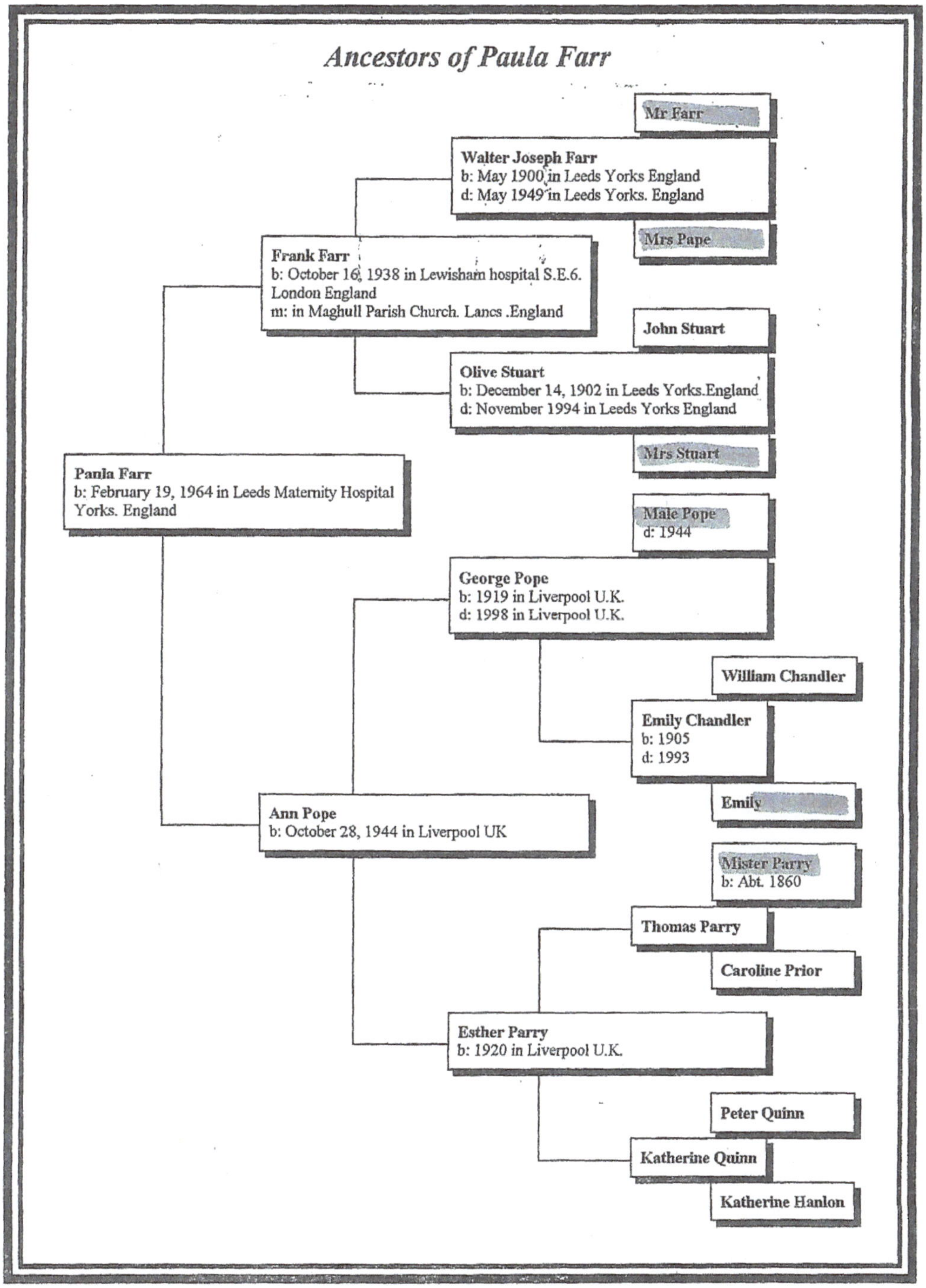

Ancestors of Paula Farr

- **Paula Farr**
  b: February 19, 1964 in Leeds Maternity Hospital Yorks. England
  - **Frank Farr**
    b: October 16, 1938 in Lewisham hospital S.E.6. London England
    m: in Maghull Parish Church. Lancs. England
    - **Walter Joseph Farr**
      b: May 1900 in Leeds Yorks England
      d: May 1949 in Leeds Yorks. England
      - Mr Farr
      - Mrs Pape
    - **Olive Stuart**
      b: December 14, 1902 in Leeds Yorks. England
      d: November 1994 in Leeds Yorks England
      - John Stuart
      - Mrs Stuart
  - **Ann Pope**
    b: October 28, 1944 in Liverpool UK
    - **George Pope**
      b: 1919 in Liverpool U.K.
      d: 1998 in Liverpool U.K.
      - Male Pope
        d: 1944
      - **Emily Chandler**
        b: 1905
        d: 1993
        - William Chandler
        - Emily
    - **Esther Parry**
      b: 1920 in Liverpool U.K.
      - **Thomas Parry**
        - Mister Parry
          b: Abt. 1860
        - Caroline Prior
      - **Katherine Quinn**
        - Peter Quinn
        - Katherine Hanlon

309

Descendants of Walter Joseph Farr

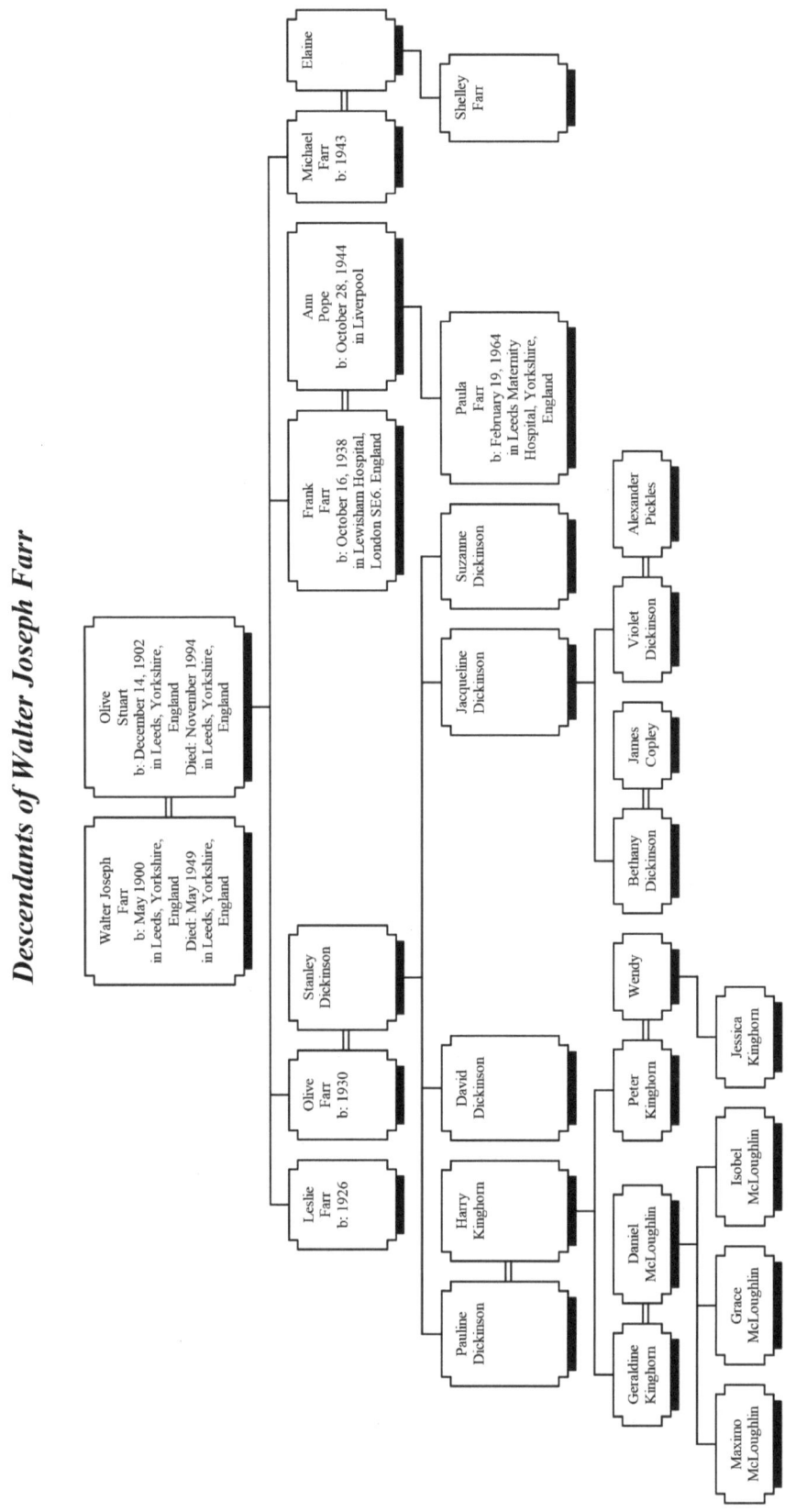

A LIFE IN STAGES

Descendants of John Stuart

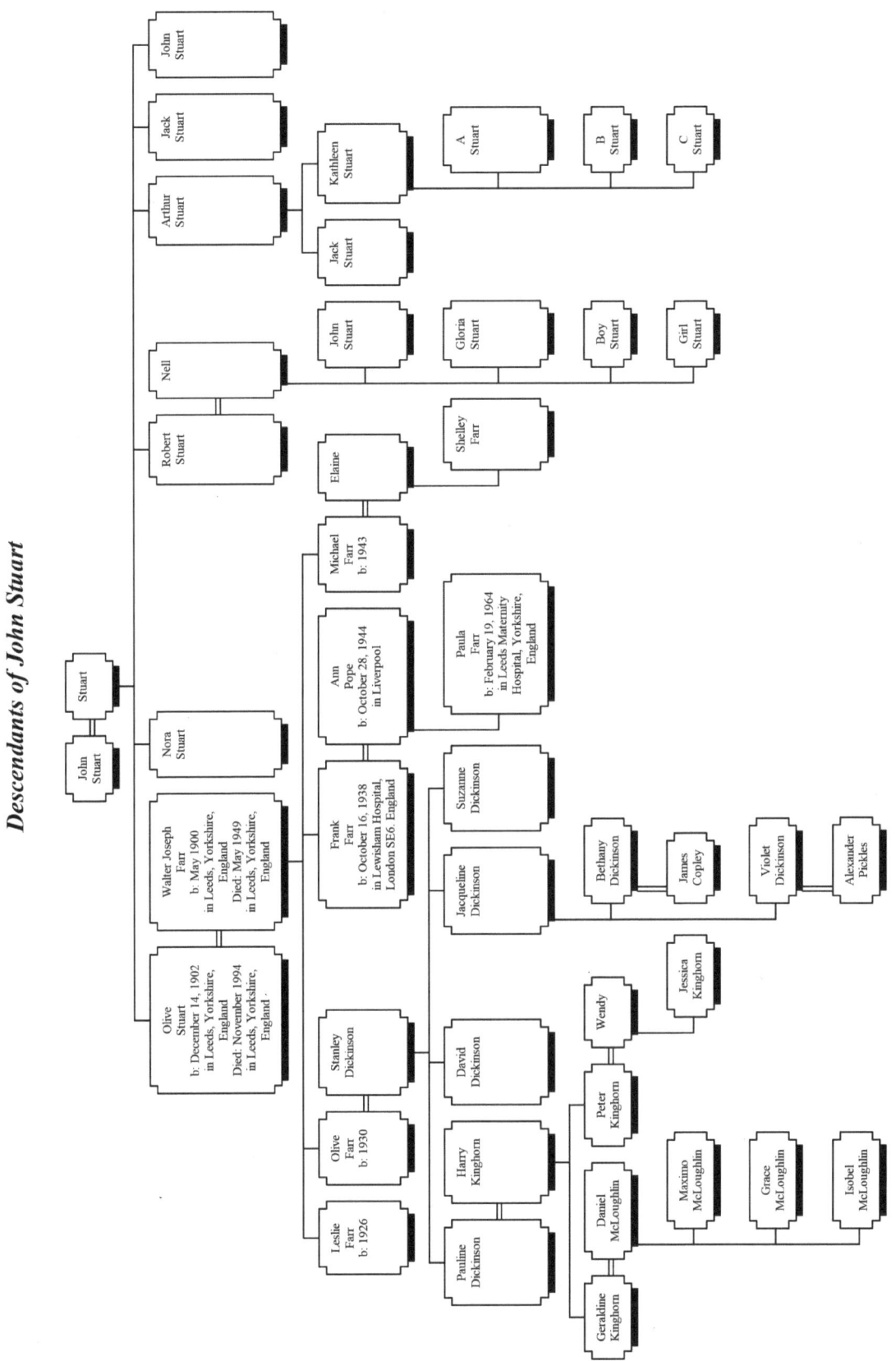

311

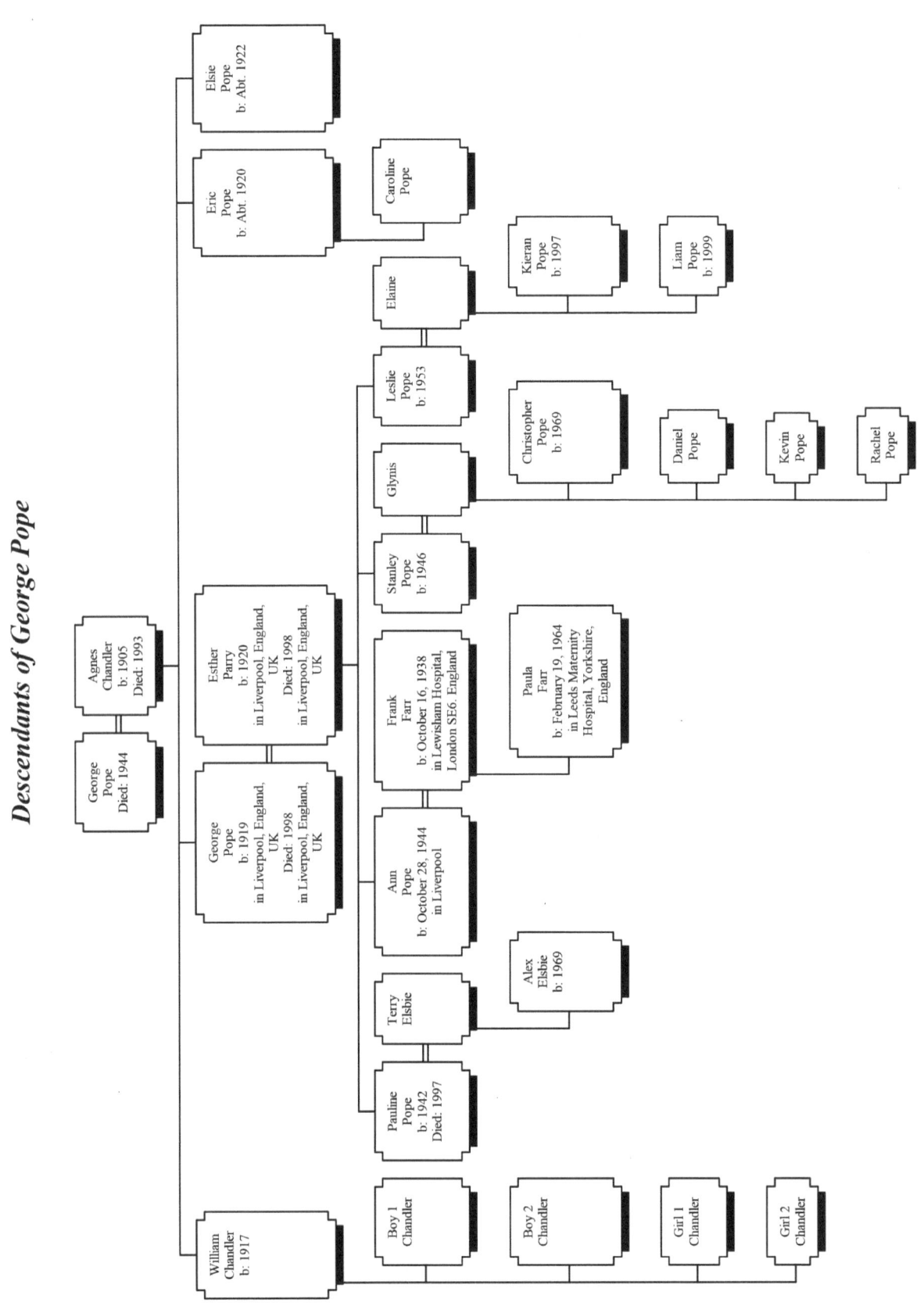

Descendants of George Pope

A LIFE IN STAGES

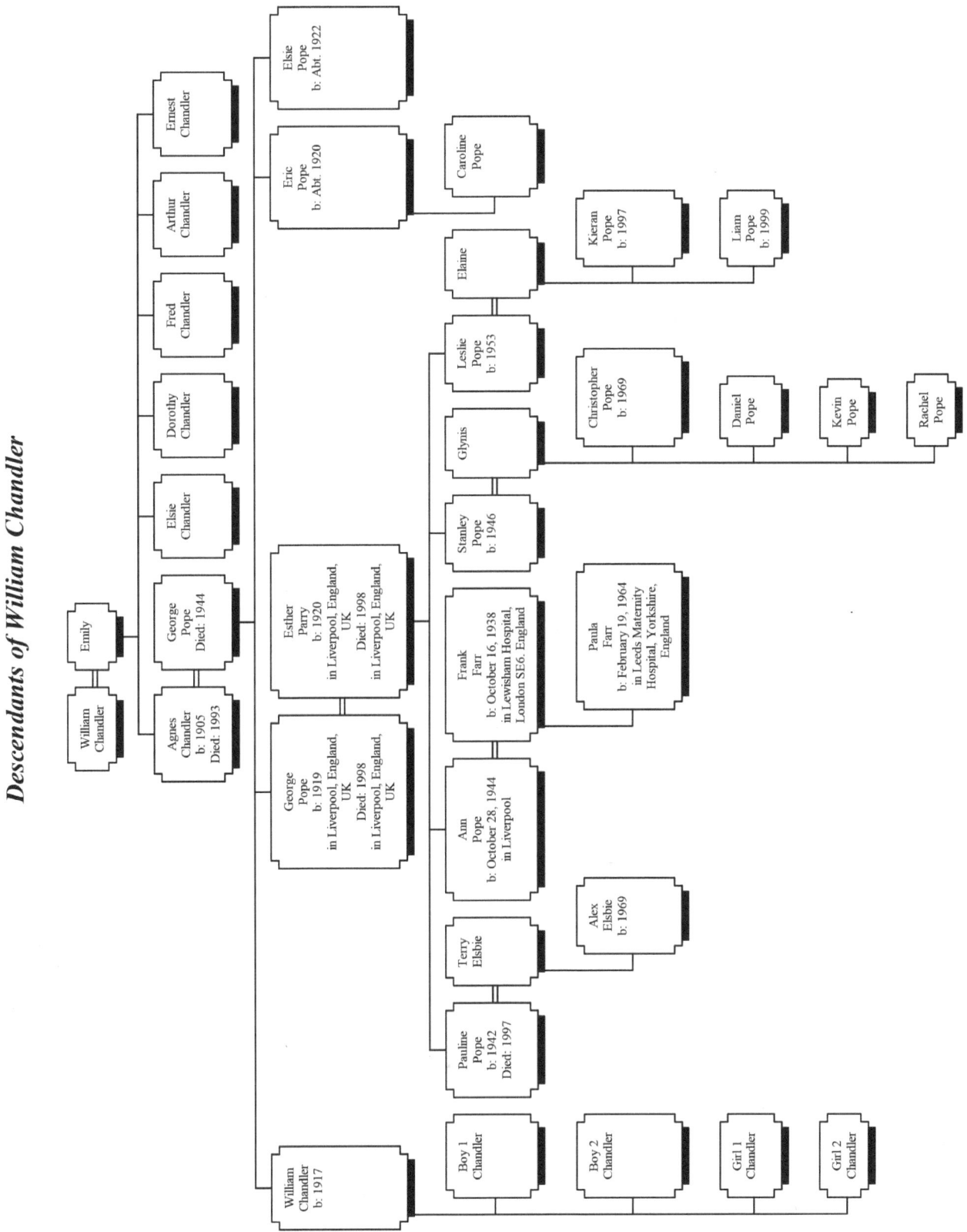

313

FRANK FARR

Descendants of Ka

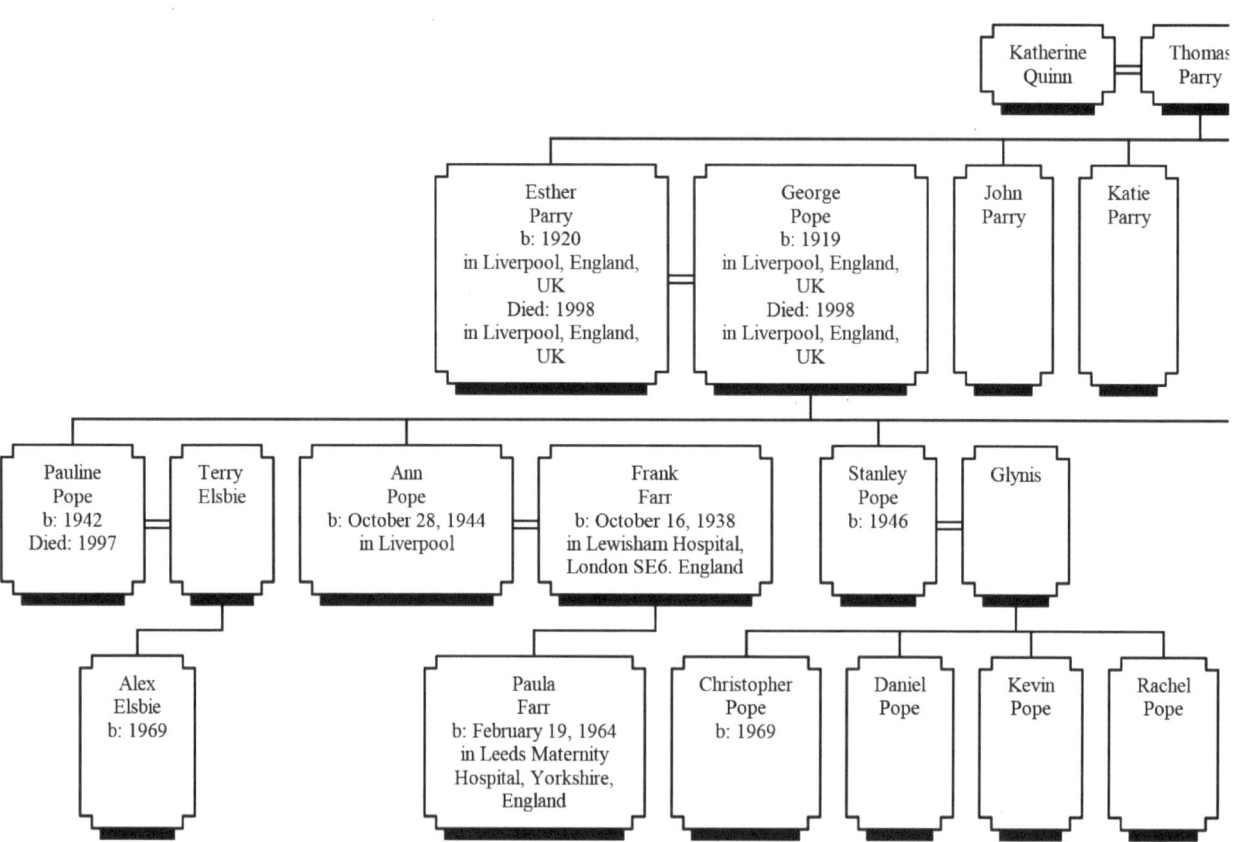

A LIFE IN STAGES

therine Quinn

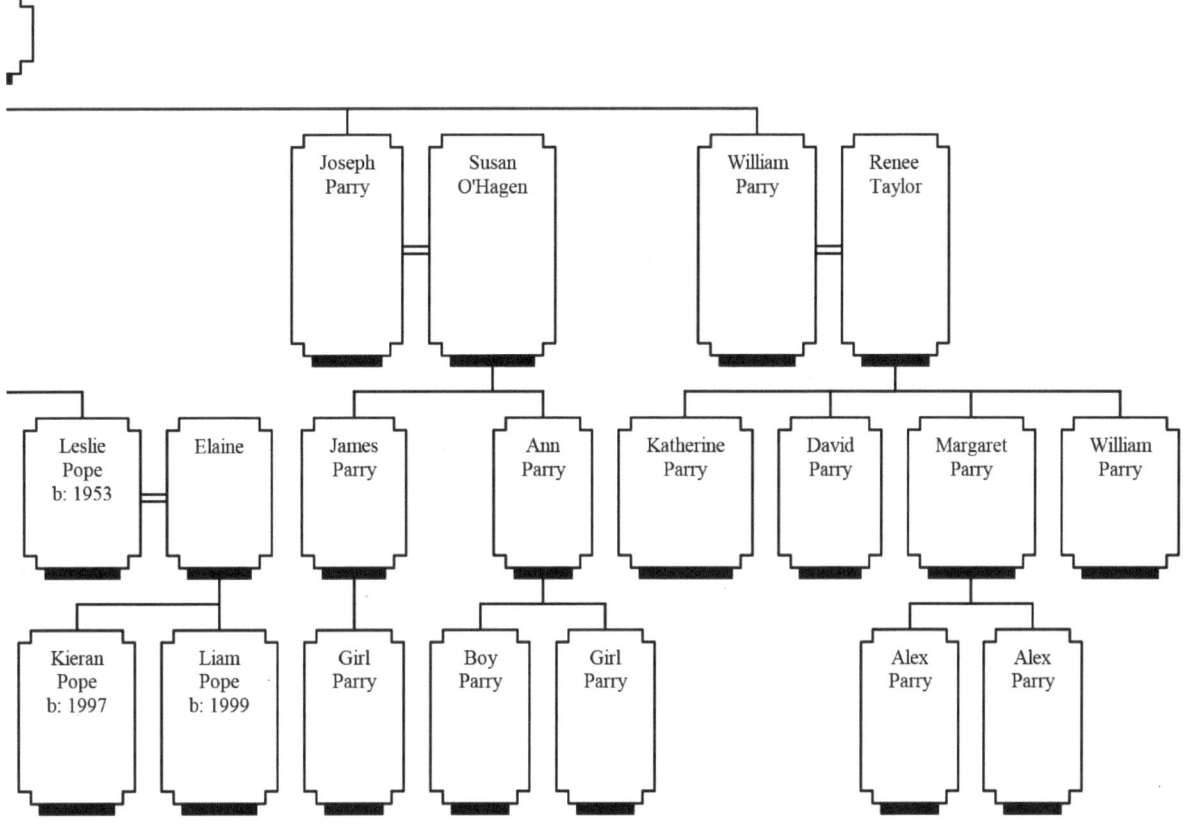

315

FRANK FARR

Descendants of

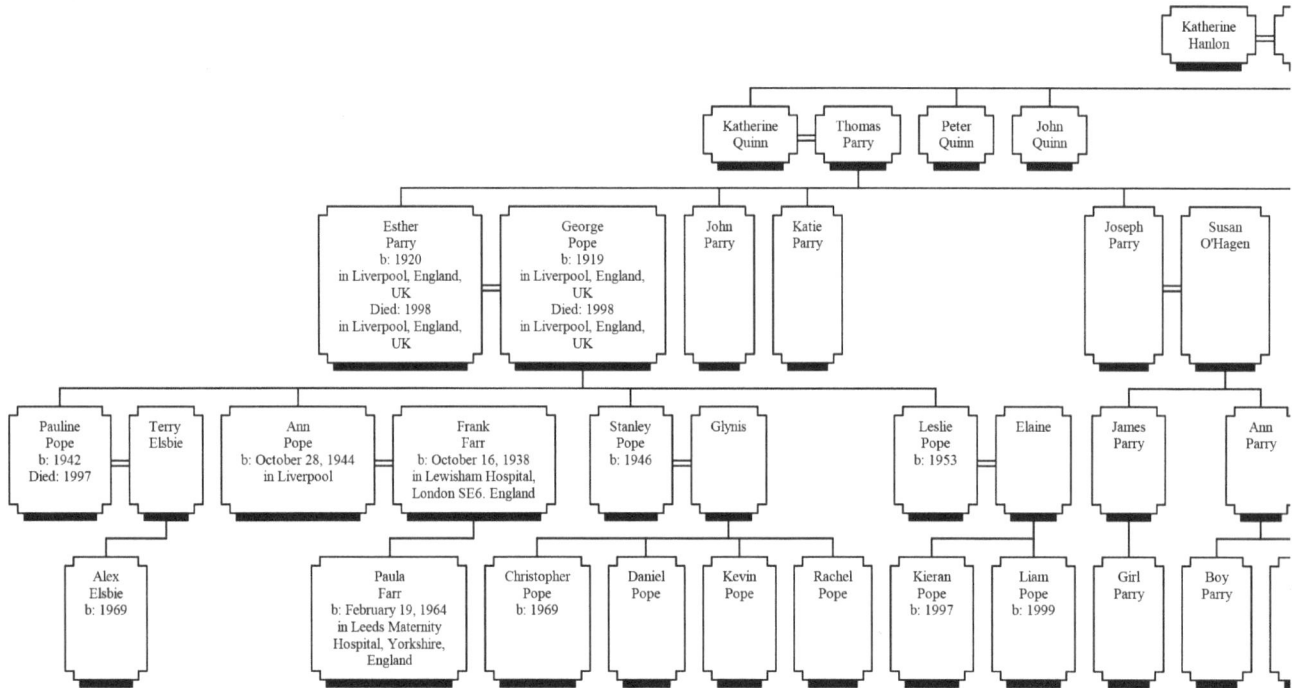

A LIFE IN STAGES

Katherine Hanlon

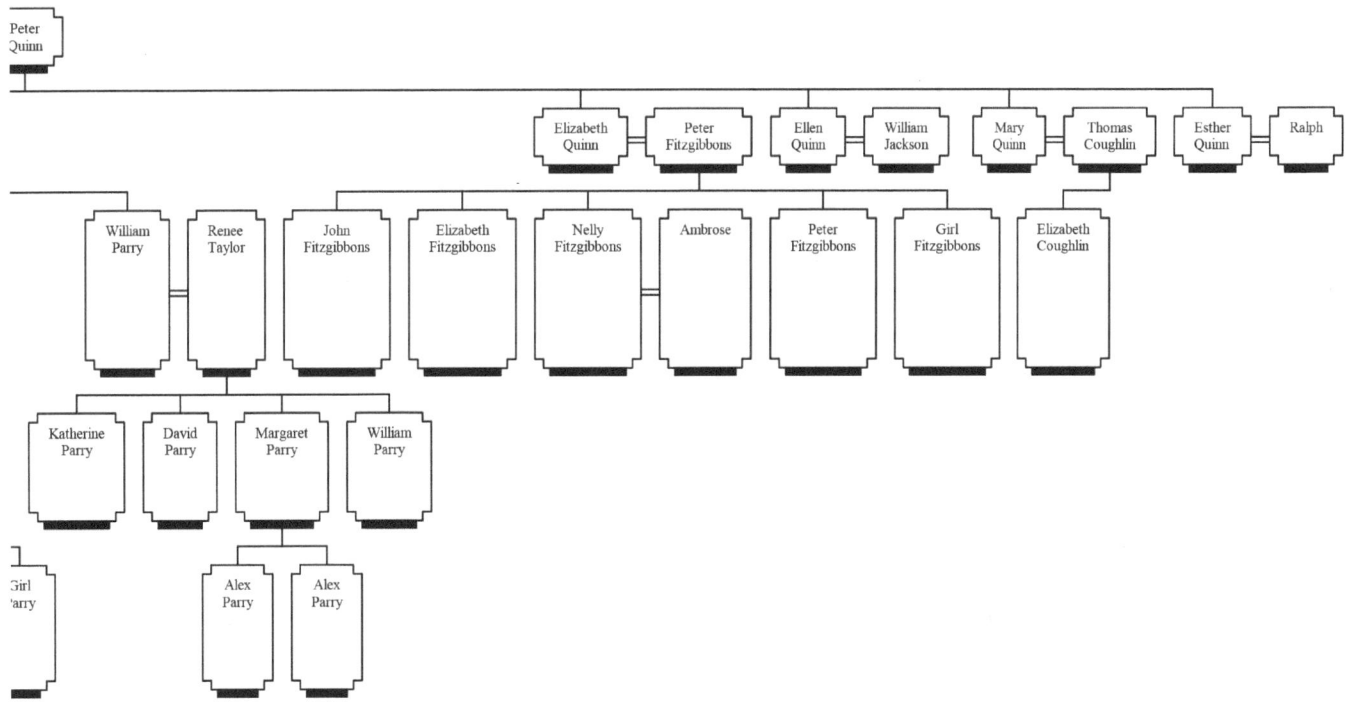

FRANK FARR

Descendants

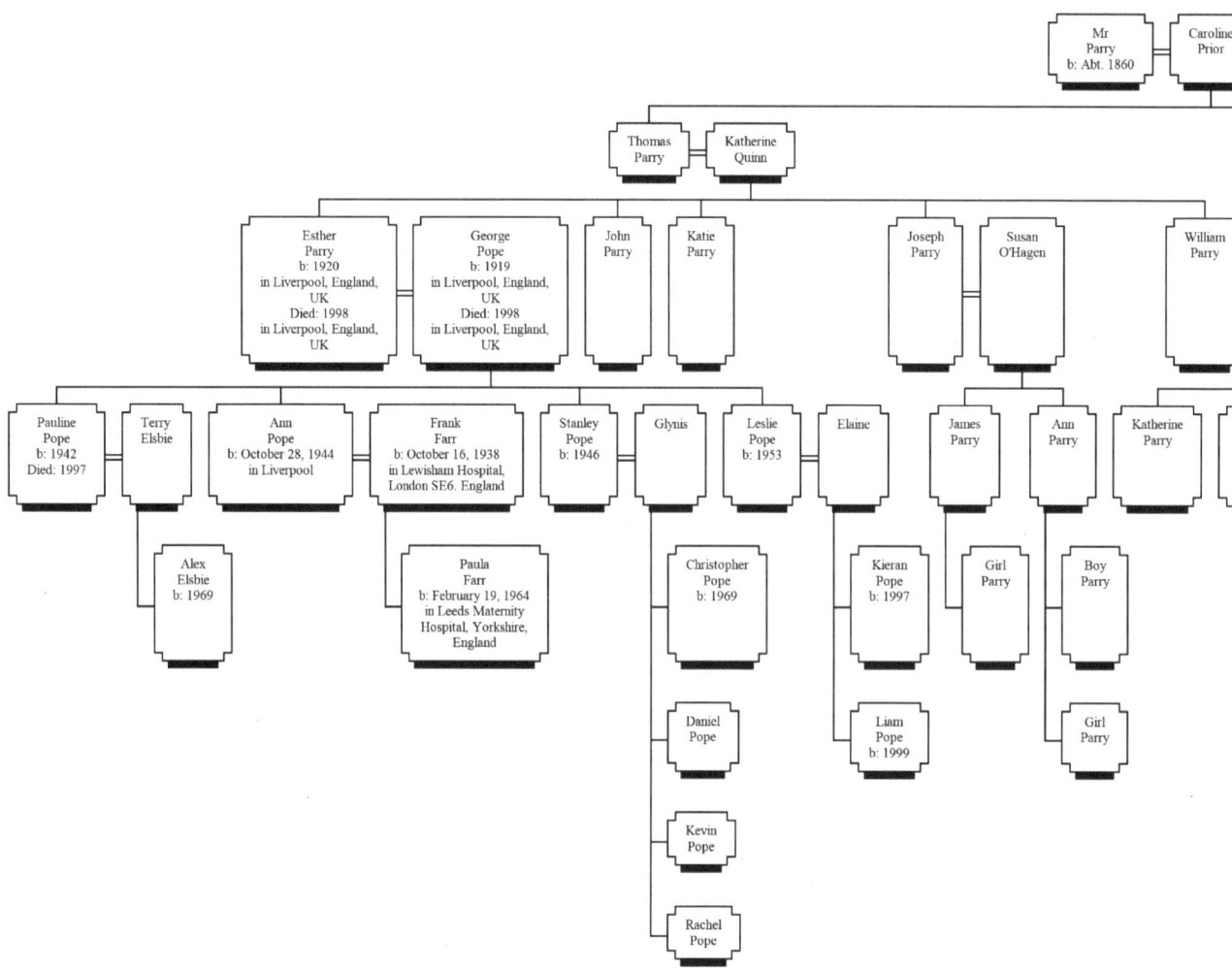

A LIFE IN STAGES

of Mr Parry

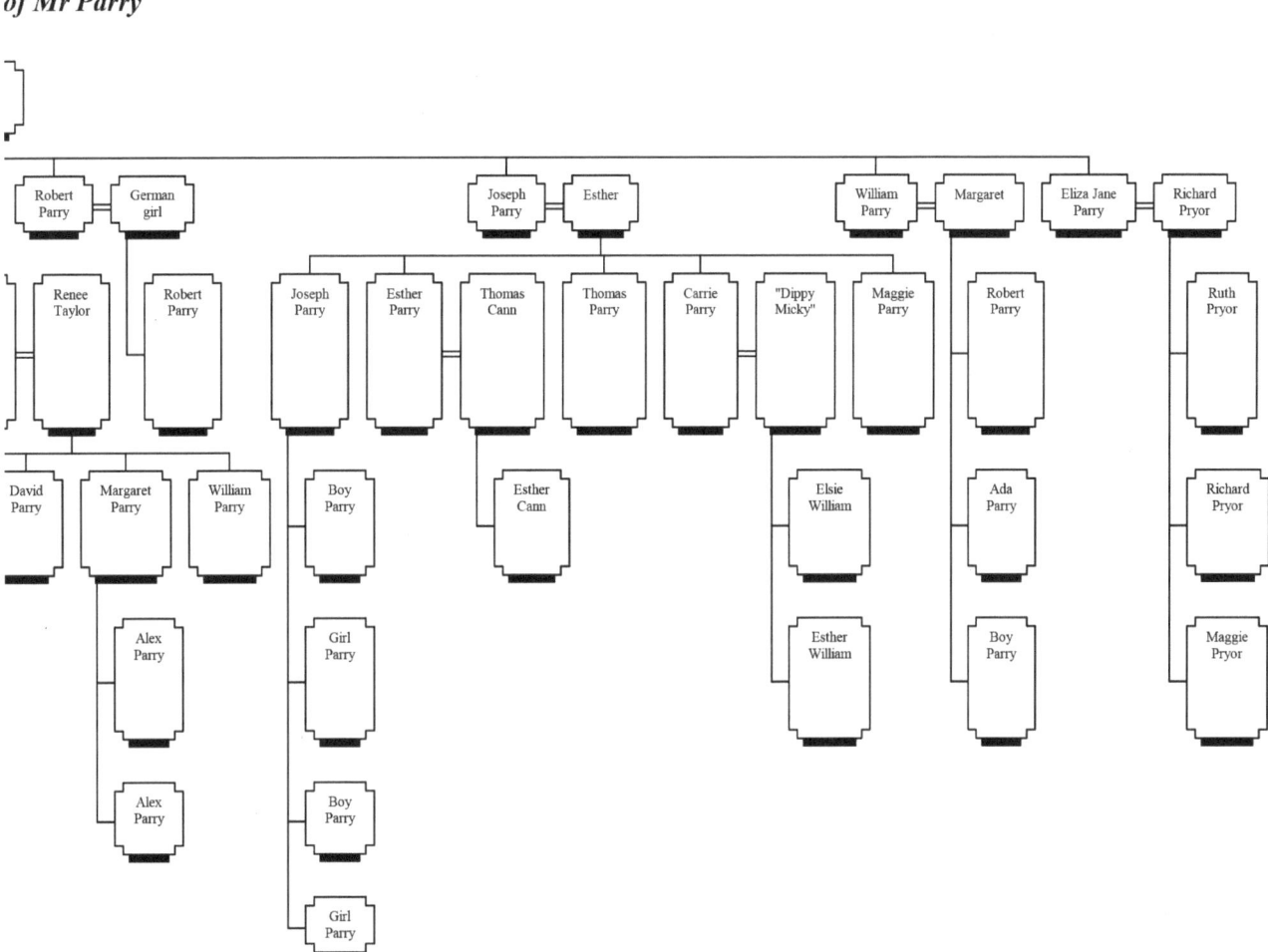

CPSIA information can be obtained
at www.ICGtesting.com
Printed in the USA
BVHW092037100122
625746BV00002B/11